From Palestine to Israel

From Palestine to Israel

A Photographic Record of Destruction and State Formation, 1947–50

Ariella Azoulay

Translated by Charles S. Kamen

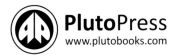
PlutoPress
www.plutobooks.com

First published 2011 by Pluto Press
345 Archway Road, London N6 5AA
www.plutobooks.com

First published in Hebrew by Resling Publishing House,
Tel Aviv, 2009

Published with the support of Zochrot – the exhibition on
which this book is based was curated by Ariella Azoulay
and first shown at Zochrot, Tel Aviv, 2009

British Library Cataloguing in Publication Data
A catalogue record for this book is available from
the British Library

ISBN   978 0 7453 3169 0   Paperback

This book is printed on paper suitable for recycling and
made from fully managed and sustained forest sources.
Logging, pulping and manufacturing processes are
expected to conform to the environmental standards of
the country of origin.

10 9 8 7 6 5 4 3 2 1

Designed and typeset by Tom Lynton
Produced for Pluto Press by Chase Publishing Services Ltd
Printed and bound in the European Union by
CPI Antony Rowe, Chippenham

CONTENTS

Constituent Violence 1947–50

Recognizing the disaster as a necessary condition for imagining the future

The war that wasn't

The photographs included here are historical documents in every sense. Analyzing them as historical documents sheds new light on what occurred in Palestine between 1947 and 1950. Although the photographs have been available to the public in the archives that preserved them (mostly State and Zionist archives) for 60 years, they have not yet been treated as archival documents.[1] This book reads them in a manner that presents a new way to write history – history through photographs. Bringing these photographs together allowed me to create a new archive: a civil archive which makes it possible to view the catastrophe they recorded.

Viewing the late 1940s from a military perspective, these years appear as a series of battles and strategic objectives whose attainment is considered the measure of success or failure. Viewing the period from a perspective of national sovereignty, it displays a series of events connected to the Zionist phantasm of establishing a national home for one people in an area occupied by a mixed population, and situates two sides at the drama's center: two mutually hostile nations fighting to the death in a conflict only one can survive. These two perspectives bury the question of whether these two sides – "Jews" and "Arabs" – in fact existed as separate, hostile parties prior to the war. This book proposes a civil viewpoint, one encompassing all the inhabitants of the country – both Jews and Arabs – that allows us to reconstruct the segregation of the two sides and the collision between them as a product of the war, which created its form and structure.

The historiography of this period is based primarily on written documents, and describes the series of events that occurred in Palestine at the end of the 1940s as a passage from "war" to "state." Critical historiography includes the "nakba" in this picture in a manner which portrays it as an additional consequence of the establishment of the state of Israel, and as a parallel narrative competing with the Zionist narrative of "independence" culminating in the establishment of the state. In analyzing the violence carried out in Palestine at the end of the 1940s, the critical narrative, like that of the Zionists, failed to question the applicability of the term "war." The civil archive that is the project of this book reconstructs the past without accepting the prior national assumptions. The unproblematic adoption of the term "war" to describe the period establishes it at the apex of the "Israel–Palestine conflict" in a manner that eliminates the complex variety of exchange and interaction between Jews and Arabs, replacing it with a narrow conception of "national conflict" that justifies an anachronistic reading of the past in which "war" between them was unavoidable. The term "war" assumes as self-evident the existence of two hostile sides which fought one another, and mistakenly identifies the violence carried out by the army with wartime "battles."

This book traces the constituent violence carried out by the Jewish military and political leadership. "Constituent violence" is understood here, following Walter Benjamin and a whole tradition of political theory, as the force used to create and impose a new political regime. The transformation of Palestine into the state of Israel was not achieved during an unavoidable war between two nations, but by the exercise of systematic and planned violence to create a clear Jewish majority that would correspond to and justify the formation of a Jewish state and the Jew-ification of the state organs. This violence was called the "War of Liberation," thereby giving rise to a persistent confusion which even today permeates Israeli and international public discourse. This confusion concerns three protagonists associated with achieving liberation: the British, the Palestinians and the Arab states. This confusion permitted the falsehood of a war for survival and justified the continued use of violence under the guise of war, and these attitudes persist today. The term "liberation" or "independence" implied a decolonization project, liberation from a foreign power, in a manner that camouflaged the colonization of Palestine by the state of Israel. The term "liberation" is inaccurate in relation to those three elements: the British left the country voluntarily, and liberation from them did not require a war. The Palestinians were certainly not the foreign power from which liberation was necessary. Rather, the Palestinians were the inhabitants of a country who were transformed into foreigners and expelled from their land by the mobilization for "war." The violent expulsion and destruction that made the declaration of Israel's establishment possible led to the acceptance of Israel as a member of the United Nations and ensured that henceforth future negotiations would take place only with other, recognized sovereign states. Ten additional months of constituent violence ended in March, 1949, with the armistice agreements between Israel and a number of Arab states, but notably the Palestinians were eliminated as official participants within the conflict. The agreements signed between the state of Israel, which imposed itself on the population of the region, and the Arab states, transformed the demand of Palestinians to return home into an illegitimate threat

---

[1]   See acknowledgements for more on this.

to the sovereignty of the newly established nation-state.

These international agreements played a role in preserving the effects of the constituent violence that imposed a Jewish state on a mixed population, while the majority of the land's existing inhabitants were expelled and never allowed to return.

Using the war as a prism through which the past is read allows us not only to read the past differently, but also to imagine a different, civil future. This book proposes to extract such potentialities from the rubble created by the nation-state's machinery of war.

From this book's civil perspective, past events cannot be split and narrated along national lines. When the fate of the entire population is taken into consideration, the expulsion, dispossession and destruction cannot be justified. The events that occurred between 1947 and 1950 appear as the struggle of a local leadership to impose its rule on the entire body politic and constitute a new regime regardless of the wishes of its inhabitants and without seeking their consent. From this perspective, the civil society as a whole was attacked. The violence toward the land's Palestinian residents positioned them as the enemy of the very people with whom they had previously shared their lives in various ways. The violence exercised by the state-making machinery against the population of citizens took place despite civil resistance of Jews and Arabs to the reality of a war and its antagonistic mobilization. These citizens tried to defend themselves by means of mutual promises, local agreements and civil contracts. By means of such civil alliances they tried to maintain neighborly relations and friendships, as well as commercial contacts, to avoid becoming enemies. Dayr Yasin, Sheikh Mouanis, Kibbutz Saris, Majdal, Sidna Ali, Miske and Rishpon are only a few of the places where Jews and Arabs tried to preserve their lives in common.

At the same time as it was undermining the Partition Plan with violence, Israel declared statehood and publicly presented itself as the expression of the world's desire for the creation of a Jewish state in Palestine. The government of Israel continued to undermine the Partition Plan by expelling hundreds of thousands of Palestinian residents of the country. These actions were not enough, however. The government even denied that the international attitude toward the Partition Plan had changed significantly. While Ben Gurion announced the establishment of the state of Israel, the US State Department was drafting an alternative plan for a solution that could be accepted by all the country's residents. The declaration of the State of Israel not only ignored the rejection of the Partition Plan by the country's Arab residents, by the Arab states and by the governments of Britain and the United States, but stipulated that United Nations recognition was irrevocable: "This recognition by the United Nations of the right of the Jewish people to establish their state is irrevocable." According to the Israeli declaration, it is not the rights of the inhabitants that are irrevocable, as has been the norm in various declarations of this kind since the American Revolution, but the recognition of the reality created by the new regime without obtaining the agreement of all those it would govern.

Again, the partition resolution was not politically valid for the community whose future it wished to establish, nor did it attempt to preserve the cohabitation that had previously existed. Military force was needed to overcome the opposition of the majority of the land's inhabitants and to realize the plan. In order to produce such military force, the civil population had to be recruited and made submissive. The might of war as an existential threat had to be imposed on the population; the dividing line between Jews and Arabs had to be constituted as essential, that is, as absolute.

Creating the dividing line

The partition plan is usually presented in Israeli public discourse as a solution to a problem and not as what contributed enormously to the creation of that selfsame problem. The plan had been rejected by the majority of the population it would affect[2] as well as the British Mandate government, the U.S. State Department, and the U.S. delegation to the United Nations.[3] In response to the massive opposition to the partition plan, the Americans – led by Secretary of State George Marshall – even presented an alternative plan for a political solution in Palestine that included the termination of the British Mandate government.[4] The alternative plan's primary aim was to come to an acceptable solution for the majority of the country's inhabitants. These alternative plans and the efforts involved in them to find a solution that would be agreed to by the entire population – Jews and Arabs – was totally rejected by the Jewish leadership. But although it rejected any alternative and officially adopted the partition plan the day after it was accepted by the UN, the Jewish leadership acted vigorously to redraw the partition lines, cleanse the land of its Palestinian

---

[2]   In fact, the partition plan was formulated solely on the basis of talks held by UN representatives with the Jewish leadership.

[3]   On the Zionist lobby for the Partition Plan among State members of the UN, see Morris, 2008.

[4]   On this plan, see Feldstein, 2009.

inhabitants, and occupy territories that the plan had originally destined for a Palestinian state.

Between 1947 and 1950, the state apparatus of the British Mandate and the institutions of the Jewish community ("Yishuv") were transformed into the apparatus of a Jewish state. They were tasked with completing the Judaizing of the region they had conquered, beginning the day after the partition plan was accepted in November 1947. They applied their logic to all areas of life in a territory which still had no permanent borders. Through some two hundred photographs this book follows the formation of the apparatus of the new state during the process of destroying Palestinian society by killing, dividing, expropriating, expelling and preventing those expelled from returning. In order for this apparatus to be stabilized, maintained and recognized as democratic it was necessary to transform the catastrophe imposed on the Palestinians into a non-catastrophe, into what I shall characterize as *"catastrophe from their point of view"* – "their," of course, referring to the Palestinians.

In order to trace the process by which the Jewish state apparatus was established, and by which the Palestinian catastrophe was structured as *"catastrophe from their point of view,"* this book puts aside two major narratives: the Zionist narrative, beginning with the dream of return to Zion and ending with its realization in the establishment of the state, and the Palestinian or post-Zionist narrative which situates the nakba as the constitutive event of Palestinian existence and identity, and ignores its contribution to the establishment of the Israeli regime and to shaping the forms of violence that maintain it.[5] Both these narratives make a rigid distinction between Jews and Arabs, not allowing us to reconstruct the origins of this division. This dividing line is still a central component of the Israeli regime's ruling apparatus. It was the means by which the disaster imposed on the Palestinians was transformed into *"catastrophe from their point of view."* The book sets aside both competing narratives, and rather than drawing a line between Jews and Arabs it seeks to understand its institutionalization as a central ruling principle of the Jewish state. It

does so by presenting the disaster imposed on the Palestinians as a *catastrophe* (from a civil perspective), and by presenting it not as the outcome of a war that preceded the creation of the Israeli regime, but as a component and as a product of that regime.

Photographic documents

The photographs in this book were preserved in archives for more than six decades, accompanied by barely a line or two of captions. Not only are these few words inadequate to describe what they show, they usually also serve to make what appears in them look like something else. The initial encounter with the photographs was, therefore, like finding orphaned documents that conceal more than they reveal. But from the moment I began treating the photographs as historical documents, and reading them in conjunction with other documents that could shed light on their contents, I found they held a tremendous amount of information and was amazed by the unexpected questions I was able to raise in their presence. Nevertheless, I was sometimes disturbed by the fact that after working for a few days with one or two photographs, and finally succeeding in reconstructing what I was initially unable to read in them, I felt my efforts didn't lead to an account substantially different from that which an honest chronicler would have attached before filing them away. It was not due to chance, however, that such accounts or traces of that chronicler were absent from the photographs, nor would they have been mere additions to them. They were, rather, essential aspects of the photographic event – as opposed to the event photographed – which is the subject of this book. The absence of such an account would therefore be part of what concerns me when reading these photographs, and distinguishes it, of course, from what that chronicler could, hypothetically, have documented, but didn't. Encountering photographs taken in a disaster zone like Palestine at the end of the 1940s, that had been preserved by a regime which had made great efforts to erase the disaster's traces and train citizens not to see it as such, forced me to broaden the range of

---

[5]   For additional discussion of constituent violence and law-preserving violence see Benjamin, 1999. In an article I wrote for a conference on the return of the refugees organized by Zochrot in Tel Aviv (2007), I characterized three groups subject to violence whose object is to maintain the Israeli regime: 1. **Non-citizens – both non-ruled (residents of the refugee camps outside of Israel) and ruled (under occupation since 1967)**. The state has waged, and continues to wage, a violent, wild, uncompromising struggle against the non-citizens' violent and non-violent resistance to a regime responsible for turning them into refugees. 2. **Non-Jewish citizens**, against whom the regime wages what is primarily an ideological struggle, including, from time to time, moderate,

measured and relatively cautious use of force. 3. **Jewish citizens**, against whom the struggle is also primarily ideological, focusing on mobilizing the citizenry to maintain the reality of a regime in which anyone not a member of the political entity that legitimates it is neither taken into consideration nor counted. The struggle includes broad nationalization of the various components of the state apparatus (both ideological and repressive), as well as of the Jewish citizens, nationalization intended to enable maximum mobilization of the Jewish population to strengthen the regime. For a more comprehensive discussion of this use of violence see Azoulay, *Sedek*, Zochrot.

historiographic tools for reading the past and add one that I call "civil imagination." In a situation where the political regime does everything possible to conceal the disaster it causes and to prevent its subjects from recognizing the disaster for what it is, civil imagination becomes a necessary tool. Without civil imagination it is impossible to reconstruct the reality of the disaster – a reality in which those who caused it came face to face with those who were its victims. Civil imagination rejects the nationalist narratives and insists on reconstructing from within the photograph the photographic event itself and asks questions about the situation in which the photograph was taken, about what the photograph might have shown had it been taken at a different place from a different angle, at a different time, thereby helping to understand why we have photographs from particular places but not from others, or what is the significance of the fact that we possess no photographs from places where we know there were cameras, and what could have been in the photographs that we don't possess.

Insistence on reconstructing the past so as to permit the emergence of a civil gaze from an encounter with photographs, most of which portray events that have remained silenced in archives, is subject to errors. Such errors offer, in my view, an invitation to a discussion involving anyone willing to risk participating in designing and developing a civil consciousness in the face of a past which seems no longer present in the world created by the nation state, to join in a conversation, add information or correct erroneous details. In a situation in which such photographs usually serve only the national discourse whose lineaments are defined by external justifications of the horrors captured in the photos, such risk-taking is necessary for the development of a new language and a conversation about the past and the future in which all who were involved participate, those responsible for the atrocities that occurred and those who were their immediate victims.

The book includes many unfamiliar photographs. Still, it would be wrong to see them as "revelations," for that would presuppose that the traces of the catastrophe were hidden and only recently revealed. Each photograph was selected because of the particular situation it records, as well as for its potential as a historical document testifying both to the catastrophe and to its transformation into non-catastrophe in the eyes of Israeli Jews. None of the photographs should surprise Israeli spectators – that is, they can't say, "We've never seen anything like this." We've certainly seen "something like this" – "we" Jewish Israeli citizens. We've seen the remains of

Arab villages on our streets as well as in photographs. We've referred to these remains in the names of the localities we live in. We've come across them as part of the urban fabric in which they've been absorbed almost unquestioningly, and in landscapes where they've appeared as ancient ruins ("khirbot"). We've mentioned the names of the refugee camps to which the Palestinians were expelled. We've used maps from which entire human landscapes have been erased. Some of us can still remember repeating as children the names of the "military operations" during which those landscapes were transformed. We've been able to see ourselves in the pages of those photographic albums documenting how the country was built – members of youth movements clearing stones from "abandoned" villages; pioneers celebrating "settling on the land" while moving into Arab houses situated against a backdrop of Arab landscapes.

Nor were images of Palestinian refugees strange to Israeli spectators.[6] In recent years, as part of the effort to preserve the history of photography in Israel, a number of Israeli museum exhibitions have included a fine selection of photographs in which various aspects of the nakba are visible. They weren't called by name, nor was any effort made to consider the significance of their presence there. Such disregard allowed many spectators to look at these photographs without noticing the catastrophe, or, at best, to view it as a "*catastrophe from their point of view*," as a marginal episode in the story of how the state was built. Nevertheless, the word itself – nakba – no longer sounds so strange in Hebrew, even if many areas of public discourse still avoid using it.

The term "nakba"

"Nakba?", Israelis would still ask today. At best, the answer they will hear will be – "Yes, that's how the Palestinians refer to what happened to them in '48."[7] The word, when it appears in Hebrew, usually does so imprisoned in quotation marks. "We" have "our" story; now the time has come to tell "their" story, as "they" see it. The word that came relatively late into Hebrew provided a heading for "their" story, even though that word existed from the moment that "our" story was created. Both these stories, entwined as distinct,

---

[6]   Most of the albums published to commemorate each decade since the establishment of the state of Israel include one or two photographs of refugees accompanied by a caption that turns them into a natural and necessary component of "building the country," as in the following caption: "Refugees – the war's terrible cost – on the road out of Ramle" (Carmi, 1997).

[7]   The first time the term "nakba" was used to describe the Palestinian disaster was by Constantine Zurayk (1956). I'd like to thank Sami Abushehada for the reference.

parallel, competing tales, are the product of the same Jewish state apparatus that operated systematically to create the line dividing Jews from Arabs and establish it as an unalterable, objective reality. This line also structured the violent events that accompanied the establishment of the state, presenting them as a tale of warfare between two sides that shared the same territory and were condemned to part.

The Arabic term "nakba," which has now become part of the Hebrew lexicon, is no longer only a concern of an organization such as *Zochrot* or a subject for academic research.[8] Even were it less prominent in public discourse, its incorporation into Hebrew has, like a foreigner refusing to be naturalized, led to a growing number of points of friction between the narrative framework it implies and the way in which those exposed to its remains during the past decade have experienced them.

The draft legislation proposed in the Knesset in the spring of 2009, the point of which was to deny funding to Israeli organizations that decided to commemorate the nakba, ended the term's relative absence from Jewish public discourse. This draft legislation was intended to re-inter the voices of the catastrophe which Hebrew, whose mendacity became second nature, swallowed up. I tried to read the photographs by narrating the photographic event in writing. I erased and rewrote each sentence dozens of times, until I was able to approximate a civil voice, a language that could describe anew what appears as a catastrophe, not only from the point of view of those who were its explicit victims but as an undeniable catastrophe from any point of view. As soon as the content of the photograph became capable of expression in Hebrew, the traces of the effort required to come to terms with it disappeared, and now nothing can again erase the blatant presence of the catastrophe, of its unbearable nature.

The Partition Plan, recognition of the nation-state and non-recognition of the catastrophe

Various historical reasons led to the adoption of this account of unavoidable war by international bodies, including those who were to have acted as unbiased "external mediators." The criticisms that were raised as part of the "Jewish–Arab conflict" against the mediators, others involved, the Mandatory Government, or UN personnel were incorporated symmetrically within the discourse as part of those two competing stories, in a manner that made it impossible to see what lay in the balance: creating the Jewish state machinery. The photographs included in

the chapter entitled "Architecture of Dispossession" portray the massive, purposeful destruction of Haifa's old city, the vestiges of the Dayr Yasin massacre and the establishment of Giv'at Sha'ul B a few months later on the ruins of the village that had not yet been erased. They serve witness to the determination of the nation-state machinery to destroy completely any possibility of creating a binational civil society. Photographs included in three other chapters – "Military Governmentality," "Creating a Jewish political body and deporting the country's Arab residents," "Borders, strategies of uprooting and preventing return" – show the degree to which this effort, most of which was carried out by military means, reflected a systematic policy.

While the nakba, "*catastrophe from their point of view*," has already become a research topic, the civil catastrophe – the destruction of the mixed society that existed in Palestine – has not yet been studied. Erasing the traces of this catastrophe, even more than erasing the nakba's traces, is the condition for naturalizing the Jewish–Israeli regime and eliminating the traces of the constituent violence that enabled its creation. In order for this catastrophe to appear as a *catastrophe*, it must be freed from its status as *their* catastrophe or *catastrophe from their point of view*. This can be done only by historicizing the dividing line between the "two sides," not letting it define *a priori* one's point of view. The appearance of the civil catastrophe as a *catastrophe*, is a pre-condition for the rehabilitation of the destroyed civil society. The book's visual genealogy of the formation of the Israeli regime and the "*catastrophe from their point of view*," is an initial attempt to do so.

The United Nations partition decision of 29 November 1947 was adopted in complete opposition to the desires of at least 70 percent of the country's Arab inhabitants. A not-insignificant number of Jews also opposed the decision.[9] From the moment that

---

[9]   No study exists that examines their scope and nature. But their traces remain in the memories of people who were alive then, and are beginning to be the subject of research. See Kamen, 1987, Kamen, 1988, and Ophir, 1999, or Zachary Lockman's (1996) book describing relations between Jews and Arabs working in Haifa in the period prior to their deterioration that began shortly after the Partition Plan was announced. Even if they don't provide an adequate idea of the extent of objections to the Partition Plan, which among Jews were undoubtedly greater than were the objections to establishing the state, they allow a glimpse into the controversy, traces of which have been almost completely erased, and blur the presumably clear division between Arabs and Jews. See an unpublished lecture by Eitan Bronstein (2006) discussing statements and actions by Jews who explicitly opposed the obligatory division between Arabs and Jews imposed by the state's institutions, or who did so by not accepting their particular political ideology. See also Yahav, 2009, and Tomer Gardi's lecture on Jewish "draft dodgers" in Tel Aviv in 1948, presented in the Zochrot Gallery as part of the symposia held in connection with the symposium "Constituent Violence" and included in his forthcoming book (Gardi, 2011). See also photographic references to the issue in Kabha and Raz, 2008 and Sela, 2001.

---

[8]   On the use of the "nakba" term in Hebrew see Musih, 2011.

the UN decided, the Zionist leadership counted the country's inhabitants along to the line dividing Jews from Arabs. The position of the Zionist leadership in support of partition and its unconditional justification of using violence to establish the Jewish regime were presented as the Jewish position. Ultra-orthodox Jews, communists, pacifists and those who supported the creation of civil society had no place in the public discourse, and almost no information is available about their struggle. This erasure is also the outcome of the action of the state apparatus as it took over public discourse, the discourse of female and male citizens, and it organized the totality of relationships among the country's inhabitants according to the destructive national and ethnic division between Jews and Arabs.

The Arabs who lived in Palestine for hundreds of years, occupying more than 90 percent of the territory, opposed from the outset the plan to partition their land, and refused to cooperate with the UN bodies that prepared it. The Partition Plan, therefore, was designed by the UN and the Zionist leadership, which thereby gained recognition as the leadership of the state-in-formation.[10] The country's Arab inhabitants had little influence, given the line-up of forces: A-(Jewish)-state-in-formation and an organization of states (the UN) supporting it.[11] The new diplomatic, military and political map that was created transformed them into "stateless persons."[12] The UN decision was a crucial moment in transforming the Arabs from inhabitants of their country into "stateless persons," even before they became literally refugees. The state that came into being in their land did not want them, nor was there any other state which did. The reason and rationale behind the opposition of the majority of the country's inhabitants to the partition plan received almost no attention. In a situation where there was room for only two competing stories, which were presented as if they both sprang from the same initial conditions, their logic was understood as an example of "irrational policy" or as "their story." The Palestinians were presented – and are still presented – as having

missed the opportunity that had been "given to them," as having made a continuous series of errors – mass flight, hostile action, cooperating with the attack by Arab states.[13] The Jews, on the other hand, were presented as seizing the opportunity offered and knowing how to make the most of it.

This book is based primarily on official Israeli state archives.[14] Its approach draws upon the ontological conception of photography which I have developed elsewhere.[15] According to this view, the photograph contains much more information than that intended by those who were involved in its creation, preservation and dissemination – photographers, soldiers, archive personnel, military and political leaders, and other participants in the various apparatuses of rule. Photographs are valuable documents through which the photographic event that left traces in them can be restored. But, of course, the photograph alone is insufficient to reveal the treasures it contains. I could not have read any of the photographs in this book in the absence of other visual and textual sources external to them. These included the important studies of the nakba and the 1948 war by historians old and new, eyewitness accounts, diaries, memoirs, newspapers from the period, minutes and memoranda. These materials often also showed the extent to which photographs are accessible under conditions of constituent violence – photographs containing traces of this violence are accessible, although what they contain might remain unacknowledged for a long time, while it is difficult to find visual evidence of non-constituent violence, violence that didn't become part of the regime, of its law. Thus, for example, although historians agree today that during the period the book documents there were at least twenty massacres of Arabs by Jews, I was not able to find even one photograph of a massacre.[16] The taking of life, therefore, had not become, in and of itself, an element of the regime.[17] But constitutionally-legalized violence – such as house destruction, looting,

[10]   This argument is based on the analysis by Deleuze and Guattri (1980) of the struggle between state institutions and nomadic society, in particular the chapter "Nomadology" in their book.

[11]   On the UN see Mazower, 2010. On the subordination of the human rights discourse to the logic of the sovereign state see Osiatynski, 2009.

[12]   This is the only appropriate use of the combination "stateless person" – a status which has been created by a particular state, rather than as a characteristic of a population, as the Palestinians in the occupied territories are commonly referred to. On the creation of stateless persons, see Arendt, 1968. On the creation of the "bare life," see Butler and Spivak, 2007, and on the category of non-citizens as an alternative to the category of stateless persons in connection with Palestinians in the occupied territories, see Azoulay, 2008a.

[13]   See Khalidi, 2006.

[14]   The book also contains a number of photographs by Ali Zaarour, thanks to the generosity of his son, Zaki Zaarour, and from the Associated Press.

[15]   For the ontological conception of photography, see Azoulay, 2008a, and Azoulay, 2011. A similar approach guided my work on the "Act of State" exhibition, Azoulay, 2008c.

[16]   For a discussion of massacres, see Morris, 2003, Yahav, 2002, and Pappe, 2006.

[17]   At least, not until the 1967 occupation. With the creation of an additional regime within the Israeli regime – an occupation regime – killing people gradually became a part of it. For more about two-regimes-in-one see Azoulay and Ophir, 2011. On targeted assassinations, see Weizman, 2007.

expropriation, dispossession and expulsion – was often photographed by agents of the state. Those acts were carried out under state auspices, under another name – evacuation, not expulsion; flight, not deportation; distribution of property, not looting; fair allocation, not dispossession. The laundered language made it possible for these activities to be immortalized in photographs that remained accessible to the public.

The discourse that did not acknowledge the disaster

During the years covered by this book (1947–50) both the catastrophe and its consequences were relatively visible to the public. Buses and trucks loaded with refugees who had been expelled from their homes drove along the country's roads in full view of its Jewish inhabitants (who sometimes even took pity on the expellees and gave them water to drink). The photographs bear traces of those Jewish observers and of the fact that everything was done openly. But despite this visibility, the catastrophe didn't appear as a catastrophe. The discourse did not acknowledge the disaster and made impossible referencing the series of violent incidents as one catastrophic event. The terms in which it was described, that sound like those we associate today with the darkest of regimes, didn't send chills down the spines of those who used them, as they would have had they felt that a catastrophe had occurred. It was only a few years later that these terms began to sound like evidence of a crime, and they were gradually replaced by others. In recent years, with the development of what has been called post-Zionist historiography, when these terms of discourse reappeared, they made the deniers (those who refused to admit that the descriptions were accurate accounts of what actually occurred) uncomfortable, as well as those who were outraged (those who felt a moral, political or civil obligation to reconstruct the story of the catastrophe). Terms like "cleansing" or "ghetto," for example, were widespread at the end of the 1940s, but someone speaking them today in Hebrew would sound as if she were being deliberately provocative.[18]

The nakba did, in fact, leave many public traces in Israel. Some remained unintentionally or inexplicably, such as demolitions whose rubble had not been completely cleared, villages and buildings that were not totally erased. But many of the

remnants were intentional, deliberate, the result of pride, administrative procedures, planning, need, preservation, policy, or image-making. The series, "Architecture of Dispossession," shows how those who carried out the nakba tried from the outset to restage some of its traces incompletely, devoid of context. They sought to incorporate these traces in the new language and ways of life in Palestine to eliminate their disturbing presence and erase the memory of the unitary, coherent world that had been destroyed. The expulsion of 750,000 Palestinian men and women from the country in which the state of Israel was established, and the subordination of those who remained to military government for 18 years, removed from the public arena those for whom those traces were from the outset both the remnants of catastrophe and part of the ongoing presence of the catastrophe.

Those who created the Palestinian catastrophe turned it into an Israeli public holiday, one celebrating the establishment of the state of Israel. The successful completion of operations "evacuating" the Arab population were occasions for the military or political leadership to raise a toast; blowing up a village was an opportunity for a photograph. Traces of the catastrophe, where no catastrophe remained, were thus merged with the state's festive celebration. The festivities were the culmination of "our" narrative, and "*catastrophe from their point of view*" was no more than a part of "their" story, the result of their error, their missed opportunity, their weakness or their abandonment by the Arab states. For decades, the Palestinian catastrophe remained "*catastrophe from their point of view,*" and thus a perpetuation of the catastrophe. Its traces remained devoid of context, unconnected to any discourse that could have made them manifest, used them to show the injustice, base on them a claim for redress and for compensating the victims. It was a catastrophe that was absent from the many traces that it left behind. A catastrophe that left no trace of catastrophe, as if the shadow cast by a man had been a shadow of a dog. These present-but-absent traces of the catastrophe were incorporated into forms of speech, landscapes, urban fabrics, political arguments, lesson plans, youth movement training programs, the structures of moral indecisiveness and historical periodization.

The term "nakba" provided a name for what had previously been present naturally, sometimes even with disturbing intimacy, in the language, the bodies, the homes and life spaces of the Israeli women and men. The nakba, which was for the Palestinians the name of the catastrophe that befell them, began

---

18   For example, the 1950 account (Lazar, 1950) of the capture of Jaffa, describes without a second thought what took place there as "cleansing." Ilan Pappe's book (2006), published in English and not yet translated into Hebrew, reads like a deliberate provocation rather than a description of the phenomenon he's addressing.

to be seen by a relatively small number of Israeli Jews as the name of a disaster which until then had no name, whose outline they had failed to recognize, and now began to appear crystal clear before their eyes. This misrecognition of the ruins left behind by colonial regimes, is called by Ann Stoler "colonial aphasia": "Aphasia is rather a dismembering, a difficulty speaking, a difficulty generating a vocabulary that associates appropriate words and concepts to appropriate things. Aphasia in its many forms describes a difficulty retrieving an available vocabulary, and most importantly, a difficulty comprehending what is spoken."[19] Bringing the term "nakba" into Hebrew not only provides a new narrative framework; it also becomes a necessary, if not sufficient, condition for recognizing these deficiencies of sight and speech. In that sense, the incorporation of the term "nakba" into Hebrew, thanks primarily to *Zochrot*, represents a milestone in the history of the catastrophe. It signifies the initial appearance of the Palestinian catastrophe as one that is *not* simply "*catastrophe from their point of view.*"

The dividing line between Jews and Arabs, that sets limits on what can be seen and what can make sense, affected the use of the term "nakba" in Hebrew. The nakba was "theirs", and a *différend*[20] – a disagreement unbridgeable in current discourse – between "ours" and "theirs" was established. This book proposes to look beyond the horizon set by this *différend* between Jews and Arabs. Rather than viewing the catastrophe from within the *différend*, or accepting the *différend* as if it had been imposed by fate, as if we had to choose between the points of view provided by the competing stories of two sides or two nations fated to fight each other unto death, it is now possible to consider this *différend* itself as part of the Palestinian catastrophe, as its continuation. Perhaps, for the first time since the term nakba came into Hebrew, it is now possible to recognize the existence of another, civil *différend* with regard to the nakba, not one between Jews and Arabs, but between those who see the disaster that befell the Palestinians as a *catastrophe* (from every conceivable civil and universal perspective), and those who see no catastrophe or, at best, see "*catastrophe from their point of view.*" The civil perspective makes it possible to understand colonial aphasia as a civil malfunction.

Civil malfunction

A civil malfunction is not an individual characteristic, the outcome of a damaged personality or moral shortcoming of the persons who suffer from it. A civil malfunction is an effect of being governed differentially with others in an entirely different way. A civil malfunction is created when the differences in the ways various groups are being governed produce a regime-made disaster that becomes a structural feature of the regime.[21] A civil malfunction is the way citizens relate to the regime-made disaster in whose continuing reproduction and preservation they participate. It is a structural malfunction characterizing the contradiction between formal civil equality and the differential way of being governed instilled in the governed population through various mechanisms of socialization and control, one that organizes and limits their visual field, restricts what they can say before they even open their mouths, and specifies which behaviors are possible. A civil malfunction refers to the manner in which citizens perceive and conduct their relations with other segments of the governed population. A civil malfunction is an effect of the regime and its governmental apparatus; the citizens participate – both consciously and unconsciously, willingly or unwillingly – in its formation and are formed by it. Civil malfunction is a structural, not a personal, failure, which citizens living under a particular regime are unable to avoid. They have no other way of paying taxes even if they object to the state increasing its financial reserves by expropriating the property of others; they can't refrain from traveling even though the roads they use have been built on land taken from others; they can't stop using the names of the places in which they live merely because they echo the names of places that have been destroyed; they can't help marveling at the architecture or the groves and orchards that have been preserved; even had they wished to redress some of the injustice and sell their homes to refugees they can't afford to do so, nor are the refugees permitted to return. But they may deal with this malfunction a little differently, insist on making its presence visible, confront others with its existence, object to it sometimes or always, explicitly, even intentionally, and make an effort to free themselves, particularly in situations in which they become accomplices to the crime. But no matter how hard individuals try to overcome this civil malfunction, full release is impossible without changing the regime responsible for it.

The photographic series, "Socialization to the State and the Mechanisms of Subordination," displays

[19]   Stoler, 2009.

[20]   Lyotard (1982) identifies various levels of discourse in which the différend appears. All are characterized by the absence of a legal instance accessible to both parties where a claim by one of them can be heard.

[21]   On the term "regime-made disaster" see Azoulay, forthcoming.

a visual genealogy of the creation of this malfunction under the auspices of state institutions. It reconstructs various situations in which traces of the fact that Jews and Arabs were being governed differentially, as well as of the creation of a rigid pattern of power relations between those Jews and Arabs (and not only between state institutions and those governed) can be discerned. Vocational training, job placement, the census, welfare benefits, mug shots, currency, ID cards, elections, festivals – all provided opportunities to make those governed aware of the differences among them, something to be accepted unthinkingly, part of a regime whose arrangements were seen as natural. The Arabs who remained were ruled differently and were almost completely excluded from the ruling circles which, prior to the end of the British Mandate, had not been closed to them, but were now exclusively in Jewish hands which were directly and indirectly responsible for the disaster that befell them. Most of them were under military government (until 1966) and their participation in the ruling circles as citizens possessing equal rights was expressed primarily through the right to vote, the act of casting a ballot. They were ruled differently with respect to everything that took place outside the voting booth, including the opportunity to be exposed to an electoral campaign that would allow them to vote after weighing the arguments presented by the competing parties.

A catastrophe from "their" point of view

The distinction between Israeli citizens who viewed the Palestinians' disaster as an actual catastrophe, in every sense, and those who see it as "*catastrophe from their point of view*," or who don't view it as a catastrophe at all, overlaps to a great degree, though not completely, the division between Arabs and Jews. The disaster, although not its traces, was quickly erased from the consciousness of Israeli Jews. Gradually, with the passage of time, more Jews became aware of it, some after 40, 50 or even 60 years of living alongside Arabs. Awareness of the catastrophe was a constitutive component of Palestinian consciousness, but reconstructing the *différend* relating to the catastrophe indicates that as a condition for Arabs who had not been expelled and had become a minority in their land, to become citizens they had to relinquish any attempt to preserve traces of the catastrophe or present it as the meaning of the traces that did remain. This was required of them both explicitly and implicitly through various practices in which they could not avoid participating, willingly or unwillingly. They were forced to sign documents in which they relinquished the right to present future claims; they had to participate in

hunting down "infiltrators" – refugees who had been expelled and attempted to return to their homes; they were required to buy produce that had been harvested from fields which had been stolen from them; they were forced to live in camps as internal refugees while Jews moved into their homes; they were employed planting forests "to reclaim the wasteland;" they were offered social services by a welfare state that had transformed them into the needy; they could democratically elect as their representatives the people who had destroyed their world and who expected them to dance at Independence Day celebrations in the forests that had been planted on the ruins of their villages. Their socialization to the state through such practices included denying the *différend* that existed between them and the Israeli Jews regarding recognition of the catastrophe.

So, despite the catastrophe that befell them, the Palestinians were expected to behave as if nothing had occurred, as if, at worst, it was "*catastrophe from their [the expelled Palestinians] point of view.*" There were, among the Jews, some individuals and groups who immediately realized that what had happened to the Palestinians *was in fact a catastrophe*, but they had to make a special effort to demonstrate this, an effort that required them to "brush history against the grain." No systematic account has yet been written about the various joint Jewish–Arab commercial, economic, social, cultural and civic ventures that were destroyed just before the establishment of the state and during its early years in order to restructure relations along the rigid divide between Jews and Arabs, between the governed and the non-governed, between citizens and citizens-under-military-rule. But the absence of an historical account does not mean that we can assume that all Jews joined in denying the Palestinian catastrophe. Such an assumption, which is unfounded, recapitulates the division between Jews and Arabs, presents the image of the disaster that befell the Palestinians as "*catastrophe from their point of view,*" and makes permanent the civil malfunction that the catastrophe has imposed upon those who brought it about and upon their descendants. Precisely because it rejects this assumption, the book proposes a way of thinking in civil terms about a place that today, under the existing political regime, appears hopeless, one where nothing can be promised, where it is impossible to dream of tomorrow.

Intangible cultural properties

Many tangible Palestinian cultural properties in what became the State of Israel were destroyed. Most of the beautiful Palestinian villages (some of them can still be seen in photographs), had been blown up, destroyed, wiped off the face of the earth. In a "state of all its citizens," this tremendous loss might not be completely irreversible. The architectural structures are lost, but what the Japanese preservation law terms "intangible cultural properties" still exist and can be restored in practice.

This distinction between the tangible and the intangible in relation to cultural properties, designates as worthy of preservation not only objects but also special skills: what is called "living treasure." Structures, no matter how unique, can always be rebuilt, their architectural design and construction materials recreated – if the skills required to rebuild them still exist. Japanese preservation efforts are, therefore, devoted also to transmitting the construction expertise used to erect the buildings that were destroyed. The Japanese might demolish in order to rebuild; thus the skills are preserved. In Israel, where destruction is already a *fait accompli*, and where most of the skills and techniques can be found today only among the refugees – the living keepers of this knowledge – the adoption of this approach to preservation might mark the beginning of a process of reparation and recompense for the refugees' loss of their place in their world. Not from the perspective of restoring lost physical objects but from that of restoring the conditions for renewing a space where the promise of a viable future might be renewed for the entire governed population.

The passage of time has made some buildings and groups of buildings worthy of preservation. These may be individual structures or entire villages. The past can't be restored. Nor can the villages be brought back as they once were. We can only demand a different kind of participation and cooperation across space and time. Cooperation and participation not only in the present, using what exists, that which violence has created, but also with the past, or at least by presenting the past in order to create the possibility of a different kind of participation and cooperation in the future. The Palestinian multi-layered presence which was violently erased, should be restored – refugees, language, homes, mosques, churches, olive presses, enterprises, partnerships, urban fabric. Not a nostalgic, impossible return that restores everything to its original location, but returning a former rich presence to today's uni-dimensional national landscape. Human skills, which built the shared world in which we necessarily live, are never simply technical skills. Those that are needed even more, though some may disappear and others be replaced, are often those relating to the manner in which people become citizens, find their

place in the world and develop ways of cooperating with each other. Many of the refugees who were dispersed in all directions are still alive. They have preserved the knowledge and skills required to recreate many of the Palestinian architectural styles, to situate them as facts in the Judaized space whose continued development will have to take them into consideration. This could be still another claim – one of many to be submitted to history's tribunal, a joint civil action by Palestinians, refugees, their descendants and Israelis of Jewish descent who can't conceive of continuing to live in Israel without rectifying the crime their parents committed.

In this book I tried not only to assemble a collection of photographs but to create an archive, a new "surface of appearance" in Michel Foucault's words, through which new discourse, a civil discourse, can emerge. This is neither an Israeli archive nor a Palestinian one, but a civil photographic archive that enables us to account for the whole governed population – Jews and Arabs – as parties to the violence that transformed their relations and imprinted their lives ever since. Narrating the past through such an archive, we can recognize, imagine or invent the unavoidable seeds of a future, a possible future where forgiveness can be asked as an invitation to restore together a universal threshold of what is unbearable, of what should not be done, what should not be violated.

ACKNOWLEDGEMENTS

I was born in the early 1960s, and for years took for granted the existence of the state of Israel. My political consciousness was formed by the 1967 occupation, the injustices it led to and the urgent need to reflect on them. As a young leftist, I was raised to believe that 1948 was a distant disaster, irreversible and less acute than the endless injustices that resulted from the 1967 occupation. Years of research on citizenship – its abuses and potentialities – and on photography made it clear that the occupation was part of the Israeli political regime, and that reconstructing its schema should start in 1948. Writing *This Regime Which Is Not One – Democracy and Occupation Between the Sea and The River* (1967–) with Adi Ophir, and creating the archive-exhibition entitled "Act of State 1967–2007," were important steps in creating the civil language needed to go beyond the common assumption about the irreversibility of 1948, which is a passive manifestation of what I call "civil malfunction." I sought a way to think of the nakba in relation to a political body which is composed of the entire governed population, the emergence of national citizenship and the renewal of processes of becoming a citizen in a way that forms a perspective from which the claim for a regime change in Israel/Palestine is justified. The English version of this book, bears traces of the passionate dialogue with Adi on forgiving, being forgiven, and about ways of restoring together the threshold of the unbearable out of which imagining a common future becomes possible again. Significant was the contribution of Zochrot's ongoing activities, by providing in recent years an increasing amount of information about the nakba's public presence in Israeli space, and above all, the determination of Eitan Bronstein and Norma Musih to involve me in the important enterprise they established – Zochrot – and my continuing discussions with them both.

This book would not have been possible without Hadas Snir's efforts to locate hundreds of photographs in the archives of institutions as well as those of individuals, and without her excellent investigatory work. Special thanks are also due to Charles S. Kamen for the English translation, Shir Hever for introducing me to Pluto Press, and Roger van Zwanenberg for welcoming me and patiently caring for this book and to Zaki Zaarour for lending photographs to the book. These photographs are the tip of an iceberg of what would have been visible had the archives of Palestinian photographers active in the country during those crucial years not been damaged.

Sami Abu Shehada, Waji Atallah, Noga Kedman, Ronnie Ellenblum, Umar Ighbarieh, Yoni Eshpar, Eyal Sagi Bizawi, Muhammad Bishar, Hillel Cohen, Tomer Gardi, Israel Gershuni, Esther Goldenberg, Fahri Jdai, Raneen Jeries, Dr. Mustafa Kabha, Walid Karkabi, Joni Mansur, Gabi 'Abed, Ilan Pappe, Neta Pasternak, Dalia Karpel, Guy Raz, Sharon Rotbard, Michael Sfard, Oren Yiftachel and Zochrot's members helped Hadas Snir and me to locate, interpret, find information and translate. We thank them all. I used various books, articles and internet sites (see Bibliography) to help me with writing the captions.

Photographers: Yehuda Eisenstark, David Eldan, Werner Braun, Teddy Brauner, Paul Goldman, Ali Zaarour, Rudolf Jonas, Fritz Cohen, Hugo Mendelson, Jim Pringle, Frank, Fred Chesnik, Zoltan Kluger, Beno Rothenberg.

Photographs were provided by: the Israel Government Press Office, the Israel State Archive, the Central Zionist Archive, the IDF and Defense Archive, the JNF Photographic Archive, the Palmach Museum photographic collection, the Haganah Archive, the Golani Museum Archive, Associated Press, Photo Art Israel, Zaki Zaarour, Nahada Zahara, AFSC Archive, Bitmunah Lab, Palestine Remembered Internet website, Meron Perach, Al Rabta/The Jaffa Arabs Association, The Monastery and School of "Jesus Adolescent" (Don Bosco) Nazareth, Jabotinsky House Archive.

BIBLIOGRAPHY

Abu-Sitta, Salman H, 2004. *Atlas of Palestine 1948*, London, Palestine Land Society.

al-Tall, Abdallah, 1960. *Memoirs*, IDF (in Hebrew).

al-Wali, Mustafa, 2001. "The Tantura Massacre, 22–23 May 1948," eyewitness testimonies, *Journal of Palestine Studies* 30(3) (Spring), 5–18.

Amir, Yisrael, 1998. *On Unpaved Roads*, Ministry of Defense, Tel Aviv.

Arendt, Hannah, 1968. "The Decline of the Nation-state and the End of the Rights of Mman," *Imperialism*, Harvest/HBJ.

Azoulay, Ariella, 2008a. *The Civil Contract of Photography*, Zone Books.

Azoulay, Ariella, 2008b. "The Governed Must be Defended: Toward a Civil Political Agreement," *Sedek* (special translated issue), Zochrot.

Azoulay, Ariella, 2008c. *Act of State – A Photographic History of the Occupation 1967–2007*, Etgar Publishers (in Hebrew) (Bruno Mondadori in Italian).

Azoulay, Ariella, 2011. *Civil Imagination: Political Ontology of Photography*, Verso.

Azoulay, Ariella, forthcoming. "Regime-made Disaster," in Yates McKee and Meg McLagan (eds.), *The Visual Cultures of Nongovernmental Politics*, Zone Books.

Azoulay, Ariella, and Ophir, Adi, 2011. *This Regime which is Not One – Democracy and Occupation between the Sea and the River (1967–)*, Stanford University Press.

Benjamin, Walter, 1999. "Critique of Violence," *Selected Writings Volume 1 – 1913–1926*, The Belknap Press of Harvard University Press.

Benvenisti, Meron, 2002. *Sacred Landscape: The Buried History of the Holy Land since 1948*, University of California Press.

Benziman, Uzi, and Mansour, Atallah, 1992. *Subtenants* (in Hebrew), Keter Publishing House.

Broyer, Moshe, 1988. *Geopolitical Aspects of Israel's Borders, Past, Present and Future*, Tel Aviv, Yavne Publishers.

Bernard, Joseph, 1948. *British Rule in Palestine*, Washington, DC: Public Affairs Press.

Bronstein, Eitan, 2006. "Local Jewish resistance to the Palestinian nakba," (www.nakbainhebrew.org/index.php?id=629) (unpublished lecture in Hebrew).

Butler, Judith and Gayatri Chakravorty Spivak, 2007. *Who Sings the Nation State*, Seagull.

Carmel, Moshe, 1949. *The Northern Campaigns*, Tel Aviv, Ma'arachot Publishers.

Carmi, Boris, 1997. *A Country in a Cradle*, Makhbarot LeSifrut (in Hebrew).

Cohen, Eitan, 2006. *Beer Sheva: Ha-ir Ha-Revi'it*, Karmel.

Cohen, Hillel, 2000. *The Present Absentees: Palestinian Refugees in Israel Since 1948* (in Hebrew, Arabic), Center for the Study of Arab Society in Israel.

Deleuze, G., and Guattari, F., 1980. *Mille plateaux*, Minuit.

Elon, Amos, 2010. *The Israelis – Founders and Sons*, Faber and Faber.

The first Israeli Knesset. Album, Ma'ariv.

Eran, Yitzhak, 1994. *The Scouts*, Tel Aviv: Ma'arachot Publishers.

Feldstein, Ariel L., 2009. "Did it Really Hang on One Vote? The Meeting of People's Administration on the Eve of the Establishment of the State of Israel," *Democratic Culture* 12, 59–72 (in Hebrew).

Forman, G., 2006. "Military Rule, Political Manipulation, and Jewish Settlement: Israeli Mechanisms for Controlling Nazareth in the 1950s," *Journal of Israeli History* 25(2), 335–359.

Gallagher, Nancy Elizabeth, 2007. *Quakers in the Israeli-Palestinian Conflict: The Dilemmas of NGO Humanitarian Activism*, American University in Cairo Press.

Gardi, Tomer, 2011. *Paper, Stone*, Hakibutz Hameuchad .

Gelber, Yoav, 1992. *Shorshey Ha-Havatselet* [The Roots of the Lili: The Intelligence in the Yishuv 1918–1947], Ministry of Defense Press (in Hebrew).

Gelber, Yoav, 2004. *Komemiyut Ve-Nakbah* (in Hebrew), Dvir, Zemorah Bitan, Kineret.

Golan, Arnon, 1992. "The Transfer of Abandoned Rural Arab Lands to Jews During Israel's War of Independence," *Cathedra*, 63, 122–154 (in Hebrew).

Golan, Arnon, 2001. *Wartime Spatial Changes: Former Arab Territories Within the State of Israel – 1948–1950*, Sde Boker, The Ben Gurion Heritage Center, Ben Gurion University of the Negev (in Hebrew).

Golan, Arnon, 2001. *Wartime Spatial Changes: Former Arab Territories Within the State of Israel, 1948–1950*, Sde Boker, The Ben Gurion Heritage Center, Ben Gurion University of the Negev (in Hebrew).

Goren, Tamir, 1995. "Administrative Actions to Integrate the Arab Minority into the Haifa Urban community 1948–1950," *Iyunim Bitkumat Israel*, 5, 304–335 (in Hebrew).

Goren, Tamir, 1998. "The Arab Leadership between the British command and the Hagana and the History of Negotiations over the Surrender of the Arabs of Haifa," in Yossi Ben-Artzi (ed.), *Haifa: Local History*, Haifa University Press, Zmora Bitan, pp. 183–214 (in Hebrew).

Goren, Tamir, 2006. *The Fall of Arab Haifa in 1948*, The Ben-Gurion Research Institute for the Study of Israel and Zionism, Ben-Gurion University of the Negev Press, MOD Publishing House, Haganah Historical Archives (in Hebrew).

IDF, 1954. *In the Enemy's Eyes: Three Arab Publications about the War of Independence*: Al-Khatib, Haj Muhammad Nimr, *Min Ath'r al Nakba [After the Catastrophe]*; Al-Sharif, Kamal Isma'il, *The Moslem Brotherhood in the Palestinian Conflict [in Arabic]*; Al-Rusan, Ra'is Mahmoud, "The Sha'ar Ha'gai campaigns", translated by S. Sabag, Israel Defence Forces, Ma'arachot Publishers.

IDF General Staff History Branch, 1964. *History of the War of Independence: The Campaign*, introduction by David Ben-Gurion, Tel Aviv, Ma'arachot Publishers.

Issa, Mahmoud, 1997. "Decoding the Silencing Process in Modern Palestinian Historiography," paper presented to the conference on *Worlds and Visions: Perspectives on the Middle East Today*, University of Århus, Denmark, December 5–7, 1997, www.arts.mcgill.ca/mepp/new_prrn/research/papers/issa_971205.htm.

Jamal, Amal, 2005. "The Palestinian IDPs in Israel and the Predicament of Return: Between Imagining the Impossible and Enabling the Imaginative," in Ann Lesch and Ian Lustick (eds.), *Exile and Return: Predicaments of Palestinians and Jews*, University of Pennsylvania Press, pp. 133–160.

Junod, Dominique D., 1996. *The Imperiled Red Cross and the Palestine-Eretz-Yisrael Conflict, 1945–1952: The Influence of Institutional Concerns on a Humanitarian Operation*, Kegan Paul International.

Jurays, Ṣabri, 1976. *The Arabs in Israel*, Monthly Review Press.

Kabha, Mustafa, and Barzilai, Ronit, 1996. *Refugees in Their Land – The Internal Refugees in Israel 1948–1996*, Givat Haviva (in Hebrew).

Kabha, Mustafa, and Raz, Guy (eds.), 2008. *Remembering a Place: A Photographic History of Wadi 'Ara, 1903–2008*. Umm el-Fahm, Umm el-Fahm Art Gallery, Alsabar (in Hebrew and Arabic).

Kadish, Alon, and Kedar, Benjamin, Z. (eds.), 2004. *War of Independence (Revisited)*, Ministry of Defense.

Kadish, A., Sela, A., and Golan, A., 2000. *The Occupation of Lydda, July 1948*, Israel Ministry of Defense and Hagana Historical Archive (in Hebrew).

Kadman, Noga, 2008. *Erased from Space and Consciousness*, November Books (in Hebrew).

Kamen, Charles S., 1987. "After the Catastrophe I: The Arabs in Israel 1948–1951," *Middle Eastern Studies* 23(4), 453–495.

Kamen, Charles, S., 1988. "After the Catastrophe II: The Arabs in Israel 1948–1951," *Middle Eastern Studies* 24(1), 68–109.

Kletter, Raz, 2006. *Just Past?: The Making of Israeli Archaeology*, Equinox.

Khalidi, Rashid, 2006. *The Iron Cage: The Story of the Palestinian Struggle for Statehood*, Beacon Press.

Khalidi, Walid, 1984. *Before their Diaspora: A Photographic History of the Palestinians, 1876–1948*, Institute for Palestine Studies.

Khalidi, Walid, 1992. *All that Rremains: The Palestinian Villages Occupied and Depopulated by Israel in 1948*, Institute for Palestine Studies.

Koren, Alina, 2008. "Good Intentions: The Policy of the Ministry of Minorities, 14 May 1948 – 1 July 1949," *Cathedra* 127, 113–140 (in Hebrew).

Lazar, Haim, 1950. *The Capture of Jaffa*, Shelach (in Hebrew).

Lesch, Ann Mosely, and Lustick, Ian (eds.), 2005. *Exile and return: Predicaments of Palestinians and Jews*, University of Pennsylvania Press.

Lockman, Zachary, 1996. *Comrades and Enemies – Arab and Jewish Workers in Palestine, 1906–1948*, University of California Press, 1996.

Lustick, Ian, 1980. *Arabs in the Jewish State: Israel's Control of a National Minority*, University of Texas Press.

Lyotard, Jean-François, 1982. *Le différend*, Minuit.

Masalha, Nur, 1992. *Expulsion of the Palestinians: The Concept of "Transfer" in Zionist Political Thought, 1882–1948*, Institute for Palestine Studies.

Masalha, Nur, 2005. *Catastrophe Remembered: Palestine, Israel and the Internal Refugees: Essays in Memory of Edward W. Said (1935–2003)*, Zed Books.

Mazower, Mark, 2010. *No Enchanted Palace*, Princeton University Press.

Milstein, Uri, 1999. *History of Israel's War of Independence: vol. 4: Out of Crisis Came Decision*, University Press of America.

Monterescu, Daniel, and Fabian, Roy, 2003. "The 'Golden Cage': On Gentrification and Globalization in the Luxurious Andromeda Gated Community in Jaffa," *Theory and Criticism* 23 (Fall), 141–178 (in Hebrew), (http://web.ceu.hu/soc_ant/faculty/docs/Link_9_Monterescu_and_Fabian_Andromeda_Hebrew.pdf).

Monterescu, Daniel, and Rabinowitz, Dan, 2007. *Mixed Towns, Trapped Communities: Historical Narratives, Spatial Dynamics, Gender Relations and Cultural Encounters in Palestinian-Israeli Towns*, Re-materialising Cultural Geography series, Aldershot, Ashgate.

Morris, Benny, 1997. *Israel's Border Wars, 1949–1956: Arab Infiltration, Israeli Retaliation, and the Countdown to the Suez War*, Clarendon Press.

Morris, Benny, 2000. *Correcting an Error: Jews and Arabs in Palestine and Israel, 1936–1956*, Tel Aviv, Am Oved Publishers (in Hebrew).

Morris, Benny, 2003. *The Birth of the Palestinian Refugee Problem Revisited 1947–1949*, Cambridge Middle East Studies, Cambridge University Press.

Morris, Benny, 2004. *The Birth of the Palestinian Refugee Problem Revisited*, Cambridge Middle East Studies no. 18, Cambridge University Press.

Morris, Benny, 2008. *1948: A History of the First Arab-Israeli War*, Yale University Press.

Mosenson, Moshe, 1960. *Elisha' Sultz – The Man and his Work*, Ma'oz Ha'im, privately published (in Hebrew).

Musih, Norma, 2011. "Angels over Manshiye", MA dissertation, The Hebrew University, Jerusalem.

Ophir, Adi, 1999. "Zero Hour," in *50 to 48*, Jerusalem, Van Leer Institute and HaKibbutz Hameuchad (in Hebrew).

Osiatynski, Viktor, 2009. *Human Rights and Their Limits*, Cambridge University Press.

Ozacky-Lazar, Sarah, 1993. *Ikrit u-Bir'am*, Giv'at Havivah: haMakhon LeLimudim 'Arviyim.

Ozacky-Lazar, Sarah, 2001. "The Military Government as a Mechanism of Controlling the Arab Citizens: The First Decade 1948–1958," *The New East* 43.

Pappe, Ilan, 2006. *The Ethnic Cleansing of Palestine*, Oneworld.

Pappe, Ilan, 2007. *The Israel/Palestine Question: A Reader*, Routledge.

Re'em, Shim'on, 2001. *Haifa in Flames: Etzel's Operations in Red Haifa, 1931–1948*, Haifa, privately published.

Rogan, Eugene L., and Shlaim, Avi, 2001. *The War for Palestine: Rewriting the History of 1948*, Cambridge Middle East Studies no. 15, Cambridge University Press.

Rotbard, Sharon, 2005. *White City, Black City*, Babel Publishers.

Salomon, Shimri, 2001. "The Intelligence Service and the Village Files, 1940–1948," [Daf me-ha-Slik] Bulletin of the Haganah Archives (in Hebrew).

Salomon, Shimri, 2005. "The Intelligence and Documentation Operations of the Haganah's 'Arab Village Files Project'," [Daf me-ha-Slik] Bulletin of the *Haganah* Archives (in Hebrew).

Sanbar, Elias, 2004. *Les Palestiniens: la photographie d'une terre et de son peuple de 1839 à nos jours*, Hazan.

Sanbar, Elias, 2007. *Les Palestiniens dans le siècle*, Gallimard.

Segev, Tom, 1998. *1949: The First Israelis*, Owl Books by Henry Holt and Company.

Segev, Tom, 2001. *One Palestine, Complete: Jews and Arabs Under the British Mandate*, Abacus.

Sela, Rona, 2001. *Photography in Palestine/Eretz Yisrael in the 1930s and 1940s*. Herzlia Museum of Art and HaKibbutz Hameukhad, 2001 (in Hebrew).

Shai, Aharon, 2002. "The Fate of the Abandoned Arab villages in Israel before the Six Day War and Afterwards," *Cathedra* 105, 151–170 (in Hebrew).

Sharet, Yaakov, 1987. *Ezra Danin – Unconditional Zionist*, Kidum (in Hebrew).

Stoler, L. Ann, 2009. "Colonial Apahsia," in Nicolas Bancel, Florence Bernault, Achille Mbembe and Francoise Verges (eds.), *La fracture postcoloniale*, La Decouverte.

Talmi, Efra'im, and Talmi, Menahem, 1982. *A Zionist Lexicon*, Tel Aviv, Ma'ariv Publishers.

Tamari, Salim, 1999. *Jerusalem 1948: The Arab Neighborhoods and their Fate in the War*, Institute of Jerusalem Studies.

Torstrick, Rebecca L., 2000. *The Limits of Coexistence: Identity Politics in Israel*, University of Michigan Press.

Vilnai, Ze'ev, 1955. *The Names of our Localities: Their Sources in Literature, in the Landscape, in Labor, in Tradition and in the Rebirth of Israel*, Tel Aviv, Massada Publishers (in Hebrew).

Weizman, Eyal, 2007. *Hollow Land*, Verso.

Yahav, Dan, 2002. *Purity of Arms – Ethos Myth and Reality, 1936–1956*, Tammuz.

Yahav, Dan, 2004. *Jaffa – Bride of the Sea, from a Major City to Slums: A Model of Spatial Inequality*, Tammuz.

Yahav, Dan, 2009. *Paths of Co-existence and the Joint Arab-Jewish Economic and Social Struggle, 1930–2008*, privately published (in Hebrew).

Ziv, Hani, and Gelber, Yoav, 1998. *The Bow Bearers*, Ministry of Defense.

Zurayk, Constantine, 1956. *The Meaning of Disaster*, Khayat (in Arabic).

OTHER PUBLICATIONS

Zochrot booklets on Akka (2005), Bir al-Sabi'e (2006), Dayr Yasin (2003-2006), Haifa (2004), Ijlil (2004), al-Kafrayn (2007), al-Lajjun (2004), al-Maliha (2007), al-Ramle (2004), Suhmata (2005), al-Ajami Yaffa (2007).

Nakba Eyewitnesses, Narrations of the Palestinian 1948 Catastrophe, prepared by Ala Abu Dheer, Palestine Media Unit (Zajel) Public Relations Department, An-Najah National University Nablus – Palestine, edited by Liam Morgan and Alison Morris, http://imeu.net/engine2/uploads/an-najah-narrations_of_the_disaster_of_1948.pdf.

Documents and articles from files deposited in the State Archives belonging to: the Ministry of Minorities; the Office of the Custodian of Absentee Property; the Ministry of Welfare; the Ministry of Health.

Articles and reports published in *Davar, Al-Hamishmar, Ha'aretz, Ma'ariv, Yediot Aharonot*, between 1948 and 1950.

WEBSITES

http://zochrot.org/en
www.un.org/unrwa
www.badil.org
www.palestineremembered.com
www.nakba-archive.org/testimony.htm
www.palestine-studies.org/enakba/Memoirs/index.html
www.suhmata.com/indexh.php
www.deiryassin.org
www.palmach.org.il/show_item.asp?itemId=8572&levelId=42850&itemType=0

CHAPTER 1

Military Governmentality

This chapter describes how, from its inception, the new regime eliminated the possibility of civil life. Reading in the photographs the new and varied forms of violence which the new regime had its army carry out, I show the implausibility of calling the period from November 1947 to March 1949, a "war." The unquestioning adoption of the term "war" to characterize what occurred, as well as the description of the military's violence using terms like "battles," overlooks the violent policies seeking to transform the politico-demographic reality in order to establish a new regime in Palestine. The chapter deals, therefore, with military governmentality and the wide range of roles the army played in managing the civilian population – as collectivities as well as individuals. I employ the term "military governmentality" to refer to the contradiction inherent in the Israeli regime from its inception: managing the civilian population – the Palestinians, certainly, but the Jews as well – according to military logic. By this logic, the Palestinian represents the potential threat to the state, and the Jewish Israeli represents the one obligated to defend it, whether by military service or by denying Palestinians freedom of movement and erecting barriers in the state's geographic, commercial, administrative, cultural or economic space. A photograph taken in Jerusalem, appearing near the end of the chapter, shows one of the last times Palestinians played a public, civic role. Crowds of Palestinians march down the road in a protest demonstration, watched by many spectators on the sidewalks, united in their opposition to the efforts by the Zionists and the foreign powers cooperating with them in their attempt to impose the Partition Plan. According to the hegemonic Zionist narrative, this moment represents "the *outbreak* of the *War* of *Independence*" – three terms whose validity as descriptions of reality this book contests: nothing "broke out" on its own, the violence did not constitute war, and ending British rule did not require violence. The Palestinians' legitimate opposition to the division of their country was defined from that moment as an unequivocal expression of the violence they were seen wishing to direct against Jewish life in Palestine. That was the justification for the constituent violence aimed at imposing on the majority population of the country a new state-political reality.

Careful reading of the many photographs in this chapter, a reading that does not restrict itself to what the picture is supposedly "about," shows that the military's presence always means the end of civil life, in particular that in which relations between Jews and Arabs were other than hierarchical. The Palestinians appear in the photographs as people uprooted from their natural surroundings who are now being classified so they can be managed according to categories of ethnicity, religion, age and sex, their individual, civil existence totally erased. But the chapter demands viewing in and through the photographs not only the population that has become an object of intervention and whose life is now controlled by others, but also those who intervened and controlled. The Jewish soldiers and police turning Palestinians into subjects are themselves being transformed in turn as rulers and perpetrators with the authority to turn others into what they will. Here, as in the other chapters, I use the photographs to show that the catastrophe they document *belongs* not only to the Palestinians. The Palestinians – the immediate, manifest victims of this disaster – paid the highest price. Those who tasted the power to shape the lives of others but did not seek ways of resisting the ease with which that power was exercised are the victimizers, but also the unwitting victims of the regime that mobilized them to become perpetrators. In the photographs one can see the emptying of Palestinian localities, the columns of expelled refugees on the road (al-Ramle, Photo 11), the buses used to transport the refugees (Bir al-Sabi'e, Photo 5), incarceration of civilians in camps (Bir al-Sabi'e, Photo 9), the military government in action (al Nasirah, Photo 26), provision of civilian services, such as medical treatment, by the army ("A village in the Negev," Photo 27), the establishment of military government in towns (Qalanswa, Photo 23), and indifference to the surrender of Palestinians that could have formed a basis for a civil compact (Lubya, Photo 10).

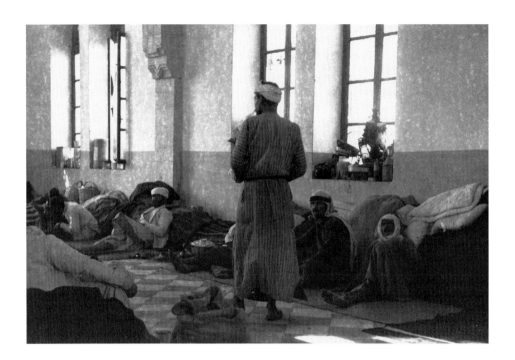

1   **Bir al-Sabi'e/Beersheba** These are the
mosque's final hours serving the town's Palestinian
residents. The new inhabitants will change its function
many times, ignoring the original purpose for which
it was built. When the photograph was taken, it was
being used as a detention camp. Most of the people
seen outside the walls of the temporary detention
camps established in public buildings are Israeli
soldiers. The army left 100 healthy, strong Arab men in
the city to help them clean up and remove rubble. Until
a few days ago they had lived in the buildings whose
ruins they're now required to clear away. During the
few hours they're not engaged in that activity, they're
shut up in the mosque with mattresses, blankets and
other belongings they've managed to save from their
homes. The official caption describes them as "Arab
prisoners of war." They'll soon be transferred to a
different prisoner of war camp in Israel.

Photographer: Hugo Mendelson, Government Press Office,
October 22, 1948

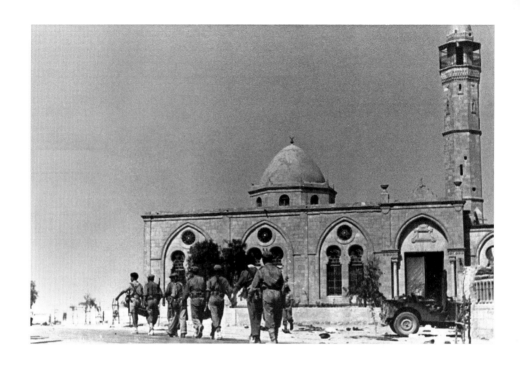

2   **Bir al-Sabi'e/Beersheba** About 3,000
Palestinians lived in the town at the end of the British
Mandate. The day after Bir al-Sabi'e was captured,
the only people on the street were armed soldiers
on patrol whose job was to prevent life in town
from returning to normal and lay the groundwork
for transforming Bir al-Sabi'e into a Jewish town.
The orders were to settle 3,000 Jews. The residents
expelled from the town won't be able to enjoy the
beautiful trees which will grow from the saplings
recently planted along the sidewalk, and the mosque
will no longer be a place for prayer.

Photographer: Hugo Mendelson, Government Press Office,
October 22, 1948

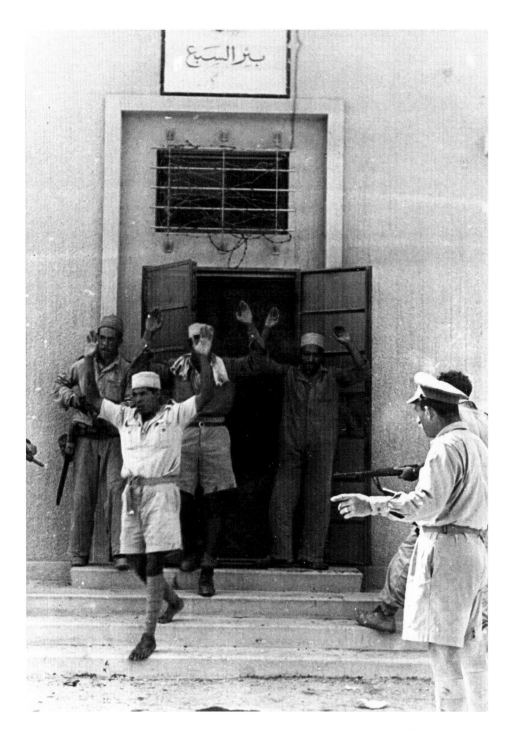

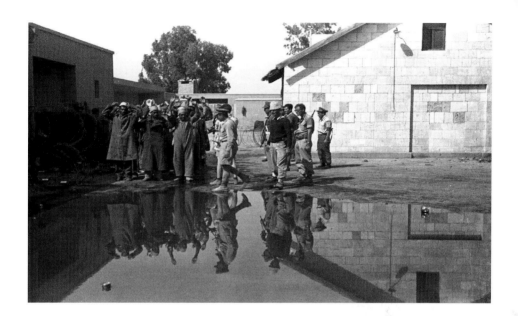

3 **Bir al-Sabi'e/Beersheba** According to the Partition Plan, seemingly accepted by the Jews, Bir al-Sabi'e was to have been part of the Palestinian state. But this was neither the first nor the last time Israel had violated the conditions set by the ceasefires that had been reached and the UN resolution (acting in the spirit of "UN – Shmoo-N," even before that policy had a name), creating facts on the ground that were inconsistent with these agreements. The conquest of Bir al-Sabi'e was an example. Men who had been captured, and who the soldiers suspected had not surrendered all their weapons, were shot. Others were transferred to prison camps. It's not possible to tell from the photograph what will happen to the captured Egyptian soldiers leaving the building.

Photographer not identified. Government Press Office, October 22, 1948

4 **Bir al-Sabi'e/Beersheba** A few hours earlier, still carefully dressed in the uniforms of Egyptian soldiers, they raised their hands in surrender and were brought to this temporary detention camp. Now, their uniforms in such disarray that it's hard to identify them as soldiers, the official caption says they're "being brought" by IDF soldiers, but it doesn't indicate where they're going. Those standing in the front row can't avoid seeing their new appearance as prisoners of war reflected in the puddle at their feet.

Photographer not identified. Government Press Office, October 22, 1948

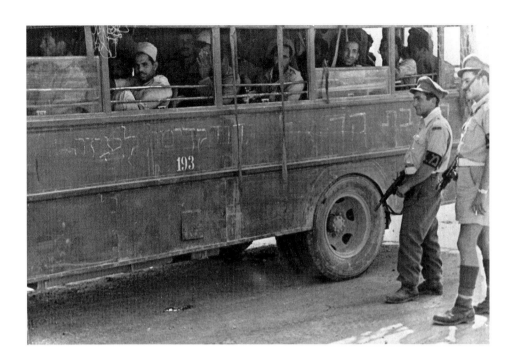

5   **Bir al-Sabi'e/Beersheba** The slogan on the
bus, "On to Gaza," doesn't refer to the destination of
the "Egyptian prisoners of war" if those sitting in the
bus are really "Egyptian prisoners of war." They'll be
exchanged a few months later, in February 1949, as
part of the armistice agreement with Egypt, and now
they're on their way to a prisoner of war camp. The
slogan might be the warcry of fighters on their way
to capture Gaza – even though, at the end of the day,
they didn't capture Gaza then – or the sign on buses
that carried the residents of Bir al-Sabi'e who had been
expelled to Gaza. Dozens of buses were put at the
disposal of the residents after the town was captured,
and the orders were clear: "If we see anyone here after
8 o'clock tomorrow, we'll kill them."

Photographer not identified. Government Press Office,
October 22, 1948

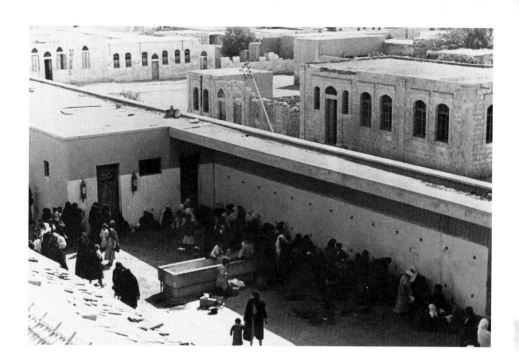

6   **Bir al-Sabi'e/Beersheba** You can get some
feeling for the town's modern appearance, planned
at the beginning of the twentieth century, from this
view through the fence surrounding the police station
courtyard – the wide streets weaving the city's fabric.
Women and children have been separated from the
men, as required by the Geneva Convention, but
despite what's written in the official caption, the
people in the photograph aren't prisoners of war,
nor Egyptians, but inhabitants of the town and their
children.

Photographer not identified. Government Press Office,
October 22, 1948

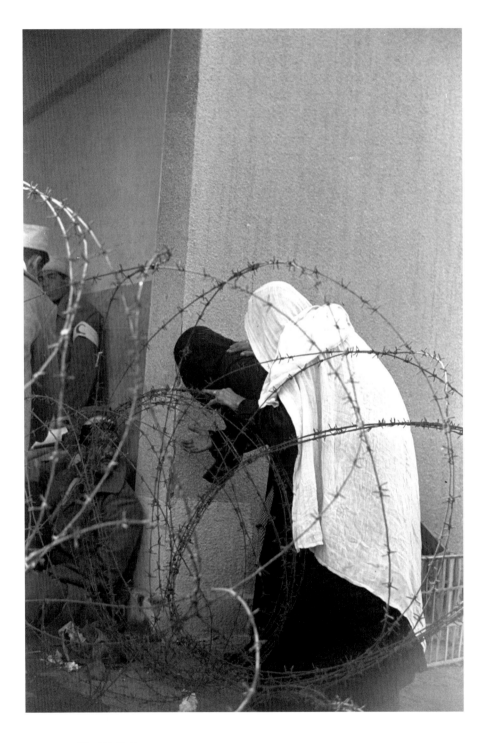

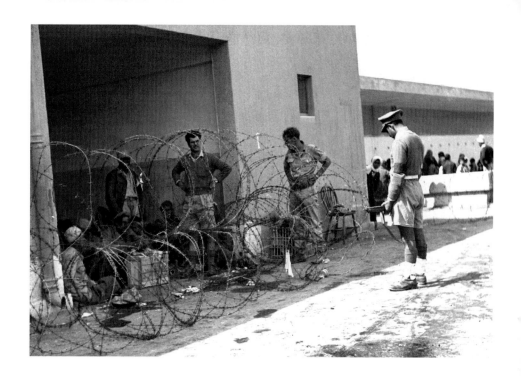

7   **Bir al-Sabi'e/Beersheba** The narrow plank
seems to separate the women and men imprisoned
in the police station courtyard. The concertina wire
is supposed to isolate the different population
groups, but the women take advantage of the gap
and talk to one of the men seated on the other side.
They've been uprooted from their homes, and their
Via Dolorosa has just begun. Perhaps they need
something, and hope that the Egyptian medics who
are also being held in that cell, and who are permitted
by the Geneva Convention to provide aid to other
prisoners, will help them.

Photographer not identified. Government Press Office,
October 22, 1948

8   **Bir al-Sabi'e/Beersheba** The initial sorting
out seems to have been conducted next to the police
station courtyard fence that is visible on the right side
of the photograph. To the left the men are crammed
into partially enclosed spaces with coils of barbed wire
in front of them. These coils mark the boundaries of the
cells, and structure the relationships between the new
jailers and the people they're guarding.

Photographer not identified. Government Press Office,
October 22, 1948

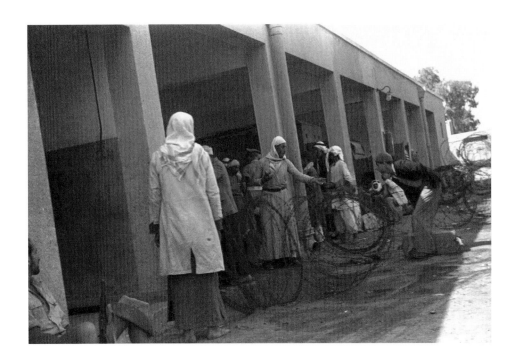

9   **Bir al-Sabi'e/Beersheba** The prisoners' needs are being met in the same improvised manner in which the detention area, whose rules and boundaries are unclear, was established. Are we seeing the distribution of rations, or peddlers to whom the soldier sitting and resting has given permission to sell their wares? Who is that peddler? How did he come to be on that side of the barbed wire coil?

Photographer not identified. Government Press Office, October 22, 1948

10 **Lubya** The photograph seems to have been taken a few hours after the white flags that are still visible proclaimed the surrender of the village. Most of its residents had left for Lebanon two days earlier, after they learned that al-Nasirah (Nazareth) had fallen. They, as well as those shown surrendering, lost their homes (there were 596 homes), which were erased from the face of the earth. Hikers in the Lavie Forest, planted on village land in the mid 1960s by the Jewish National Fund, may come across old wells and hedges of prickly pear decorating the landscape, which are now only ancient remnants of the past. Some of the refugees from Lubya made their way to Dayr Hana, in the central Lower Galilee. To this day they have not been allowed to return to their land.

Photographer not identified. Golani Museum Archive, no date

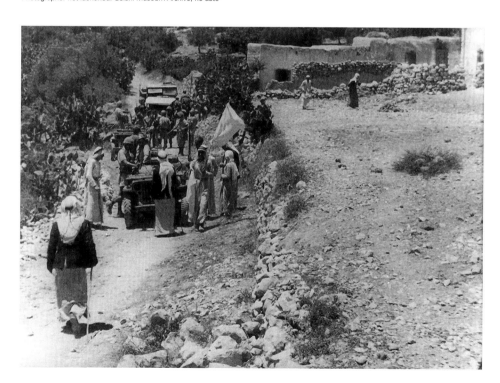

11   **al-Ramle** The photograph shows the result of the violent process that was frequently repeated in most places that were captured: uprooting the local population (which the army concentrated in temporary fenced-off areas) from their homes in order to deal separately with people ("The Committee for Transferring Arabs from Place to Place") and with property. Those who are still seated and watching the military trucks evacuating their fellow residents are beginning to understand that they won't be returning home from here. It probably didn't occur to them at this moment that their return would be prevented for generations. Only a few Palestinians succeeded, after considerable effort, to return to their homes. Most lost them forever.

Photographer: Beno Rothenberg, Israel State Archive, 1948

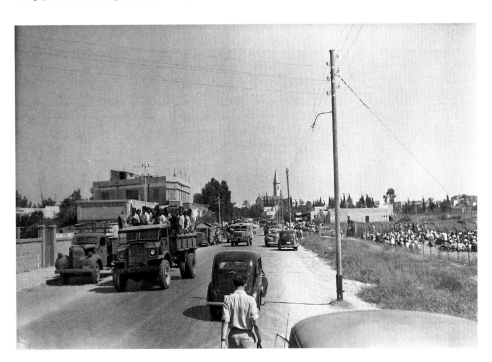

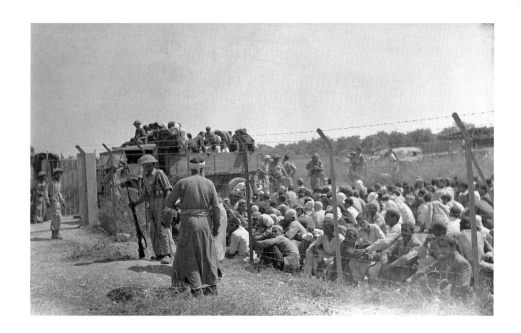

12　**al-Ramle**　Separating the Palestinians from
their homes was usually accompanied by separating
men from women. The photograph shows hundreds of
men penned on the roadside. Their homes have been
broken into; the fate of their women and children is
still unknown. Protocols of cabinet meetings refer to
reports that when the refugees were penned behind
fences, women in town were raped and the city was
plundered. The government, troubled by the looting,
discussed it, but didn't take the rapes seriously, as
the words of one minister during those meetings
indicated: "There are reports of rape in al-Ramle. I can
forgive rape, but not other, more serious behavior.
When people come into a city and remove rings
from fingers and jewelry from the neck, that's a more
serious business." By condemning one type of behavior
they legitimized the other, though the behavior they
condemned didn't necessarily cease. Held behind
barbed wire, without blankets or food supplies, men "of
military age" were taken by truck to detention camps.

Photographer: Beno Rothenberg, Israel State Archive, 1948

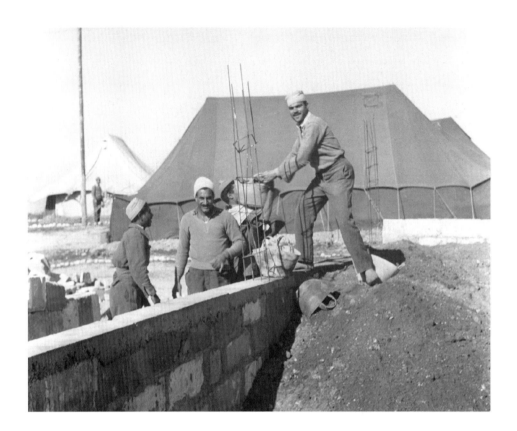

13   **Ijlil** Before it was turned into a prison camp, about 700 Palestinians lived in the village of Ijlil. "Prison Camp 791" operated for eleven months, and held about 2,000 people. Every Palestinian male "of military age" was to be detained. In the camp they were employed in various activities, and were a source of cheap labor. Some of the camp commanders didn't hesitate to use them as such, and to extend their period of "incarceration." In order to transform the village into a prison camp, the prisoners were required to work in construction. While they were doing forced labor in the camps, their families struggled to survive in the absence of their breadwinners. The chance that a photograph of them might reach members of their family, which sometimes occurred through the mediation of the Red Cross, must have been enough of a reason to smile for the camera. Or perhaps they had other reasons.

Photographer not identified. IDF and Defense Archive, 1949

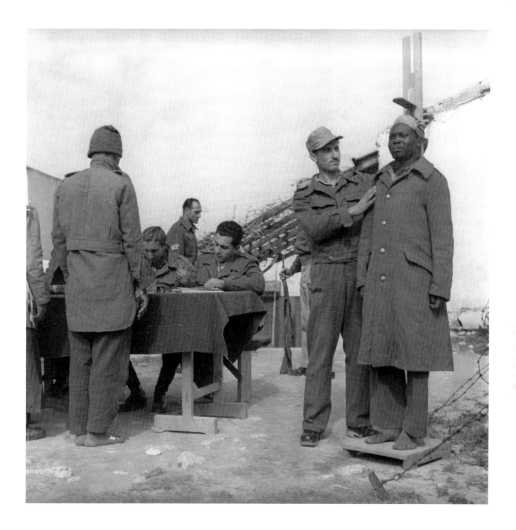

14   **Ijlil** Camp No. 791. Managing the population,
like managing its property, required accurate
record-keeping. The "prisoner" was forced to
remove his shoes in order to facilitate collection
of information about his physical characteristics.
These were, without a doubt, useful in deciding
what work to assign him. The location is described
on the sign as the "Office of Prisoner Registration."
In fact, the office also handled the registration
and administration of the unpaid labor in which 65
percent of the prisoners in the camps were forced
to engage.

Photographer not identified. IDF and Defense Archive, 1949

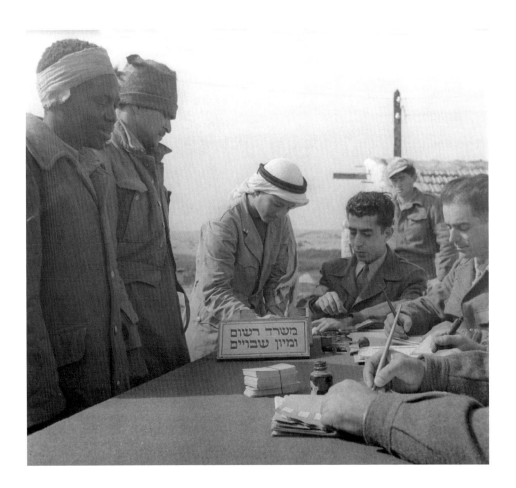

15   **Ijlil** Camp No. 791. The camp still received
new "prisoners" in 1949. All that was needed were
three clerks, an ink bottle, pen, rubber stamps, blank
documents, forms and lists, and soon everyone had
his own prison document containing the relevant
information about him. It was important to those who
organized the photograph to make clear that the camp
held only prisoners of war. The sign, "Office of Prisoner
Registration and Classification," wasn't intended for
the prisoners, most of whom couldn't read Hebrew,
and it was easy to move it a few times so it would be
readable in each of the photographs taken that day.

Photographer not identified. IDF and Defense Archive, 1949

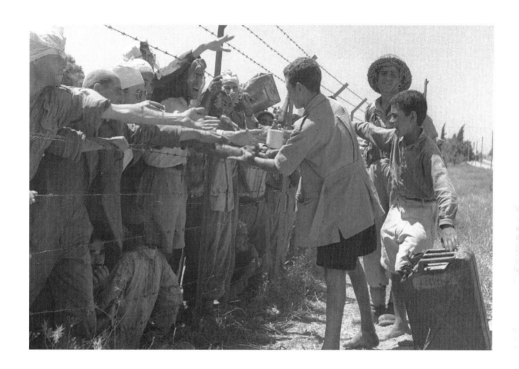

16 **al-Ramle** The same people whom Beno
Rothenberg photographed (cf. Photos 11 and 12)
were characterized by the Government Press Office
archive by the term then commonly used to describe
Palestinians who had been uprooted from their homes
– "prisoners of war." Who sent the two youths to ration
out the water? Did they do so at their own initiative,
or was it the idea of the Israeli army? Are they now
obligated to someone because they were allowed to
move around freely with the water?

Photographer: David Eldan, Government Press Office, July 11, 1948

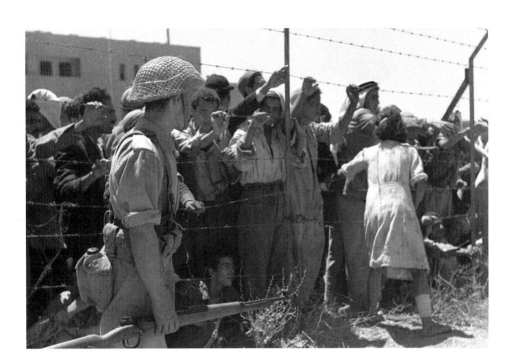

17 **al-Ramle** Imagine a town that has just been occupied, where only women, elderly men and children have remained, after armed combatants filled its streets and arrested all the younger men who appeared strong enough to represent potential resistance to the new rule imposed on the town. Imagine these women on their own, their plight, exposed to Jewish combatants who treat anything they find as their own – who demand to be served food, drink, sex. Barefoot, she hurried here to search for him among the thousands of prisoners – perhaps she had something urgent to tell him or maybe she heard a rumor that the men won't be here much longer. Fortunately, she seems to have found him. But in a few hours they'll be separated again. He'll be transferred to a prison camp, and she'll be sent elsewhere. If her luck holds, in a year or two the state will approve her application for "family reunification." In most cases, approval of the application will be conditional on their being reunited "beyond the country's borders."

Photographer: David Eldan, Government Press Office, July 7, 1948

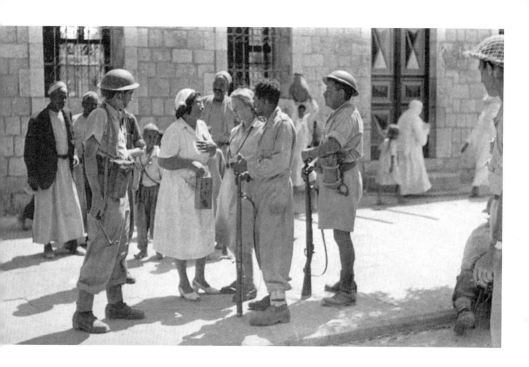

18 **al-Ramle** The picture taken in the courtyard of the monastery that was turned into a welfare and treatment station bears some traces of the demographic convulsion that shook this Arab town, and the transformation of its internal balance of power. In an Arab town of 18,000 residents (most of them Moslems) making an honest living, employed as railway station managers, government officials, merchants, landowners, school principals and physicians, only about 1,175 remained, including internal refugees, most of them Christians. Men "of military age" had been taken to prison camps, and most of those remaining were "invalids, the chronically ill, the elderly and women with children." They had to be taken care of. The soldiers are also implementing the welfare policies coming into effect in the midst of the violent acts that transformed those whose needs must now be met into an indigent minority in their own land. We don't know what the Palestinian nurse and the Jewish nurse are talking about, but the power relation between them is pretty clear. The conversation with the Jewish nurse takes place in the presence of at least five armed soldiers.

The Palestinian nurse is appealing on behalf of her patients. In making her appeal she places her hand on her heart as part of her effort to convince the Jewish nurse to agree to her request, or perhaps even to thank her for her efforts. Behind them, waiting to see the outcome of the discussion, stand children and elderly men who have been dispossessed of whatever status and power they had to affect their own lives, and are now reduced to being spectators awaiting the words of a Hebrew nurse. When, one year later, a field representative of the Ministry of Minorities will speak "as a civilian" to those who've remained, they'll formulate their complaints fluently and protest the fact that their homes have been requisitioned by the military authorities or by Jewish settlers, that some have been destroyed or demolished, that they've been restricted to living in a small area, behind barbed wire, lacking freedom to move about, and that they're under a nightly curfew from eight in the evening until six the following morning.

Photo scanned with the compliments of Beno Rothenberg, from the photographic album ("Our Finest Year") which he edited, 1948

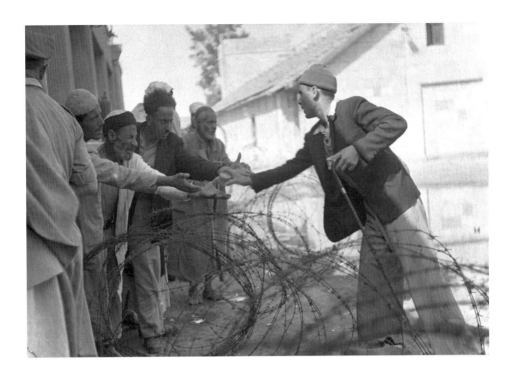

19   **Bir al-Sabi'e/Beersheba** Many hands reach through the coil of barbed wire, pleading for food. Who is that person who doesn't have enough biscuits to distribute (or sell) to everyone? The prisoners are not only learning subordination; they're also learning to be dependent on others, to be transformed into people who can no longer meet their own needs.

Photographer not identified. Government Press Office, October 22, 1948

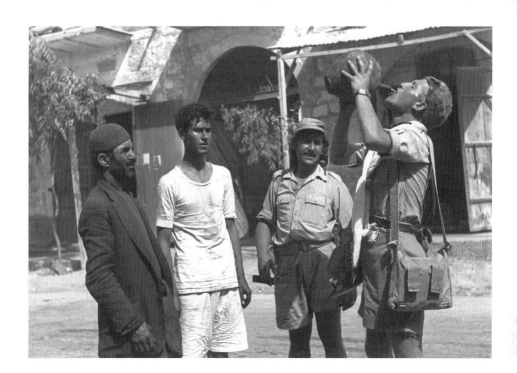

20 **Bir al-Sabi'e/Beersheba** A kaffiyeh is tied carelessly around his neck. He captured their town and now drinks their water. Both stand tensely, hands extended slightly. When he lowers the water skin from his lips they'll quickly take it from him. The official caption eases their discomfort: "An IDF soldier and local Arabs rest for a moment after the surrender of Be'er Sheva." The way of the world.

Photographer: Hugo Mendelson, Government Press Office, October 22, 1948

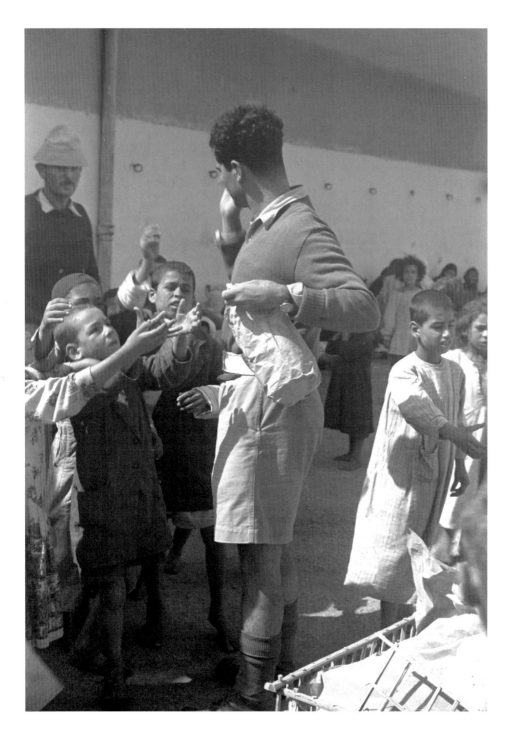

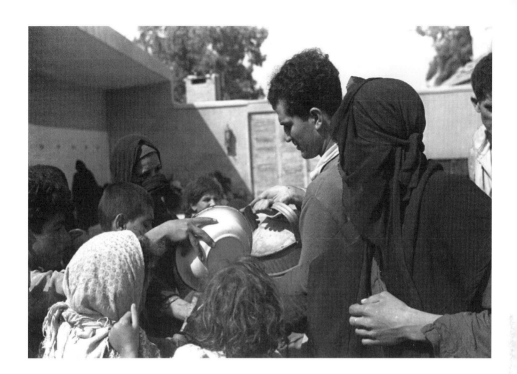

21   **Bir al-Sabi'e/Beersheba** The official caption reading, "An IDF soldier distributes food to Bedouin children in Bir al-Sabi'e, after the town's surrender," has no room for the soldier's disciplinary gesture with which, in response to the outstretched hands pleading for food, he teaches the children manners.

Photographer not identified. Government Press Office, October 22, 1948

22   **Bir al-Sabi'e/Beersheba** The more one reads the testimony of refugees, both men and women, about the thirst from which they suffered on the roads, the harder it is to devalue this "humanitarian" gesture of slaking the Palestinians' thirst, which served as the basis for so many photographs. While he's distributing water to the children, she, standing to his right, searches his features, trying to discover who he is and what he represents.

Photographer not identified. Government Press Office, October 22, 1948

23   **Qalanswa** No rule, including military rule,
is possible without the cooperation of the local
population. One of the men on the right already wears
an armband embroidered with the Arabic word for
"Guard," setting him apart from the others. Nor can
a conquered population manage its affairs without
participating in some manner in the regime that rules it,
even if that regime frequently acts against its interests.
At the end of the street, observing from a distance,
are people the officer hasn't included in the new
arrangements.

Photographer not identified. Government Press Office, May 10, 1949

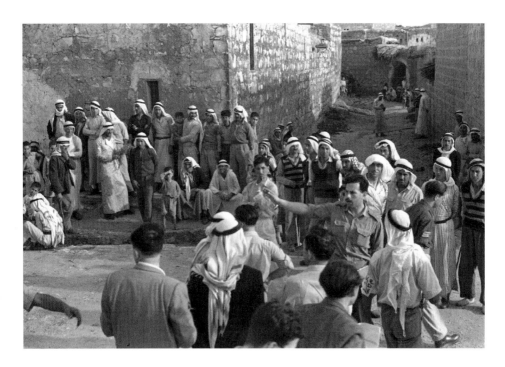

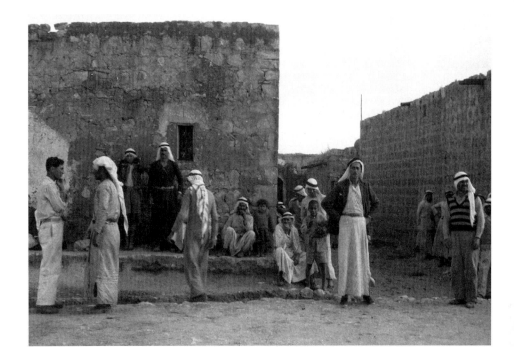

24   **Qalanswa** Most of the people are watching
the conversation one of them is having with the officer.
Some look suspicious, others smile, some seem
indifferent and one looks directly at the photographer.
The image of an Israeli soldier talking privately –
confidentially – with one of their own will accompany
them for at least 17 more years, until military
government is abolished. The policy of "divide and
rule" reflected in the photograph is emblematic of how
the military government operates. Military rule always
divides the population into collaborators and those who
don't collaborate, into desirable local residents and
internal refugees who are a burden and a threat, into
those who stayed and those who "infiltrated." From the
day the photograph was taken until the end of June,
a few thousand "internal refugees" were deported
from the "Triangle" with the help of the local residents.
At the end of June, the military governor of the area
could report that "today there are no more refugees
in the area, other than a few who merited special
consideration, or had been recommended." According
to estimates, 4,000–8,000 internal refugees had been
deported.

Photographer: David Eldan, Government Press Office, May 10, 1949

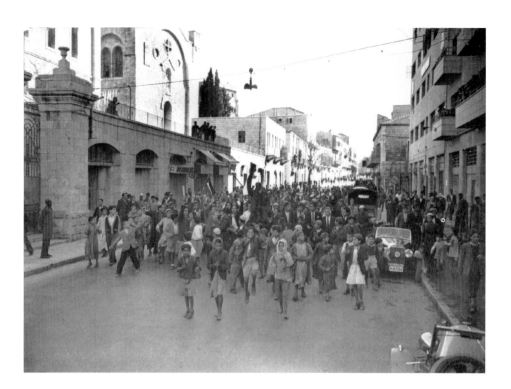

25   Mamila neighborhood, al-Quds/Jerusalem
The procession filling the road apparently was held on December 1, 1947, as part of the three-day general strike called by the Supreme Arab Council in response to UN Resolution 181 approving the Partition Plan. The shops are shuttered, and the street has become the locale in which Arabs act as political subjects and express in the public arena their determined opposition to the imminent transformation of their country's regime without their consent. Since the beginning of the British Mandate the Arabs opposed plans to divide their country between them and the Jewish immigrants. After World War II they refused to cooperate with UN members preparing the plan, who continued drafting it in coordination with the Zionist leadership. According to the plan that was adopted, the Zionists received 55 percent of the country's land (though actually controlling less than 10 percent). But it was not only the injustice involved in the way the country was divided, but the very declaration of partition, that led to the massive Palestinian street demonstration. This political procession, of a governed people objecting to the new regime that outsiders threaten to impose upon them, thereby transforming the political entity of which they are members, ended the following day in violence and mutual reprisals that quickly deteriorated into what was portrayed and treated as a war. One month before the partition decision and the response it engendered, a correspondent for the *Palestine Post* had reported the Jewish Agency's assessment that most Arabs in Palestine preferred coexistence to violence. From the moment the plan undermining their political rights was adopted, Arabs began to be denied their status as political subjects. During the period of military government to which they were subordinate in the Jewish state established on the territory which had been allotted to it, as well as on most of the territory that had been allotted to the Arab state, they were also denied their right to use the streets to express their views.

Photographer not identified. Central Zionist Archives, 1947

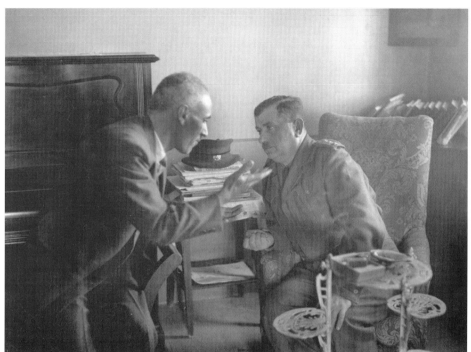

26 **al-Nasirah/Nazareth** Office of the Military
Governor. The official caption reads "Conversation
with a local Arab notable." Travel permits, visits to
prisoners, release of prisoners, applications for family
reunification, obtaining work permits, permission to
establish transportation routes, judicial procedures,
re-establishing the educational system – any of these
could have been the reason for their meeting. Are they
leaning toward one another because they want the
photographer to immortalize their relationship? Or are
they, perhaps, trying to conceal something from him?

Photographer not identified. Central Zionist Archives, 1948

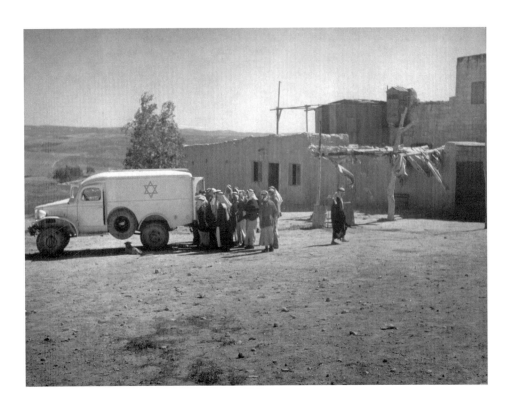

27   **A village in the Negev** This photograph is an
excellent example of how the neglect of Palestinian
citizens of Israel went hand in hand with concern for
their welfare. The military government made certain
to provide citizens, who were guaranteed equal rights
by Israel's Declaration of Independence, with a weekly
visit by a government physician in a mobile clinic.
This clinic provided important services, but there's no
need to emphasize that these services were limited,
and the crowd of those needing them around the
entrance of the vehicle shows the degree to which
they were forced to expose their medical distress
to others. But there were even more critical issues,
such as the language in which the services would

be provided. The mukhtars appealed to the Ministry
of Minorities, arguing that they can't understand the
Hebrew instructions in the circulars they received,
which in turn contacted the Ministry of Health on their
behalf. In the adjacent Jewish localities, on the other
hand, all of them officially recognized and given names
(which would have made it impossible for photographs
taken in those localities to be filed in the archives
simply under the name of the region, "Negev"), most
health services had been established by the 1950s and
were provided in buildings staffed by what were the
equivalent at the time of HMOs.

Photographer not identified. Central Zionist Archive, 1950

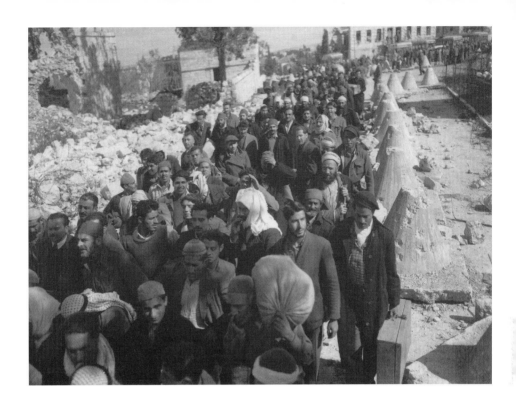

28 **The Mandelbaum Gate** The Armistice
Agreement with Jordan included a prisoner exchange.
Most of the released Jewish prisoners returned to their
homes. Those who had formerly lived in the part of
Jerusalem which became "East Jerusalem," and could
not go back there, returned to a country that protected
them and helped them establish their homes. Most
of the Palestinian prisoners, on the other hand,
were released at the Mandelbaum Gate (which had
become the only crossing point established under the
agreement between the two parts of the newly divided
city of Jerusalem/al-Quds) and were sent to refugee
camps in Jordan. The Palestinian photographer stands
where he can see the flood of released prisoners
getting off the trucks and continuing eastward on foot.

Photographer: Ali Zaarour (with the kind permission of Zaki Zaarour),
1948–49

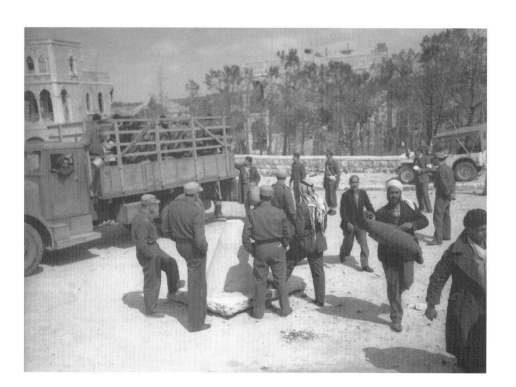

29   **The Mandelbaum Gate** Israeli and Jordanian
commanders insure that the uprooting of the
Palestinian refugees, who now arrive as liberated
prisoners, will be carried out without interference and
according to the official and unofficial agreements
between them. "From the entrance to Jerusalem, past
Lifta-Romema, through Mahane Yehuda, King George
Avenue and Mea She'arim – there are no foreigners.
One hundred percent Jewish." Thus Ben Gurion, at a
meeting of the government, summarized what had
happened in Jerusalem.

Photographer: Ali Zaarour (with the kind permission of Zaki Zaarour),
1948–49

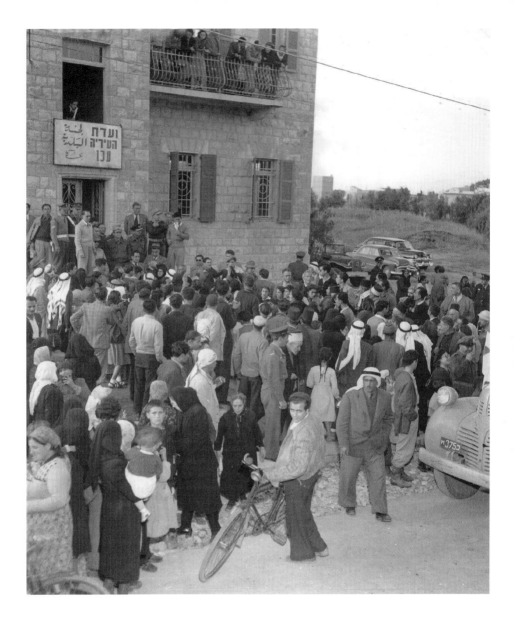

30　**Akka/Akko** Officers and military government personnel stand at the building's entrance. Local residents gather on the plaza in anticipation of the arrival of refugees or prisoners whom they hear are returning to the city. A few thousand Palestinians who had been held in prisoner of war camps were released in 1949. Some of them were returned to Akka, which had meanwhile become Akko. Were any of them among the people for whom the large crowd was waiting that day? The official caption laconically describes what the photograph doesn't show: "Arab refugees returning."

Photographer not identified. Central Zionist Archives, 1949

CHAPTER 2

Socialization to the State, and the Mechanisms of Subordination

This chapter traces how the citizens of the new state were mobilized to accept the civil disaster that occurred in Palestine at the end of the 1940s as a natural phenomenon, and to view the injustice it created as a necessary evil. Some of the photographs are stamped with the seal of military governmentality and could have been included in the first chapter. But this chapter stresses one moment of military governmentality – the gradual withdrawal of visible and naked military force from public space and its replacement by apparently civilian control mechanisms. This withdrawal and replacement allowed the new agents of democracy – the new state's Jewish citizens – to use such photographs in order to disseminate the tidings of democracy and be proud of its existence, ignoring the ubiquitous evidence of the violence by which it had been established. The scene, presented as something to be proud of, showing Arab citizens at the voting precinct on election day holding Israeli ID cards in their hands, conceals the fact that al-Nasirah was under military rule. Another photograph, of Palestinians asked to join "Independence Day" celebrations and wave Israeli flags, isn't meant to add insult to the injury of expulsion and dispossession, but expresses the openness of Israeli society. Even in the photograph at the beginning of the chapter, where the military presence is visible, the atmosphere is of a meeting between equals, Arab leaders from the Kafr Qassem area and army officers (Photo 31). Jews and Palestinians were each socialized differently, incorporating them in this military "democracy" and the mendacious language it used to describe, legitimize and conceal the violence it carried out. The Jews socialized to the differentiations established by the new regime easily adopted the institutionalized distinctions between themselves and the Palestinians, and erased from their consciousness the regime's violent dispossession of Arabs from equal citizenship. The Palestinians were socialized to subordination and learned to accept their place, but never made the mistake of believing that the regime imposed on them through violence was legitimate or democratic. They didn't think they had to thank Jews for allowing them to participate in "their" democratic regime, as if democracy belonged only to one group. The basis of socialization to the new regime was training citizens to view the various distortions as something other than what they in fact were. So, for example, elections supervised by the army were described as "free elections" (Photo 40); Arab participation in ceremonies and celebrations of their subordination was called "Independence celebrations"; their land which was taken over and expropriated was called "abandoned land" (Photo 61). The chapter pays attention to the body language of Jews who gained civil privileges by subordinating Palestinians, while they forget or repress the fact they've become perpetrators, as if that played no role in their relations with their subordinates. Among the photographs – one person proudly looking at the camera while providing humanitarian assistance to a dispossessed, needy Arab (Photo 45); lordliness while preparing the Arab for "modernization" (Photo 52); journalistic professionalism and "neutrality" while covering the expulsion (Photo 57); invading and settling in homes of expelled Palestinians while the question of their return had not yet been decided (Photo 56). The photographs display traces of economic exploitation, the extension of subordination to all areas of existence, neutralization of Palestinians as political subjects, willingness to accept the exclusion of Palestinians from public space and their subordination to military rule.

31   **Kafr Qassem** According to the agreement signed by Israel and Jordan in Rhodes, the "Triangle" was to be transferred to Israel, which promised in return not to harm the local population. Leaders of the Arab villages in the area, seated on primary school chairs, receive instructions from representatives of the military government. The civil equality they were promised was denied them at the very moment they were subjected to military rule. The military government had not promised to refrain from harming the internal refugees, and one of its main tasks was to deport them. "When we moved into the area," said the military governor, "we announced that refugees have no right of residence in the area nor any right to assistance or benefits. We prohibited people from employing them. We did not prevent them from obtaining necessities distributed by the Red Cross, or making use of goods in their possession, but we prevented anyone from organizing permanent relief supplies for them." Without the cooperation of the local Arab leadership, the military governor would not have been able to deport a few thousand internal refugees over the course of a few weeks.

Photographer not identified. Government Press Office, May 6, 1949

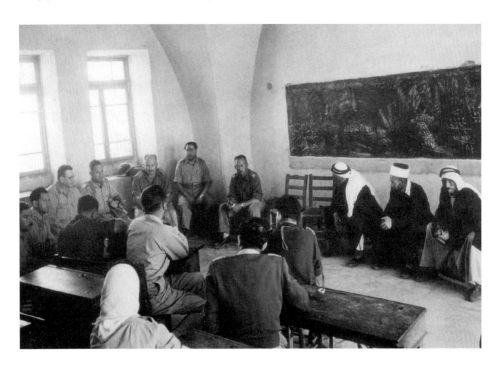

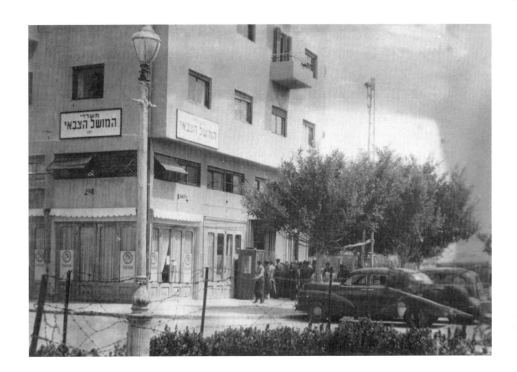

32　**Yafa/Jaffa** Only official photos show what occurs inside the offices of the military government, primarily polite discussions with the Military Governor. The interrogations and the injuries these caused to the residents leave no photographic traces. The long line at the entrance to the Military Governor's office on Jerusalem Boulevard is only one spatial expression of the military administration of the city following its capture. That also included separating men from women, concentrating the men in a special area, identification line-ups, sealing shop entrances, laying barbed wire along the sidewalks, establishing zones, distributing (or denying) permits and differentiating between civilian areas that were open and military areas that were closed. The military government, which established itself in the office of the city's Arab mayor, and was responsible for the administration of the Arab population, in fact devoted its attention to regulating the movement of that population in and out of the open public space controlled by the Jewish citizens. This regulation was aimed at preventing Arabs from actively participating as equals with Jews in the distribution of resources, property and other goods. While they struggled to obtain a permit to travel to the other side of the city, or to leave the Ajami ghetto, most of their property was being looted or distributed to others. *Tnuva* is already marketing its products in the corner restaurant.

Photographer not identified. IDF and Defense Archive, May 1, 1948

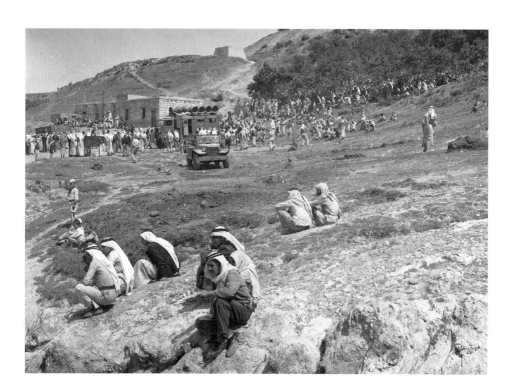

33   **Wadi 'Ara** The foreign sounds coming from
the loudspeakers on the military vehicle were
already familiar to local residents. They heard songs
("Hatiqva" – the Israeli national anthem and songs of
the Palmach); "Voice of Israel" broadcasts in Arabic;
announcements that a curfew was in effect, or had
been lifted; and various other orders such as, for
example, the one instructing residents to leave their
homes while the town's new military government staff
selects the buildings in which they will establish their
offices.

Photographer: Beno Rothenberg, Israel State Archive, May 1949

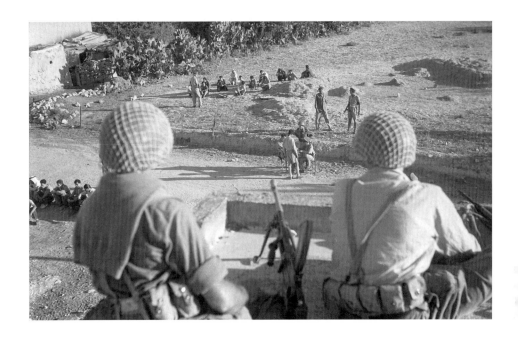

34   **al-Nasirah/Nazareth** Out in the open, opposite
two soldiers seated on chairs, observed through the
sights of guns pointed at them from an observation
point higher up where two other soldiers sit, residents
of al-Nasirah and the surrounding area are counted
and forced to hand over their weapons. This must
have been the local census conducted in al-Nasirah
at the end of August, intended to identify those who
were present in the city (13,609 residents and 4,185
refugees) and differentiate them from those who might
wish to return.

Photographer: Beno Rothenberg, Israel State Archive, 1948

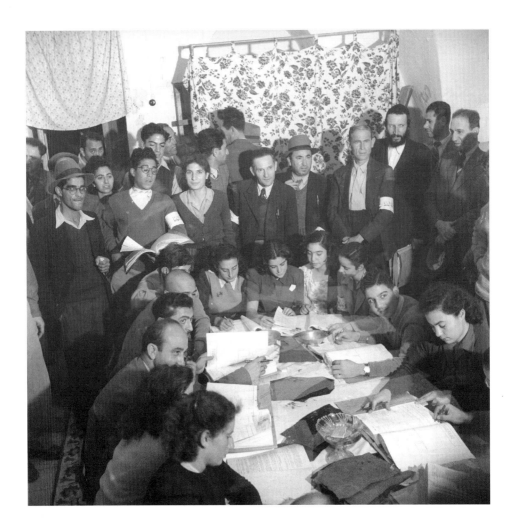

35   **Beit Hakerem** In a relaxed, festive, solidary atmosphere, many registration clerks, identified by their armbands, sit around a table in the Jewish neighborhood of Beit Hakerem, demonstrating for the camera how they enter information in the ledger. Each person, or pair of people, is accompanied by a registration clerk who helps them fill out the forms. It isn't clear from the photograph whether these are people who are actually being enumerated during the census, newly appointed clerks rehearsing how to conduct the census or simply clerks playing a role for the camera. Many of those crowded around them for the photograph subsequently left to conduct the census from house to house in the neighborhood. To insure maximum accuracy of the census results a full curfew was imposed throughout the country from 5 o'clock in the afternoon until midnight. The census would be the accurate reflection of the newly created body politic with a Jewish majority. The census results will not, by themselves, enable those who use them to reconstruct the violence by which they were produced.

Photographer: Yehuda Eisenstark, IDF and Defense Archive, November 1948

The official JNF caption: "After the Bedouin inhabitants of the Negev have been registered, they're photographed holding their registration number."

36 **"The Negev"** Every citizen of the country has a registration number, but only prisoners will sometimes be photographed with their number across their chest. Perhaps because they were afraid that the kaffiyeh might make it hard to identify the person whose picture was taken, the authorities established a special rule for the unfamiliar faces of the Bedouin, in unidentified localities – "the Negev." Their pictures are taken outside, in the open, exposed to everyone's gaze, in a setting lacking that degree of intimacy created between a photographer and a subject who come together to take an ID photo.

Photographer: Fred Chesnik, JNF Photographic Archive, November 1949

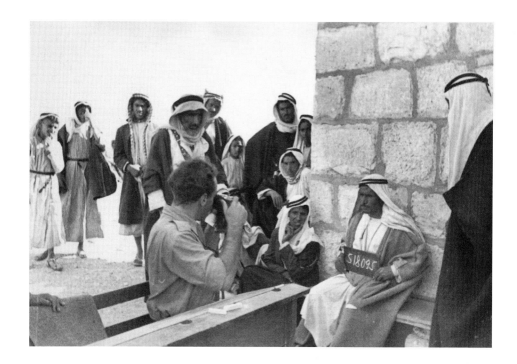

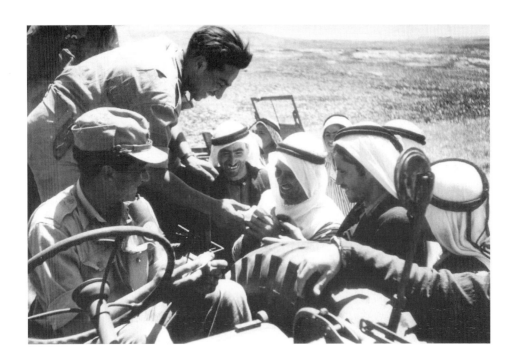

37   **Kafr Qassem** No one – neither those displaying the currency nor those watching them – is able to contain his excitement or suppress a smile at the sight of the new banknote they will use from now on. They had no necessary connection to the previous version of the currency, so why should they complain about the new one, so long as it doesn't become a symbol of how they're discriminated against.

Photographer not identified. Government Press Office, May 6, 1949

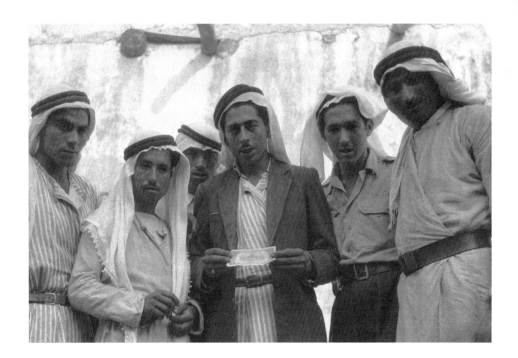

38   **Qalanswa** Unlike later banknotes, on which
only the denomination and name of the bank is printed
in Arabic, the new Palestinian pound with which they're
having their picture taken was completely tri-lingual
(Hebrew, Arabic and English). Still, the photographer
thought it was worth taking a picture of a Palestinian
holding an Israeli banknote up to the camera.

Photographer not identified. Government Press Office, May 6, 1949

39   **Yafa/Jaffa** Until 1948, Yafa had been a
lively Arab city. The expulsion of some 70,000 Arab
residents and the resettlement in the city of 45,000
Jewish immigrants prevents us from viewing Jews
and Arabs waiting together for the bus as a symbol
of modest but reasonable coexistence. The Jewish
immigrants could move freely about the city, while
the 5,000 Arabs remaining after it was captured –
some originally from Yafa, others refugees from the
surrounding villages – were concentrated in the Ajami
ghetto, closed off under military rule. They couldn't
leave without a special permit.

Photographer: Zoltan Kluger, Government Press Office,
March 1, 1949

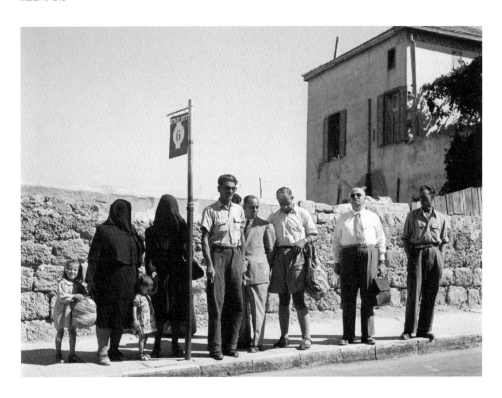

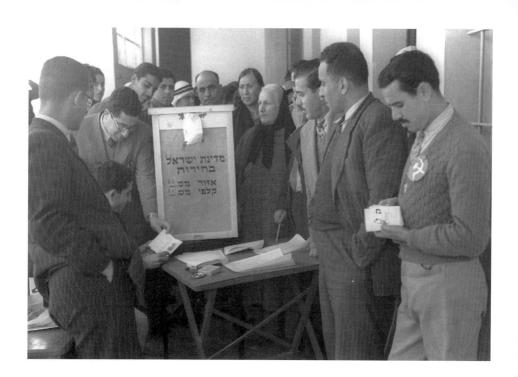

40 **al-Nasirah/Nazareth** The makeup of the city's population changed dramatically: Some of its residents were deported, while thousands of internal refugees streamed in from various localities. There was utter chaos at the beginning, and the military governor, who did not allow the Arabs to administer municipal affairs by themselves as they had been accustomed to doing, had difficulty dealing with it. Despite overt and covert efforts to prevent the residents and refugees from coming into contact with representatives of the Communist Party, on election day, the ultimate expression of democratic government, the military governor permitted a representative of the party to stand at the entrance to the polling place with a party symbol on his lapel, holding the party's ballots in his hands. When the head of the Communist Party asked why distribution of campaign literature in the city was forbidden, the Minister of Interior replied: "This is the first time a government gives the right to vote to members of a nation with which it is at war. Therefore, even though the Arab inhabitants of the state enjoy full civil rights, they won't be allowed to freely distribute campaign material, just as its distribution is prohibited in the army." The Communist Party's ideas, and its leadership's analysis of the existing situation, were a threat to the relatively uniform image that was disseminated everywhere regarding the conditions required for the establishment of a Jewish regime.

Photographer not identified. Government Press Office, January 25, 1949

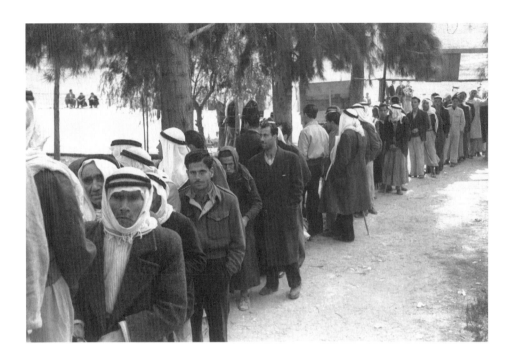

41 **al-Nasirah/Nazareth** They arrive at the polls hoping to have an influence. But even when their votes are counted, the results of the State of Israel's first elections will reflect the violent transformation of the local population's demographic structure – the uprooting and transfer of 80 percent of the Arab population beyond the new country's borders, and the creation of a Jewish majority.

Photographer not identified. Government Press Office, January 25, 1949

42 **al-Nasirah/Nazareth** Election Day. If, even now, after all the injustices the Jews managed to inflict on the Arabs, a radical change had occurred in the way in which the Jewish state apparatus treated Arab citizens, men as well as women, and its officials recognized the unconditional right to citizenship of the country's Arab inhabitants, rather than viewing citizenship as a gift that was theirs to grant, this photograph could be read differently. And perhaps we might even have been amazed by the fact that "Identification Card" is written on the cover in Arabic and Hebrew letters of equal size.

Photographer not identified. Government Press Office, January 25, 1949

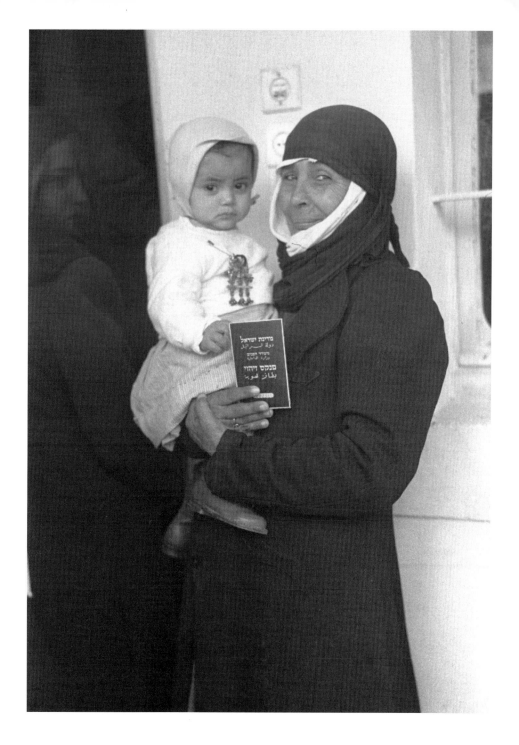

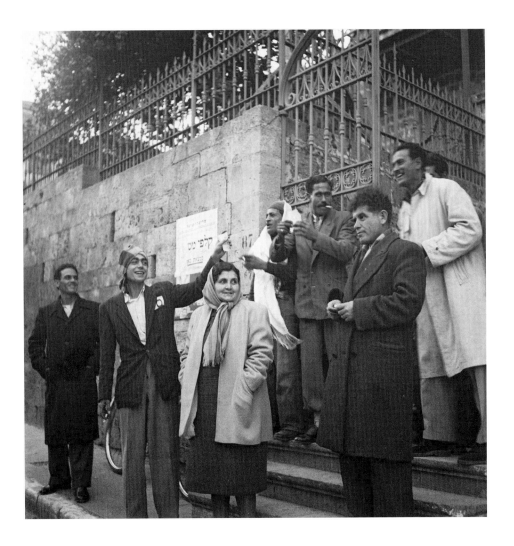

43   **Yafa/Jaffa** Elections to the First Knesset. Jews and Arabs stand outside the polling place, delighting in their civic duty, asking the people coming to vote to support the list they represent. One holds a ballot with the letter "ס" – *samekh* – "The National Union of Sfaradim and Eastern Communities"; the man standing on the steps holds a ballot printed with the letters "יא" – *yod alef* – "The Arab Workers Bloc" (al Kutleh al'Amileh). The characteristic urban sight of Arabs wearing suits in public became very rare after the destruction of the Palestinian towns, and the image disseminated in the press was primarily one of backward fellahin.

Photographer: David Eldan, Government Press Office, January 25, 1949

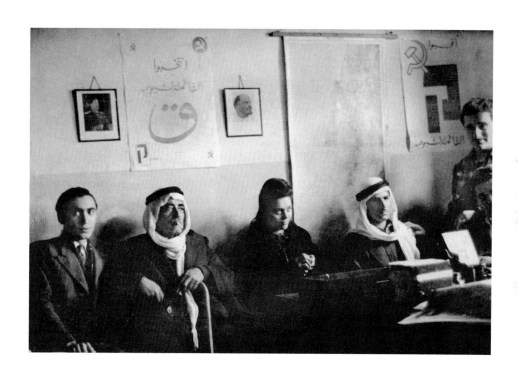

44   Election Day, elections to the First Knesset
Below the posters in Arabic, portraits of Lenin and
Stalin and a map of Palestine, members of the
Communist Party sit in their office preparing for the
future. With the establishment of the state of Israel
their shared vision – a binational state or a two-state
federation recognizing "the right of the two peoples
for independence in a unified, free and democratic

Palestine, based on the principle of full equality of civil,
national and political rights" – had been defeated. Their
stubborn efforts to salvage their dream and continue
to organize activities involving meaningful cooperation
between Arabs and Jews pushed them to the margins
of the political map, and sometimes even beyond.

Photographer not identified. Central Zionist Archives, 1949

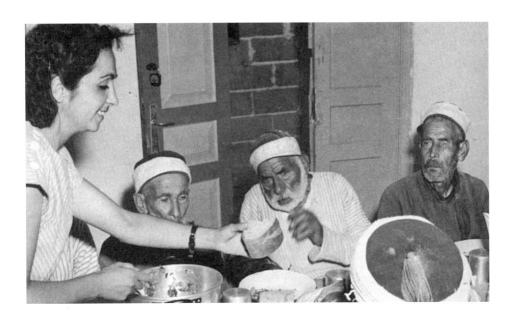

45   **al-Ramle** Blind persons were among those
on the list of "Destitute people in Ramleh" (which
also include those who were ill, elderly, handicapped
and women with children) prepared by an official in
the Ministry of Minorities who urgently appealed
to his superiors to "provide them with free food."
"We wish to call your attention to the urgency of the
matter," the official wrote in his letter, "because these
families have been left with no means of subsistence
and each passing day brings them closer to complete
destitution." No pictures of "families literally starving to
death," such as those described in one of the internal
memos, have been found in the archives. Only pictures
like this one, taken at food distribution locations in
the town, showing a welfare worker providing food.
Her broad smile for the camera is chilling against the
background of the solemn expressions of the blind.
Even though they can't see the camera, they surely feel
the presence of the photographer who's taking their
picture while they receive food from the state.

Photo scanned with the compliments of Beno Rothenberg, from the
photographic album ("Our Finest Year") which he edited, 1948

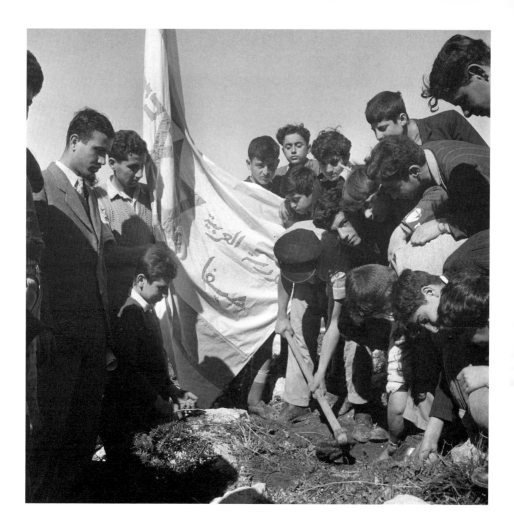

The official JNF caption: "Haifa tree-planting ceremony – Municipal school pupils from minority communities plant trees."

46   Haifa Even before the state of Israel was established, the Yishuv's institutions transformed the Tu B'Shvat festival into a day in which trees were planted all over the country as a way of strengthening the connection of the foreign-born population to the land. After the establishment of the state, Israeli boys and girls in festive white shirts continued to participate in tree-planting ceremonies. Only later would some of them discover that the trees they planted were intended to conceal crimes committed at that location, and bury the ruins beneath them. The national flag, on which the name of the school was written in Hebrew and in Arabic, provides the auspices under which "children from minority communities" participated in the ceremony. The children in the picture were old enough to have felt Haifa's shock when some 60,000 of its residents were expelled. As they crowd around the hoe to dig a hole in the earth, it's difficult not to imagine them peering into it as part of their attempt to reconnect with that catastrophe.

Photographer: Rudolf Jonas, JNF Photographic Archive, February 1950

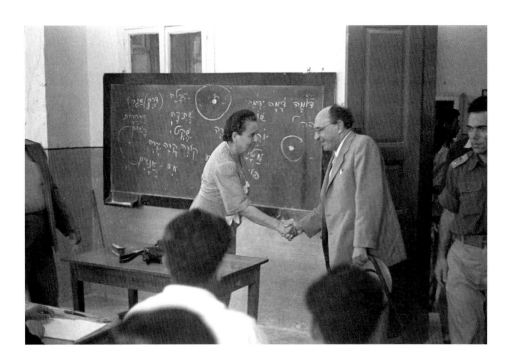

47   **al-Nasirah/Nazareth** The Minister of Education
shakes hands with the woman teaching Hebrew to
Arab educators. Hebrew instruction was carried out
under the auspices and supervision of the military
government, one of whose staff can be seen at
the right. Only teachers whose views had been
investigated and approved by the military government,
and who were not suspected of disloyalty to the state,
were allowed to enroll in the classes.

Photographer not identified. Government Press Office, July 27, 1949

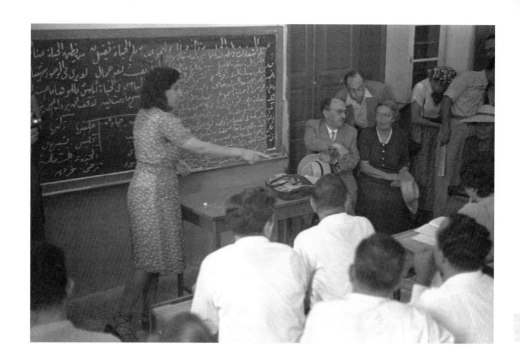

48   al-Nasirah/Nazareth Jewish teachers learn
Arabic. The Minister of Education and his wife are
seated with their backs to the blackboard. Even today,
60 years after the establishment of the state, few
Jews learn Arabic as a normal component of their
citizenship, while many in the political leadership and in
the population continue to ignore the language. There
are some exceptions, those few who see their future
in the security services, where knowledge of Arabic is
a necessary tool, as it was for the military governor of
al-Nasirah.

Photographer not identified. Government Press Office, July 27, 1949

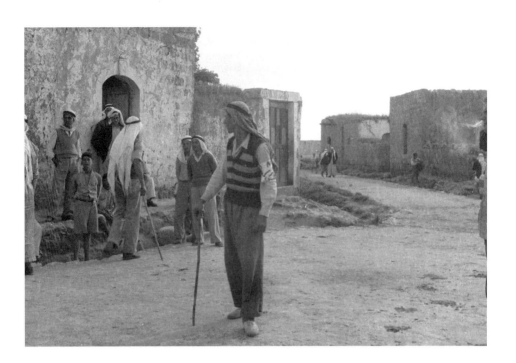

49   **Qalanswa** The many tasks of policing and
control required of the regime in order to administer
the population of Arab subjects for whom the new
regime symbolized the destruction of its society were
more than could be met by the Jewish manpower that
could be recruited to carry them out. Thus, guided by
liberal egalitarian ideas, and the military concept of
security, Arabs were included right from the beginning,
if only to a limited degree, in the apparatus of
supervision and control. The look one of their own gives
them, as he wears an armband identifying him with the
state apparatus, will no longer be the same look. The
military government that appoints him hopes that, at
the moment of truth, when one of those deported from
the village tries to return, he'll feel sufficiently obligated
to the regime that he too will define the returning
refugee as a foreign infiltrator.

Photographer: David Eldan, Government Press Office, May 10, 1949

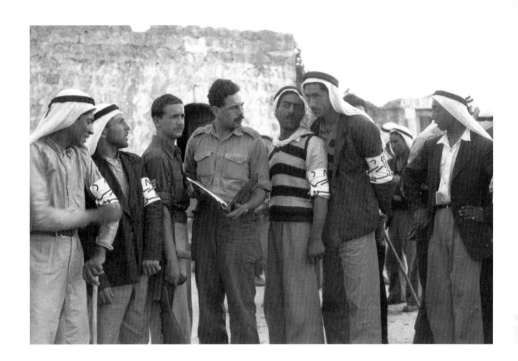

50   **Qalanswa** The man on the left, wearing
an armband, can't keep from smiling excitedly. The
attributes of power, the authority they provide, can be
exhilarating. The people standing to the right of the
officer who explains their new role seem somewhat
uncertain about his instructions, wondering among
themselves whether what they understood is what he
actually meant. The guard on the right, busy studying
his neighbor's armband, may be trying to see in it his
own reflection as a guard who is part of the military
government.

Photographer: David Eldan, Government Press Office, May 10, 1949

51   **Western Galilee** Druze, Bedouin and
Circassians already began joining the Haganah in 1947.
In August 1948, their operations were unified in the
"Minorities Unit," and the Israeli army uniforms they
wore, appropriately displayed by the soldiers during
this roll call, included a traditional kaffiyeh. They were
kept standing on the threshold – not actually inside,
but not completely outside, either. They were, in fact,
assigned to guard the threshold, to locate Palestinian
refugees trying to return home and view them as illegal
infiltrators to be deported.

Photographer: Frank, IDF and Defense Archive, June 1, 1949

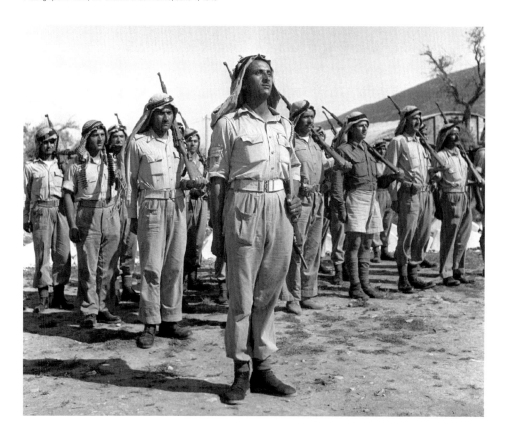

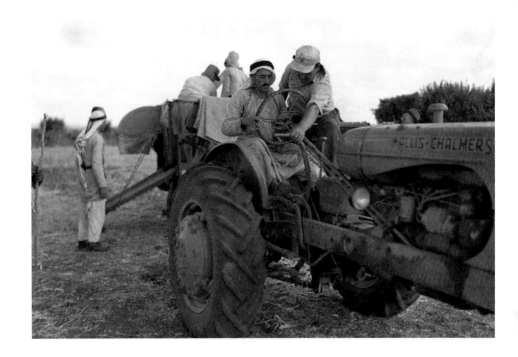

52   **Jaljulya** After 13,200 dunums were
expropriated from Jaljulya's farmers by declaring
their land to be the "property of present absentees,"
despite the fact that they were not only present but
also citizens of the state, leaving only 800 dunums
in their hands, the state could afford to improve their
means of production without fearing that a few new
tractors would allow them to compete with Jewish
farmers. In addition to expropriating land, the state
took many other measures to prevent Arabs from
freely competing with Jews in the market for labor
and for goods. The photograph shows Ministry of
Agriculture staff, wearing baseball caps, teaching Arab
fellahin to operate a modern tractor. The discourse of
modernization structured the hierarchy of relations
between Jews and Arabs, but also helped integrate
Arabs, always as inferiors, into the new market
arrangements in which they would participate.

Photographer: Teddy Brauner, Government Press Office,
August 10, 1949

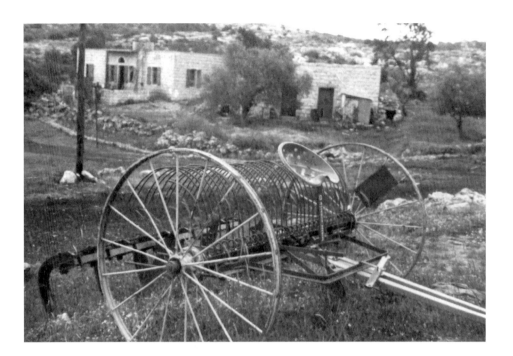

53 **Kufr Bir'im** The settlement group that would eventually establish Kibbutz Bar'am found itself with thousands of dunums of land. They also needed new equipment to work it.

Photographer not identified. The photograph was given to Nahida Zahra, a member of the second generation of those dispossessed from Kufr Bir'im, by a member of Kibbutz Bar'am (scanned with the compliments of Meron Farah, who is also one of those dispossessed from Kufr Bir'im), 1948

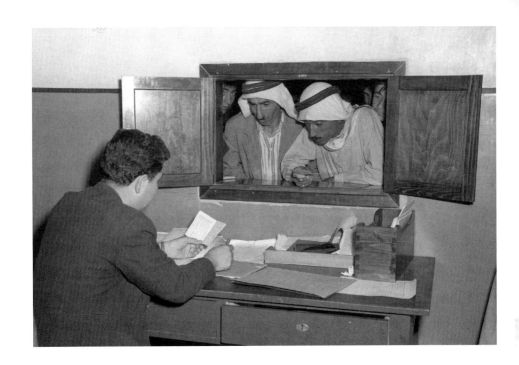

54   **al-Nasirah/Nazareth** Arabs needed travel
permits to work for Jewish employers, where pay
was higher than what they could receive working
for an Arab. The economic and national advantage
inherent in Arab willingness to work for less pay
and for longer hours than usual had to be balanced
against the national interest in preserving Jewish
labor and reducing Jewish unemployment. The
military government was responsible for preserving
this delicate balance, granting few travel permits
and thereby regulating the flow of Arab job-seekers
reaching the Employment Service's narrow counters.
Arabs were sent more than once to work on land
adjoining their villages, land that had once been theirs
but was now in the hands of Jews who received
the income it generated, while the Arabs were paid
only a modest wage, and sometimes received only a
portion of the harvest, but no money. The men in the
photograph have already overcome the first hurdle on
the way to a job – obtaining a permit – and now they're
anxiously watching the clerk, hoping he'll find in the
papers he's looking at confirmation that the permit
they're showing him is valid.

Photographer not identified. Government Press Office,
September 1, 1949

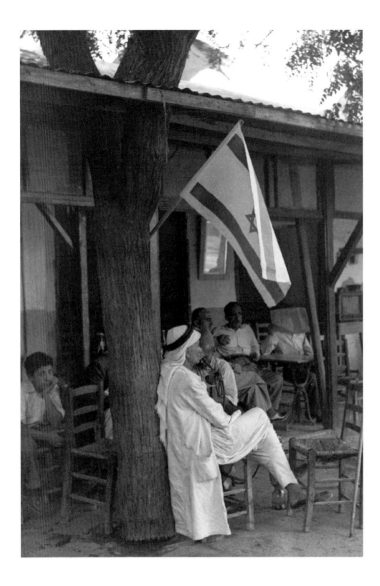

55   **Akka/Akko** Usually the relaxed posture of people sitting in a café can't tell you anything about what's happening a few yards outside the frame. After the disruption that was caused by Acre becoming a way-station for thousands of refugees, and by the spreading typhus epidemic, rehabilitation proceeded fairly slowly. The flag stuck on the front of the café could be part of the effort to stabilize life in the town and come to terms with its new circumstances. The law passed five months earlier, defining where and when the national flag should be displayed, prohibited its commercial use, but neither required nor prohibited its display anywhere other than on public buildings. Though it isn't possible to know whether the owner of the café was forced to display the flag, or whether he did so at his own initiative, its presence seems not to have deterred locals from continuing to gather and sit on its front terrace in chairs of woven reeds.

Photographer: Fritz Cohen, Government Press Office, June 1, 1949

56. Kufr Bir'im Socializing the Arabs involved a double socializing mechanism in every area of life, subordinating the Arabs and transforming the Jews into masters. Youth movements and "Nahal" settlement groups served as hothouses that made the relations of dominance, and the neglect that accompanied them, second nature. "Good deeds" played a large part in making the crime possible. Thus, for example, when members of settlement groups moved into the village houses, they stored away most of the possessions of those who had been deported, thereby signifying their explicit intention to refrain from looting. Thus it was easier to lose sight of the act of looting of houses and land in which they participated. Members of the youth movements lived in the houses of Kufr Bir'im's residents, while those who had been expelled were sleeping at night on the hillside; they'd prepare food for themselves in the expellees' kitchens while the latter didn't have enough to eat and drink; they would enjoy the fruits and vegetables grown by the people who had originally lived there; they'd sit down to dinner together on their terrace and discuss how to construct a just society while the former inhabitants of the house had been excluded from that society's sphere of justice. Wearing white shirts and speaking socialism, most contradictions evaporating, this segment of the population, playing the role of leftists-with-a-conscience, developed most of the formulations legitimizing the plunder.

Photographer not identified. The photograph was given to Nahida Zahra, a member of the second generation of those disposed from Kufr Bir'im, by a member of Kibbutz Bar'am (scanned with the compliments of Meron Farah, who is also one of those dispossessed from Kufr Bir'im), 1948

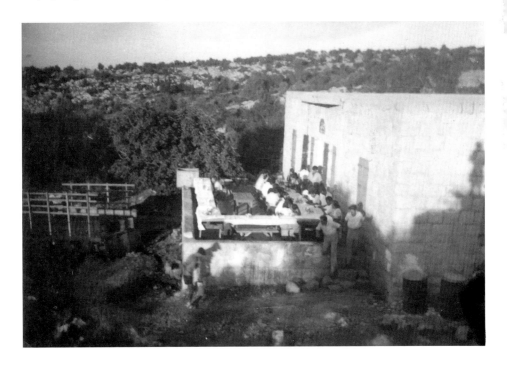

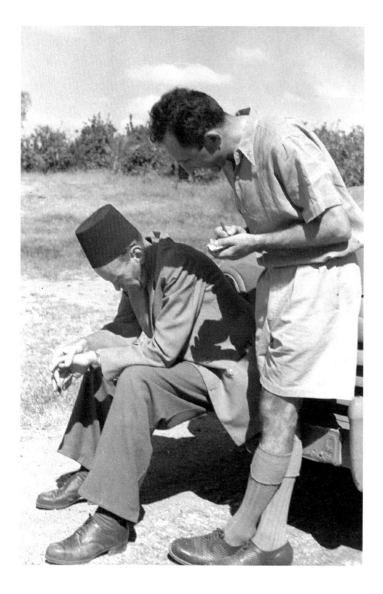

57   **al-Ramle** A few hours after the city had surrendered. Anything the journalist – if he was, indeed (according to the official caption), a journalist – was able to learn from the Arab, who is obviously unwilling to cooperate with the interrogation, will become irrelevant in a few days when the expulsion of people from the city begins. Meanwhile, if he changes his mind and decides to talk, he'll already be able to tell the journalist that young men have been arrested and gathered together in locations from which they'll be taken to prison camps.

Photographer: David Eldan, Government Press Office, January 11, 1948

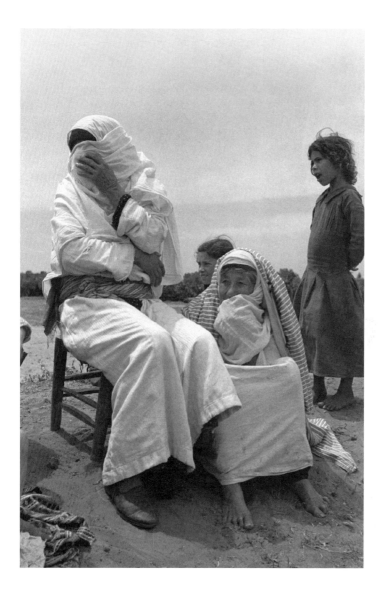

58   **al-Tira** The woman in the photograph might have had many reasons not to cooperate with the Government Press Office photographer, but the stereotypical view of Arab women, like the view of Arab men, narrows them down to "religious reasons" (according to the official caption accompanying the photograph). This makes it possible to distance the Jewish photographer and the employees of the archive for which he's taking the photographs from the female Arab subject. Gathering information on the local population often involved confirming the framework in which it was viewed. She, moreover, like the girls next to her, turns her head to the right, toward the ceremony celebrating the first anniversary of the official transfer of their village to Israel as part of the armistice agreement with Jordan.

Photographer: Fritz Cohen, Government Press Office, May 7, 1950

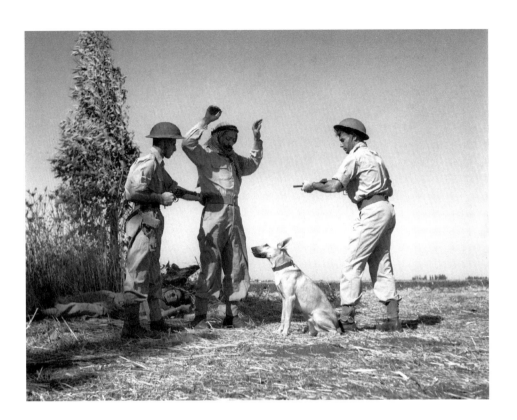

59   In addition to the military benefit of simulating
"How to capture an Arab prisoner," the exercise shows
how the Arab's response is imagined, or at least
the way the soldiers want it to be displayed for the
photographer documenting the exercise. The people
running it had the help of "half" an Arab: he's either
a Jew who glued on a mustache and wore a kaffiyeh
in order to become an Arab, or he's a soldier from the
Minorities Unit who in any event is viewed by Jews
as resembling what they imagine an Arab looks like.
Whatever the case, the "Arab" in the performance
looks down at the ground, raises his hands in
surrender, and the two soldiers standing by don't have
to use any force at all. The third soldier, who's lying
on the ground, can take a nap; maybe he's playing a
"casualty" in this show.

IDF and Defense Archive (Source: IDF Maps and Photographs
Service), November 9, 1948

60   This photograph displays one of the many
ways the rich repertoire of methods for gathering
information about Arabs operated: taking the "stoolie"
for interrogation. Some interrogations were violent,
some were conducted pleasantly and involved building
deceptively friendly relationships with the people being
questioned. The intelligence noncom in the photograph
(Scouts Department, Fourth Battalion "HaPortzim," Fifth
Headquarters Unit) and the Arab from whom he wants
information seem, in the photograph, to be smiling
pretty broadly. Will the Arab still look that way after the
interrogation?

Photographer not identified. Palmach Photographic Collection
(Har'el Brigade album. Photograph provided by Abraham Ben Porat,
from Even Yehuda), 1948

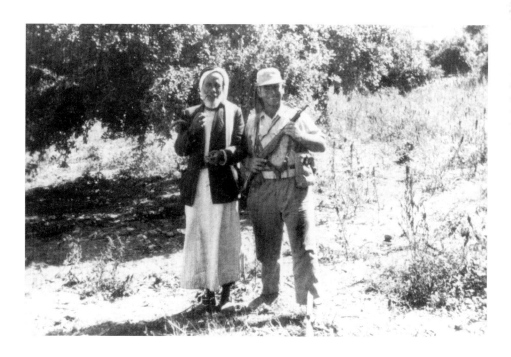

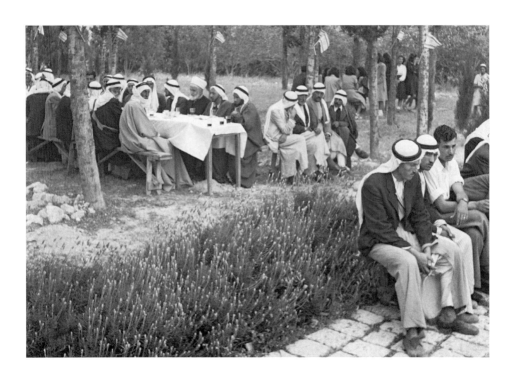

61   **al-Nasirah/Nazareth** The Government Press
Office sent a photographer to document "Guests of the
Military Governor on Independence Day." The event,
held outdoors, shaded by trees decorated with the
national flag, provided an opportunity to see whether
the Arabs were willing to publicly display their loyalty to
the state. Those who failed to attend had their absence
noted. So, everyone must have shown up.

Photographer: Fritz Cohen, Government Press Office, April 23, 1950

CHAPTER 3

Architecture of Destruction, Dispossession and Gaining Ownership

The ruined landscape visible in the photographs is the most compelling testimony to the fact that what occurred here between November 1947 (after the Partition Plan) and March 1949 was not a war but rather policy, carried out by many and various means. The policy readily evident in the photographs is one of destruction – destruction of Palestinian society, habitat and landscape, together with the destruction of the delicate forms of cooperation that were gradually constructed, to different degrees of closeness, between Jews and Arabs from the nineteenth century to the end of the 1940s. The massive destruction shown in the photographs is not the result of a war for survival, of battles, of existential distress. This destruction was unnecessary, intentional, straightforward, systematic, utilitarian, harsh, alienated, premeditated, indifferent and, in particular, intended to socialize the population to the new political regime. From its inception until today, as the state of Israel continues to demolish Palestinian homes with a wave of its hand, this unnecessary destruction has been understood as a legitimate means in "special cases," in a manner which conceals the fact that it is an end in itself. The reasons and justifications put forth to socialize the country's Jewish citizens to view this destruction as *a legitimate means* were many and varied: the buildings were occupied by "terrorist cells," they were on the verge of collapse, Palestinian construction does not meet modern standards, they were not hygienic, there were problems, needs of immigrant absorption, Jews have different requirements from the locals, the threat of refugees returning – the "infiltrators," as the Palestinians expelled after May, 1948, were called – if their homes are left standing. A few of these reasons, if offered off-handedly and in particular and limited cases, might seem to be to the point, but when they are repeated again and again they can only be direct expressions of power, violence and racism. They were freely substituted for one another as needed, and the sum of them transformed the brutal, unnecessary destruction of people's homes into an available tool that many were authorized to employ. In that sense, the destruction was an excellent means of socialization for Jewish citizens whom the regime wished to turn into collaborators with its actions, to make them accept the destruction and recognize its necessity. Not only the dispossession of the Palestinians from the landscape of their lives was written on the surrounding desolation, but also a fundamental basis of the Jewish citizens' habitus – wrapping the disaster that befell others in an array of justifications and arguments that made it bearable and, usually, seeming other than it was. In a few cases, Jewish citizens actively participated in the destruction, but they usually found themselves looking at mounds of what-once-had-been-homes. It was sometimes difficult to reconstruct the living room wall from the stones removed by schoolgirls sent to the "abandoned villages" (Photo 97). The "abandoned" home in Ayn Karim that was given to new immigrants seemed to them like a miracle, and the question of who had been the previous owners was only irritating (Photo 92). Elsewhere, existential needs were so urgent that questions about the destruction simply did not arise. The massive destruction took place in a brightly illuminated arena, so it was impossible to deny or assign responsibility for it to others (as blame for the "refugees" was assigned to "Arab states") (Photos 68 and 85). The destruction required a new vocabulary from which its unbearable aspect had been removed, one that normalized it. Destruction and more destruction and more destruction, and as it continued the initial hesitant questions were no longer asked, those that had no answers were forgotten, and as time went by it became part of a past there was no point in awakening. Thus the demolition of a house whose inhabitants had been expelled or fled no longer sent a chill down the spine and raised no moral quandary. The justification ceased to be a problem; destruction became part of the landscape. Everyone helped remove the rubble – kindergarten children, elementary and high school pupils, laborers and volunteers, all were enlisted to build the country. Clearing the rubble of demolished Arab homes simply became synonymous with building the land (Photo 93).

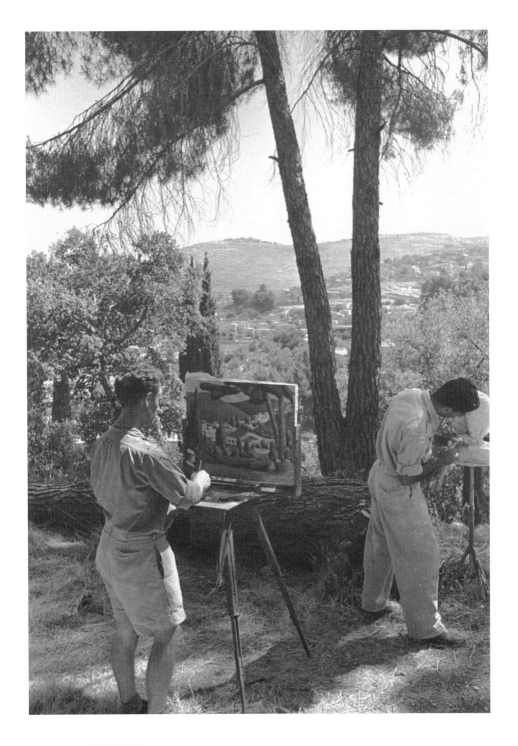

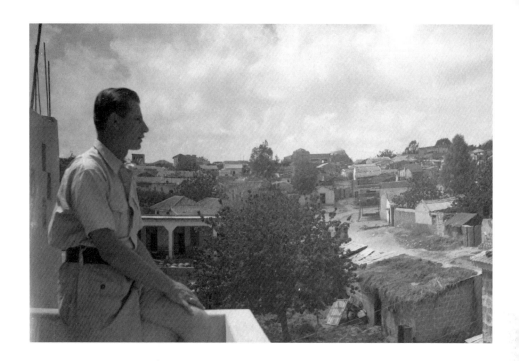

The official JNF caption: "Ein Karem Jerusalem – Kibbutz artists' course in Ein Karem."

62   Ayn Karim So many buildings in each village had been destroyed that the few which remained standing were now isolated jewels from the past which could be reset in what had become "new." Since most of the country's villages had been depopulated or destroyed, Ayn Karim, whose buildings were left standing, survived as a pearl from days gone by. So, despite the fact that Jews were already living in the homes of those who had been expelled, artists could come and paint in an authentic Arab village. In the 1970s, when I studied art in high school and we were asked to look at this landscape, it no longer signified an Arab village. We were asked to paint a view of Jerusalem, inspired by the Jewish artists who had done so before us.

Photographer: Werner Braun, JNF Photographic Archive, July 1, 1950

63   Salama The village is already deserted and emptied of its inhabitants, who were expelled, and there's no one left to ask "Who moved into my house?" No one will intrude on the picture-postcard scene of a desolate village, the background to a meditative portrait of an unobstructed view all the way to the horizon.

Photographer: Beno Rothenberg, Israel State Archive, probably late April/early May 1948

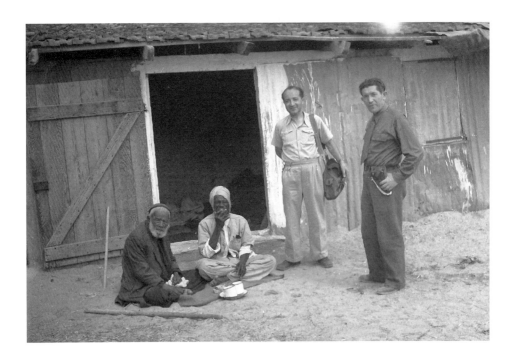

64   **Salama** 6,670 Moslems and 60 Christians
lived in the village before it was captured. Ben Gurion
arrived immediately after it fell, and to emphasize that
it had been emptied of Arabs he noted in his diary
that, other than an old, blind Arab woman, he didn't
see a living soul there. How many other old women
or men who could no longer see anything (or report
what they saw) were still at that moment in the village,
which was starting to look like a stage set ready for
dismantling, its dilapidated buildings to be replaced
by new construction? Soon they were also removed
from their homes, and their lands swallowed up by the
development of Tel Aviv.

Photographer: Beno Rothenberg, Israel State Archive, probably late
April/early May 1948

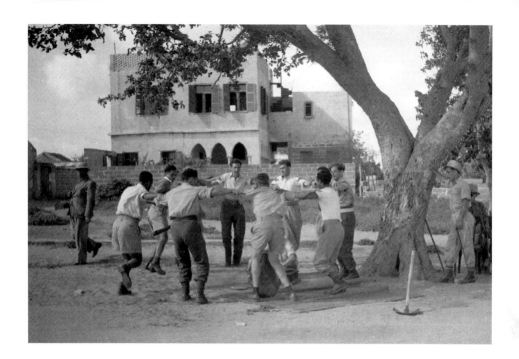

65   **Salama** The Arab house with the arches, the
hoe (the implement, but also the use of its Arabic
term "Turia"), the phonograph the soldiers removed
from one of the houses, folk dances, including those
of the Bedouin and the Arabs, the large clay storage
jar (again, the implement, but also the Arabic term
"Jara") – all these, chosen sparingly, combined
with "their own western" culture, signify to them
authenticity. Thus, the new urban textures they had
a hand in creating on the ruins of the villages they
had a hand in destroying won't appear hollow, but
will possess historic depth. With the help of these
attributes, the expropriated history will be transformed
into a signifier of the past deprived of history.

Photographer: Beno Rothenberg, Israel State Archive, probably late
April/early May 1948

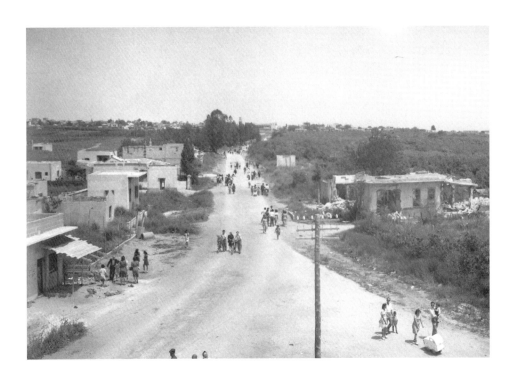

66   **Salama** Not a soul lives here. The Arabs
have been expelled, and Jews have not yet been
permitted to move in. The place has been designated
a closed military area because of fears of looting and
uncontrolled expropriation of property by individuals
but, as the picture shows, large numbers of Jewish
visitors streamed in to view the place that newspapers
had for months described as a "village of murderers."
They were very surprised to find the same things
they'd expect to find in normal homes – a phonograph,
records, newspapers, dolls and toys, pictures hanging
on the walls, schoolbooks, cups of coffee, dough that
had fermented and risen, attractive dishes, furniture
and clothing. In order to allay any suspicion that these
800 houses were not simply dwellings for 6,730
people but military outposts, the walls had "This
courtyard was inspected by the N. bomb squad"
written on them. When the bomb squad had finished,
the civilians in charge of distributing the property
"fairly" among Jews began their work, and wrote on
buildings not slated for demolition, like the one at the
left, "Jewish house."

Photographer: Beno Rothenberg, Israel State Archive, probably late
April/early May 1948

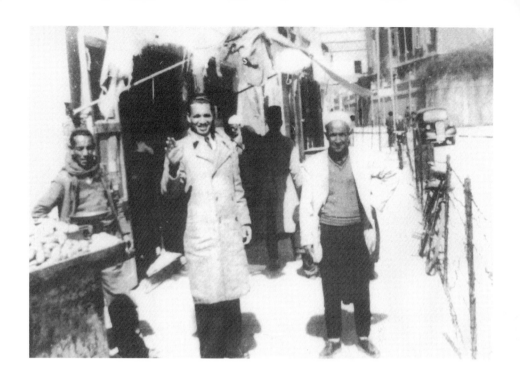

67   **Yafa/Jaffa** This is what a ghetto looks like.
Those imprisoned behind a fence smile and wave at
people looking at them from outside, hoping this time
to be rescued; among those on the other side are
people for whom this sight seems natural or justified.

Photographer not identified. With the compliments of "The Jaffa
Arab Committee" (al-Ratba 'L Ra'ayit Sha'un 'Arab Yafa), 1949

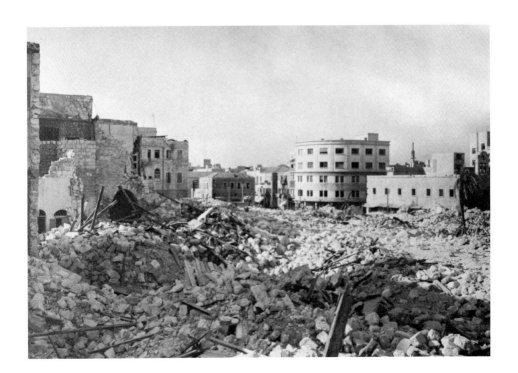

68   **Haifa** The destroyed city shown in the photograph
recalls Dresden, bombed for three consecutive days until
its buildings were in ruins, pulverized into stones that
blocked the streets. Haifa, in a series of photographs one
of which is displayed here, also has that appearance. But
this scene of destruction is inconsistent with descriptions
of the battle for Haifa, and is the result of a political
decision by a leadership determined to erase the Arab
towns so that refugees expelled from them would have
nowhere to return to and those who remained would feel
like strangers. Many workers and many days were needed
to clear the rubble left from the merciless destruction of
220 buildings in Haifa's old city. Jewish workers weren't
enough. They were joined by Arabs, most of them from
Haifa, who came to work each morning from the newly
created ghetto in Wadi Nisnas that had been established
for them after they had been expelled from their homes.
Isolated structures were seen as less threatening,
which was how the Carmelite Monastery or the circular
building in the center was saved. When the new regime's
institutions moved into these ancient buildings, they were
able to impose, on those who accepted it, an authority
that was partially based on some abstract ancient past.

Photographer: Jim Pringle, Associated Press, April 1948

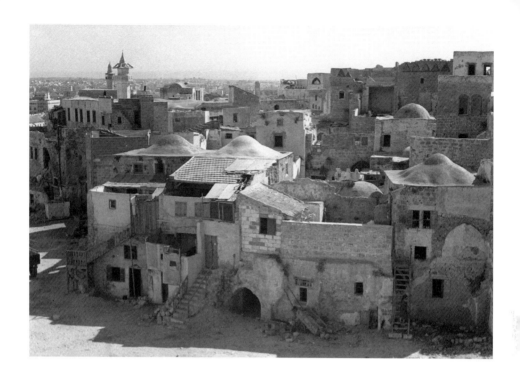

69   **Yafa/Jaffa** In the absence of any justification based on reasons of security or of settlement, the Jewish political and military leadership talked about "safety" – the buildings were defined as slums and marked for demolition. The experience gained from dynamiting tens of thousands of buildings during the war created a body of new knowledge. The "Mishor Ltd." cooperative, established by demobilized soldiers, used explosives to demolish neighborhoods and villages, saving, they claimed, dozens of man-days. The destruction of unique neighborhood fabrics, like that in the picture, which tourists from all over the world drive on narrow, winding roads to see, was described by members of the cooperative as fulfilling "extremely important, constructive goals." After 18 mosques and entire city neighborhoods were destroyed, it was a simple matter to seal Yafa's fate as an Arab town and annex it to Tel Aviv, for reasons like those stated by the Minister of Interior: "Yafa played no role in world history, nor in the history of Israel; it has no ancient cultural remains from any period."

Photographer: Teddy Brauner, Government Press Office,
October 1, 1949

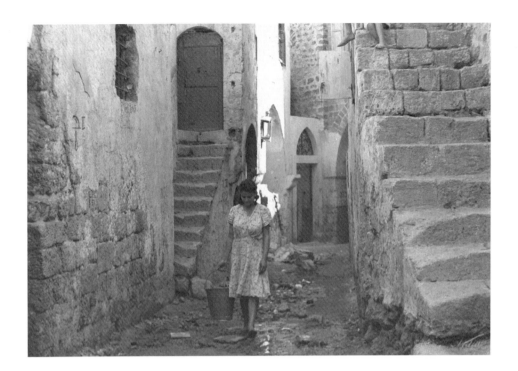

70   **Yafa/Jaffa** Had these buildings been spared
from destruction, Jewish artists would probably
also have been placed in them, painting typical Yafa
cityscapes. Captions such as the one that accompanied
this photograph, "A Moroccan immigrant is happy to
move out of these dilapidated Jaffa neighborhoods,"
prepared both the ground and the hearts for their
demolition.

Photographer: Teddy Brauner, National Photographic Collection,
October 1, 1949

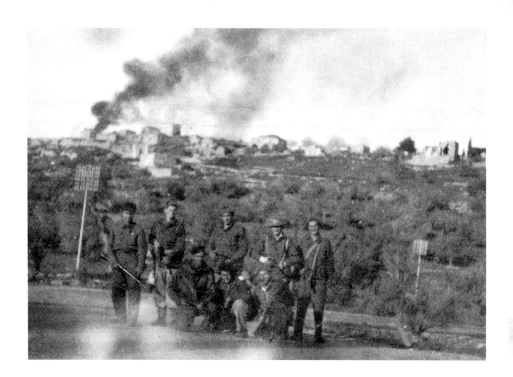

71   **Saris** The caption of the photograph in the
Palmach Archive reads, "Capture of Saris; sappers
'deal with' the houses." Linking the capture of Saris
to "dealing with" the houses is part of a systematic
effort to portray the destruction of Arab villages as a
necessary consequence of the war, and to conceal
the political reasons of state which motivated it.
The "sappers" in the photograph don't appear to be
"dealing with" the houses, but gather for a group
portrait at some distance from them, against the
backdrop of the village from which smoke still rises.
Those who sent them to "deal" with the houses
included some who already saw that a new Jewish
locality would arise on the ruins of the village, for
whom the village and its homes and mosques
represented "an important location from the security
standpoint." When this photograph was taken, the
residents evacuated from Saris were waiting not far
away, after having been taken from their homes as "the
houses were cleared one by one," and had become
unwilling observers of their own disaster.

Photographer not identified. Palmach Photographic Collection
(Album of the Har'el Brigade, Fourth Battalion. Photograph provided
by Meir Bareket), probably April 1948

72   **Salbit** The third soldier from the left puts
his hands over his ears to muffle the sound of
simultaneous explosions at a number of locations.
He and the other "sappers" ("khablan" – that's how
they're described in the original caption in the Palmach
Archive, and that's what we've learned to call them, so
that we don't get confused and forget they're not the
same as terrorists – "mekhabel" – Hebrew variations
on the same word) are watching the success of their
operation. This apocalyptic scene of burning villages
and earthshaking explosions is also visible to the
inhabitants of nearby villages. It complements the
rumors soldiers whispered to some of the residents
after the villages were captured but before the
inhabitants were expelled, so they would leave on their
own and the claim could be made that they'd fled.

Photographer not identified. Palmach Photographic Collection
(Album of the Har'el Brigade, Fourth Battalion), probably April 1948

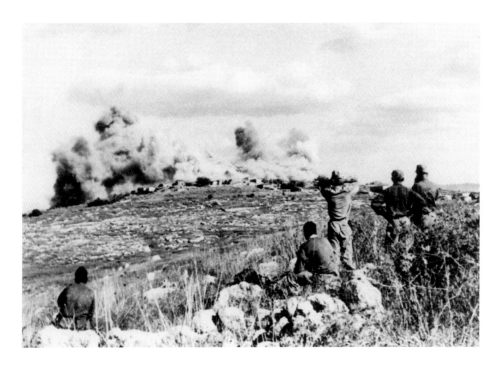

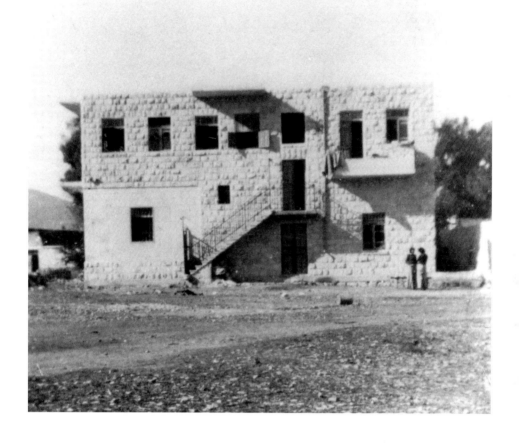

73   **Bisan** Bedding that hasn't been brought back
inside is still airing in the window. The house, like the rest
of the city, has already been emptied of its inhabitants.
The official caption that reads "Beit She'an abandoned,"
doesn't refer to what the photograph shows, but to
the achievement that created a "valley that's entirely
Jewish." The two women in the photograph don't give
the lie to that description, for they are present as internal
observers sharing the field of vision with the authors of
the official caption which serves to display for us a town
abandoned, rather than one whose inhabitants are to be
returned, a town that no longer belongs to those who
built it or who, until yesterday, lived there.

Photographer not identified. Palmach Photographic Collection
(Album of the Yiftah Brigade, Third Battalion), no date

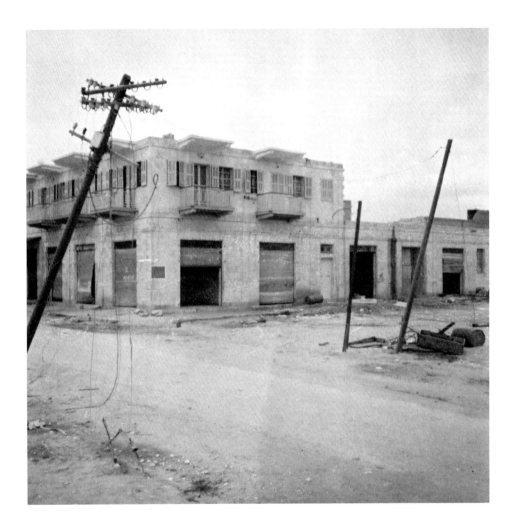

74   **Bir al-Sabi'e/Beersheba** The actual capture of the town during what is officially described as a "war" was only the first in a series of non-military occupations that validated the army's behavior and played their part in expropriating the town from its residents. These began with the caption's official wording that, in one version or other, was on everyone's lips – "The town is empty of inhabitants" – until, a few days later, this building became the JNF House. The owners of the shops on the ground floor, like the owners of the apartments above, must have been among the 450,000 refugees who in the 1960s filled out property-claim forms for the UN Reconciliation Commission that prepared an estimate (published on April 28, 1968) of the value of "abandoned" Arab property. There's no need to mention that Israel rejected the document and ignored its implications.

Photographer not identified. Palmach Photographic Collection (Album of the Har'el Brigade, Fourth Battalion), January 1949

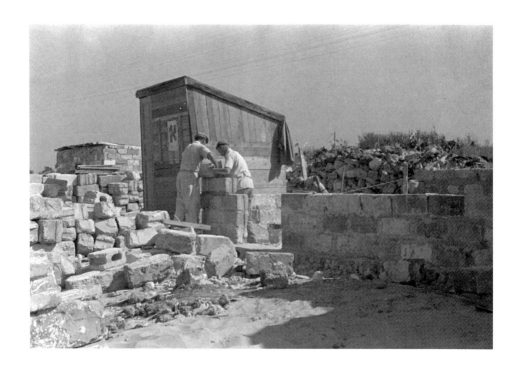

75   **Yazur** Jewish immigrants sent to live in Yazur worked to transform it into Azur. The photograph shows two of them building a new house for themselves. Construction of new housing units, while others stood empty nearby (most had been demolished because they had been classified as failing to meet Jewish building standards), was part of the systematic effort to transform the landscape and destroy the characteristic form of the Arab localities so refugees wouldn't be able to return, not only because of Israel's refusal to let them back but because the country would no longer be the same as one they had left. Various activities were undertaken to completely transform the landscape – a confusing mixture of construction and destruction. There were concrete structures built by Arabs in Yazur prior to its destruction, before that material had become identified with the expansion of Jewish construction in the 1950s.

Photographer not identified. Government Press Office, June 20, 1949

76   **'Aqir** The series of protests by the British and by MAPAM members against evacuating the village didn't help the 3,000 inhabitants confronting those imposing the transfer policy on the complex set of relations between Jews and Arabs. Later protests by the Ministry of Minorities against moving immigrants into the village didn't help either, and it was made ready for Jewish settlement. As part of the preparations for populating the village, the new settlers were required to remove piles of rubble that seemed to be part of the new settlement's inventory, and bore no indication they had once been people's homes. The language of the official caption is spotlessly clean: "New immigrants remove broken stones from the abandoned village of 'Aqir." "An abandoned village," its land covered with "broken stones," becomes yet another entry in the glossary of neighborhoods. In those days the use of the term "abandoned" sometimes still preserved traces of the violent transformation required to turn an inhabited locality into one that is "abandoned" – "The [military government] wishes to turn it into an abandoned place." It didn't take long for "abandoned" to be used as an adjective describing the physical condition of buildings and environments.

Photographer: Zoltan Kluger, Government Press Office, October 1, 1949

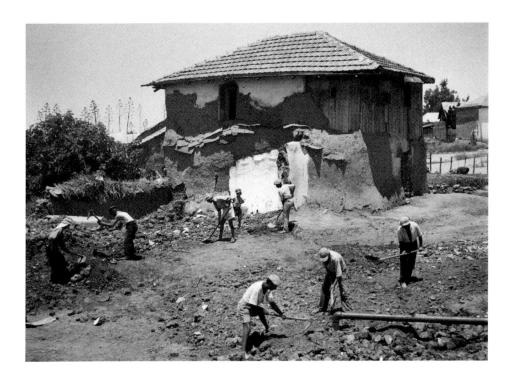

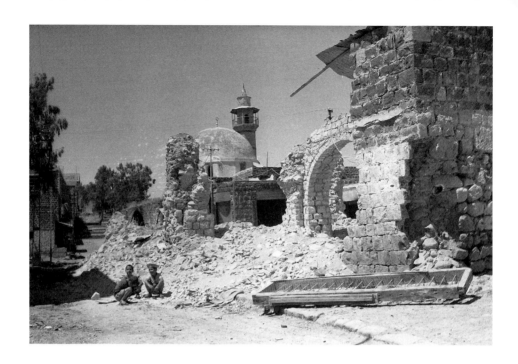

77   Tabariyya/Tverya 2,500 Arabs and 1,000 Jews lived in the old city of Tabariyya before it was destroyed (the total population of the town included 4,000 Arabs and 6,000 Jews). At first a small number of buildings were demolished "for security reasons" (even houses that belonged to Jews). The Jews who wanted to return to their homes were prevented from doing so with the excuse that their houses were unsafe. These houses, too, had suddenly become an obstacle to implementing the army's plan for transforming the face of the city. Generals don't like ancient towns in whose winding streets they find it hard to get a foothold. Very soon the ancient buildings were replaced by a broad avenue, around which a new urban fabric developed, more transparent to the military gaze. The Jewish inhabitants of Tabariyya had from the beginning opposed the military operation – including the expulsions and demolitions – that had been imposed on them, and carried out on their behalf as Jews. They, like the Arabs, had also been dispossessed, but unlike them, had been given in exchange homes belonging to Arabs in other neighborhoods of the city.

Photographer: Beno Rothenberg, Israel State Archive, April 1948

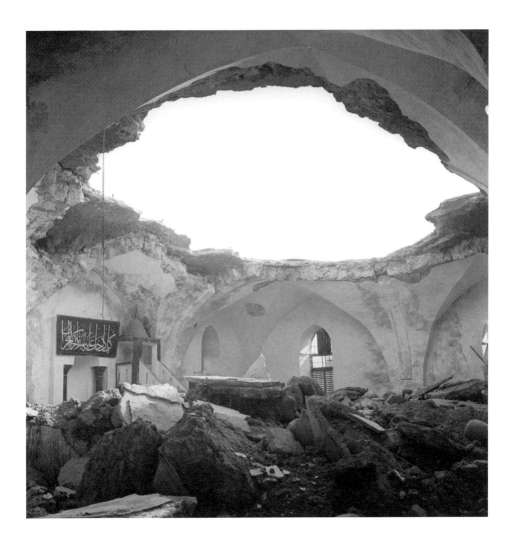

78   **al-Majdal** The orders not to demolish holy sites were widely disseminated, but the fact that dozens of mosques were in fact destroyed indicates that their more important purpose was to publicize the message that Israel did not damage holy sites. Of 160 mosques found in the area that became part of the state of Israel, about 40 remained standing. "Our soldiers don't destroy mosques," became a kind of leitmotif in the purity-of-arms legend. In December 2008, the Israeli government was still considering (without deciding) whether to rehabilitate 18 of the mosques it had partially demolished in 1948 and then done nothing to preserve them so their condition had further deteriorated. Although the al-Majdal mosque had been severely damaged and its dome was gone, its walls and their treasures were not damaged: the inscription, "While Zecharia visited her at the al-Mihrâb" (the prayer niche) to which the inscription refers, and the *Minbar* (the small platform on which the imam stood to preach) were still there. They could be rehabilitated.

Photographer: Frank, IDF and Defense Archive, June 10, 1949

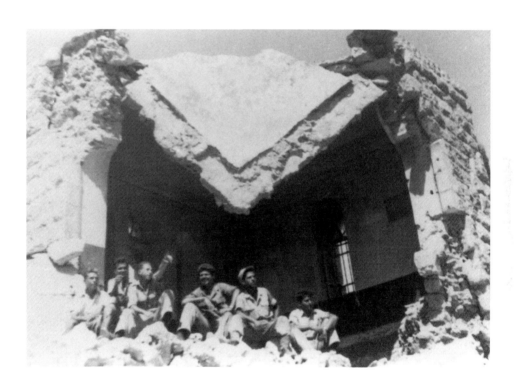

79 **Saris** A martyrs' forest (a memorial to Jewish victims of the holocaust) stands today in place of the village of which the demolished house in the picture was once a part, but there's no longer any other indication that it ever existed. Inspired by those who sent them, the soldiers who "cleared" (as they said) the village from house to house saw a strategic site "important from the point of view of security and of settlement," rather than a village where people live. The justification for bombing the village in April 1948 was that otherwise its buildings would be turned into a "fortified position." Sitting for a photograph, their backs to one of the demolished buildings, the soldiers can enjoy their view of the other buildings they destroyed, and point out to each other the marks they left on them and on the landscape.

Photographer not identified. Palmach Photographic Collection
(Album of the Har'el Brigade, Sixth Battalion. Provided by
Dov Keren, C. Glickson), 1948

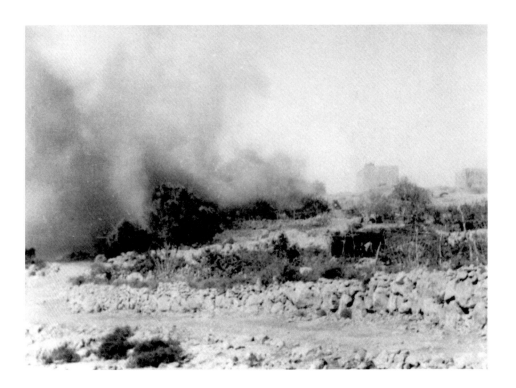

80   **Bayt It'ab** The 626 residents of the village
were expelled, and nothing remains of it but a
ruin that was spared. What probably saved it from
destruction was the belief that it's a Crusader
structure, and the desire to preserve the "location's
historical past." The vast amount of information
the fighters collected about the villages during
the 1940s allowed them to carry out "pinpoint" or
"intelligent" destruction," damaging only what was
necessary. That's how 193 houses were carefully
blown up, while this distinguished structure
was preserved. Historians later argued over the
attribution. Today, in any event, as it stands solitary
on the hill, this ruin has already accumulated
sufficient historical value even if it turns out to be
"only" a native Palestinian house.

Photographer not identified. Palmach Photographic Collection
(Ha'el Brigade album, obtained from Meir Shamir), 1948

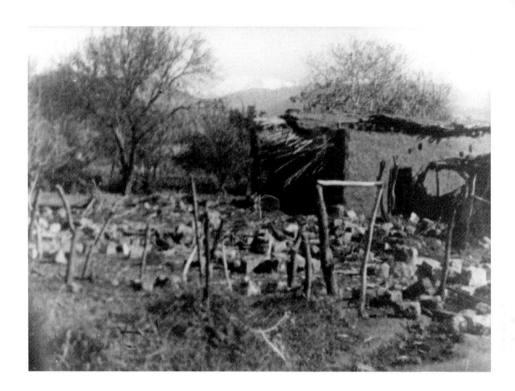

81   **al-Khisas** A few broken-down shacks and a few buildings were destroyed while the people living in them were still inside as an "act of reprisal" for the attack on a member of Kibbutz Ma'ayan Baruch, who died later from his wounds. It cost twelve dead including four children. Throwing grenades into a house in which a baby is crying (as reported by one of the participants), a person has to make a great effort to convince himself in the justice of "acts of reprisal." Shortly after the "reprisal," it was discovered that the attackers weren't from al-Khisas. An improvised field tribunal doesn't need proof in order to do justice. Contradictory evidence sometimes strengthens its authority and encourages turning more hypotheses into facts: "It is very unfortunate that children are put to bed in this small military outpost and fall victim to this kind of attack" (senior member of the Haganah, a few days after the massacre). At a meeting with Ben Gurion, in response to criticism of the attack, Moshe Dayan and Yigal Alon formulated Israel's political strategy: "Expressing a desire for peace will be interpreted as weakness." Afraid to be suspected of weakness, Israel continued attacking. When the fighters had completed their work, one of them took out a camera and documented the house; the photo in the archive still bears the initial caption – "A building blown up in an act of reprisal." In June 1949, the residents of al-Khisas, Qitiyya and al-Ja'una were expelled. In response to a question in the Knesset about the reasons for expelling the residents of these villages, who had "always been friendly," Ben Gurion replied: "Only the residents of Khisas deserve to be described in the terms used by the questioner ... and even so, the headquarters of the northern command had sufficient military justification for transferring them."

Photographer not identified. Palmach Photographic Archive (Yiftach Brigade album, provided by Yisrael Rashtik), December 18, 1947

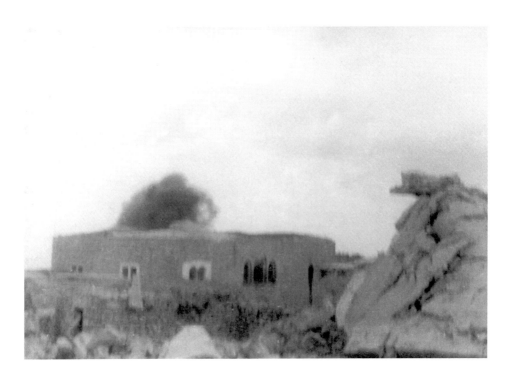

82   **Bayt Mahsir** This village had 2,784 inhabitants, living in 654 houses. Almost all the village buildings were destroyed "immediately following its capture," according to the official caption, and the few that remained standing were incorporated as jewels from the past in the new plan for the Jewish settlement of Beit Meir. The expelled villagers have lived since then in refugee camps outside of Israel. Their dispossession from their homes began a few years before they were expelled when, in the guise of lovers out for a stroll, or classes on nature walks, members of the Haganah went around openly with cameras (and sometimes with concealed cameras), collecting information and photographing the village's buildings and residents. Their homes were transformed into strongholds "having strategic and tactical topographical and political significance."

Photographer not identified. Palmach Photographic Collection
(Har'el Brigade album, provided by Dudu Sheni), May 1948

83	**Tel Aviv** Scouts who took the Haganah's training courses learned many skills, each of which was linked to an item whose explicit purpose was to generate information – a camera (photography), compass (navigation), ruler (diagrams and cross-sections), pencil (preparing maps) or binoculars (fieldcraft). But all these tools notwithstanding – any one of which could have indicated their profession – they chose something else for the class photograph – the kaffiyeh, which was existentially central to their being. Though they used it as camouflage, it served them even more importantly as a way to "know the enemy" and draw close to him. Excitement shows on their faces, and each of them tries to find the right expression. The kaffiyehs they're wearing connects them to the image of the Arab that fired their imagination, simultaneously an authentic local figure and a potential enemy. The photograph presents what is almost a primer to the variety of textiles and the ways of wrapping them around the head, as if it were intended as a guide – who wears which cloth, in what fashion, when it should be worn. As they worm their way into the Arabs' lives in order to prepare the "village files," they'll display their expertise in wearing kaffiyehs and making coffee. That will help them get friendly with the Arabs and collect personal information about the inhabitants and their lives – "how they go back and forth to work," "political opponents," "ethnic groups," "titles and nicknames."

Photographer not identified. Haganah Historical Archive, 1944

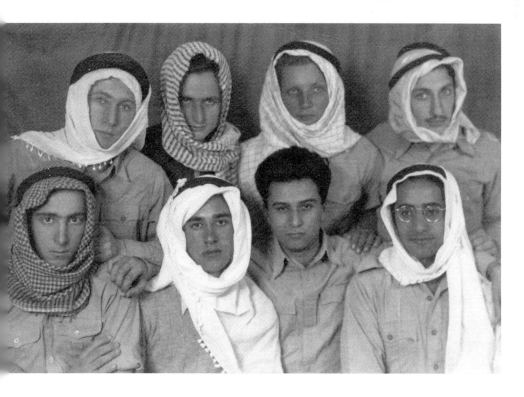

84 **Salama** The fact that this photograph was taken in order to prepare a "village file" – files prepared by the Haganah containing social, geographic and strategic information on each Arab village – explains why the photographer "failed" to center the subject in the frame, and "failed" to focus correctly. A souvenir snapshot from a trip camouflages the fact that the photographer is really interested in the main street running through the village, how the village space is organized, how people move through it. Photography was studied together with camouflage in the Haganah scouts' course, and could provide valuable topographical information that would be used "when the day arrives." The slight deflection of the camera away from the subject, to the main street, might not be noticeable to the untrained eye. A few years later, the information collected in Salama's village file helped capture the village and expel its residents.

Photographer not identified. Haganah Historical Archive, 1945

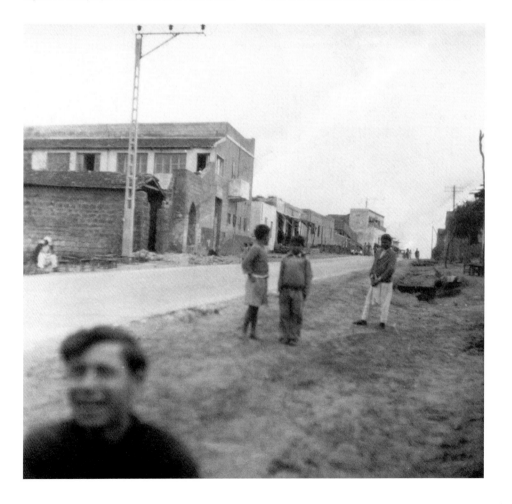

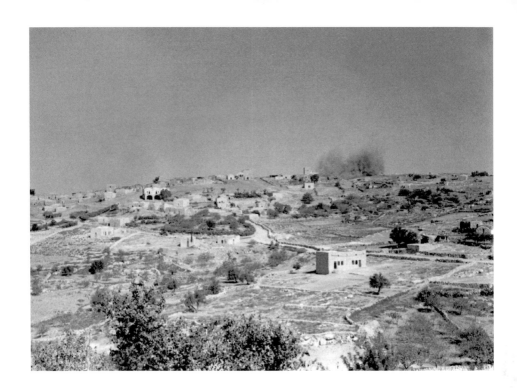

85   **Bayt Natif** Most buildings weren't blown up
haphazardly. Each demolition had its own justification,
one that allowed ordinary people to destroy the homes
of others without this being too much of a problem for
them. In the absence of such justifications, it's likely
that at least some of the soldiers who were part of
these actions wouldn't have participated in them. The
justification wasn't always "justice." From the moment
the Palestinian house lost its right to exist in and of
itself, and was perceived only in relation to Israeli
needs, a phrase like "Expanding the transportation
corridor to Jerusalem" was enough to eliminate any
doubt regarding demolitions. Each explosion, each
destruction required redrawing the map. And so, little
by little, over the course of almost two years, a new
map was created, reflecting not only a change in land
ownership but a total transformation of the face of the
country.

Photographer not identified. Palmach Photographic Archive
(Har'el Brigade album), no date

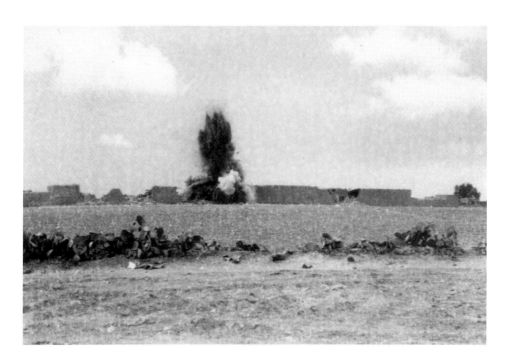

86   **Bir al-Sabi'e/Beersheba** Veteran residents, the
people who gave the order to blow up buildings in Bir
al-Sabi'e and elsewhere in the country, are the same
ones who later chose their own homes from among
the few they hadn't destroyed, later to be valorized as
"ancient." Intimate familiarity with them will lead some
of these residents to develop an interest in architectural
preservation and in later years even sue in the High
Court of Justice to prevent the demolition of buildings
"dating from the Ottoman period," and organize
guided tours of these neighborhoods. Nonetheless,
these precious houses will never be described as
"Palestinian."

Photographer not identified. Palmach Photographic Archive
(Yitzhak Sadeh album, received from Yoram Sadeh), no date

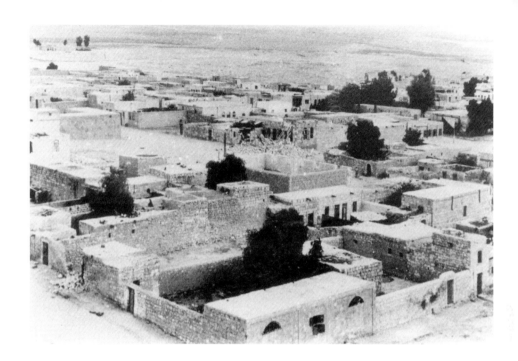

87 **Bir al-Sabi'e/Beersheba** Many accounts of
Bir al-Sabi'e's capture describe plunder and looting.
Ben Gurion and the Custodian of Absentee Property
were among those criticizing looting of homes. But
everyone was silent about the systematic plunder of
land and buildings. Imagine the urban landscape shown
here, dating to the beginning of the twentieth century,
preserved and transformed into the ancient center of a
cosmopolitan, multicultural Beersheba.

Photographer not identified. Palmach Photographic Archive
(Negev Brigade album), 1948

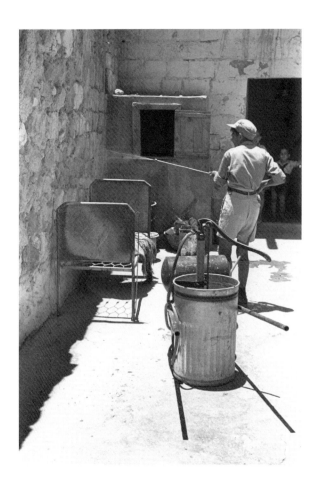

88   **Bir al-Sabi'e/Beersheba** Military occupation was not enough to turn Bir al-Sabi'e, which was to have been included in the Arab state, into a Jewish town. Civil occupation was also necessary. Beginning in October 1948, after extensive areas had been captured in military operations in the south and in the north, feverish discussions were held regarding the appropriate procedure for taking over Arab land. These discussions occurred in various committees established for that purpose – the Transfer Committee headed by Yosef Weitz, the Ministerial Committee for Abandoned Property, the Committee for Distributing Lands, the JNF – as well in conversations and discussions between the Prime Minister and his associates. The solution eventually found, after many revisions, was for the state to "legally" sell the "abandoned" lands to the JNF as part of a "development plan" so that the rights of the original owners would allegedly be preserved. In May 1949, when Israel was accepted as a member of the United Nations, the hairsplitting ceased, and all the territory which was "held" became part of the sovereign state of Israel. It was now important to quickly get the buildings ready for new Jewish immigrants. During the early years, the state used DDT to fumigate both the bodies of Jewish immigrants from North Africa so they wouldn't transmit disease, and the walls of the Arab houses before the Jewish immigrants moved in. If the boy has already learned Hebrew, and knows how to ask what the man holding the large, noisy apparatus is doing, the proud reply would certainly be that he's preparing a lovely, disease-free home for him.

Photographer not identified. Government Press Office, June 1, 1949

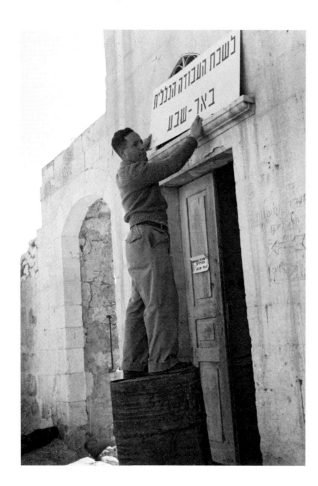

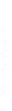

89   Bir al-Sabi'e/Beersheba Something of the excitement one feels in moving into a new house comes through in this photograph – the belongings scattered about, the pictures and other evidence that the new occupants are making it their home. Something on the order of, "Here, we've only just arrived in this desolate town and we're already overcoming all the difficulties, improvising ladders out of barrels, and even establishing a local labor exchange to provide welfare services to the new residents." It was only natural to locate government offices in the old buildings, in order to give the new regime an appearance of stability and permanence. The clerk places the sign on the window ledge, which seems to him as if it had been constructed for that purpose. One day someone might tell him, or his superiors, that it's totally absurd for the sign to conceal the building's beautiful arch. The sign will be moved elsewhere, and everyone will be amazed at the handsome structure. But they'll forget how beautiful it is when someone asks them about Palestinian culture before 1948, and reply, "No, no – most of the people here were primitive fellahin." And, of course, no one knew the name of any of the Palestinian architects who designed the various buildings, in different styles, that existed here, of which only a few traces remain.

Photographer: Zoltan Kluger, Government Press Office,
April 30, 1949

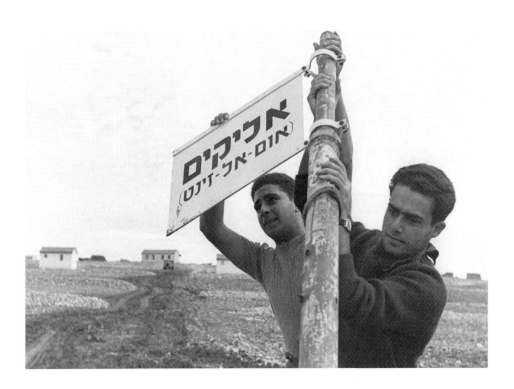

אילים
(אום אל-זינת)

90   **Umm al-Zinat** A new settlement – Elyakim – springing up *de novo* beyond the sign. If you look at the piles of earth along the road, you can see that they're mixed with the rubble of Umm al-Zinat's 209 houses, crushed into bits after their 1,470 residents were expelled. Beginning in the 1930s, the JNF's Names Committee took steps to Hebraize the country's map, with Ben Gurion's enthusiastic support – "Just as we refuse to recognize Arab political ownership of the land, we also refuse to recognize their cultural patrimony, or their place names." Had it been solely up to the committee, Arab names would have been completely erased from the lexicon – "Since the places referred to no longer exist, the names of these places are also to be eliminated." But how could the history of the "War of Independence" be written if the names of villages in which the soldiers fought were completely erased? How will new immigrants find their way when old-timers, a significant part of whose lives were connected to a detailed knowledge of Arab Palestine, still referred to the villages by their original Arab names? In 1950, Yemenite immigrants, on the lands of Umm al-Zinat, could erect a sign at the entrance to the village on which both names appeared. Since 1952, thanks to an intensive "informational and educational" campaign, the Hebraizing project had been successful and the new names took root. Signs that bore Arabic names were removed. Old-timers would pronounce the Hebraized names of certain locations as if they were in Arabic in order to identify themselves as natives (for example, "Zakkariya" rather than "Zecharya").

Photographer: Teddy Brauner, Government Press Office, 1950

91   al-Yahudiyya When these immigrants registered at the local branch of the Workers' Party of *Eretz* Yisrael (MAPAI), they probably had not yet become aware that the country's workers' movement had been completely transformed from one based on class and concerned with workers throughout the world ("Unite!") into a national movement that dispossessed most of the country's Arab farmers and workers from their lands and their jobs. Nor did the veteran Jewish members of MAPAI consider this transformation – "from a class to a nation," as Ben Gurion memorably characterized it in 1947 – nor what transpired in its aftermath and in its name, the dispossession of the Arabs from their land and the expropriation of their property and their means of production – to be a watershed moment, a shock, a betrayal of the original idea. The many moralizing arguments that accompanied this crime, always focusing on issues that were marginal to the main criminal act, served to legitimize it and made it part of the local socialist discourse. How could the new immigrants have even noticed anything if the previous signs, which must have been written in Arabic, had already been removed from the lintels of the buildings, and no trace of them remained? A new sign, smaller than its predecessor, replaced them, announcing the socialist future and even expressing concern for the welfare of the new immigrants.

Photographer: Beno Rothenberg, Israel State Archive. Photo taken around the time that people moved in.

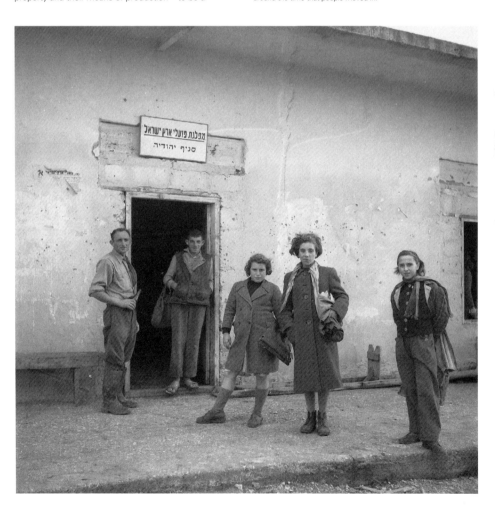

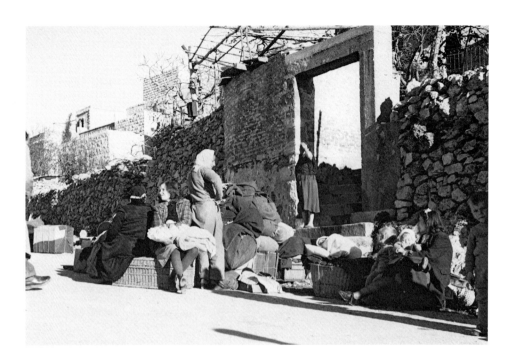

92   **Ayn Karim** Not knowing the local language, children by their side, the large suitcases and blankets tied in bundles indicating that this isn't their first stop in Israel, these new immigrants wait to receive the housing they've been promised by the Jewish Agency, which encouraged them to come and handled their immigration. A long, burdensome process, uncertainty about their future here, the children's complaints, thirst, harsh sunlight, urgent questions like how will they earn a living, what will they eat. They weren't aware of the reservations that were expressed (and rejected immediately) about the decision to allocate houses to them in Ayn Karim. Their present distress, the result of their immigration and their having to make their way in the new country, certainly left them no time to wonder for themselves at gaps in the story they had been told

regarding the partially furnished homes (much of the furniture had already been looted or distributed in an organized and "legal" manner) they were moving into. While waiting to be taught how to work the plots of land adjoining their houses, so they can also participate in the general effort to increase Jerusalem's food supply, they'll enjoy the abundant fruit growing in the surrounding orchards. They and the other families who came with them will move into 150 of the 555 houses in Ayn Karim whose inhabitants had been expelled, houses which the army did not destroy, unlike its usual practice. Two new settlements were established on the village's lands – Beit Zayit and Even Sappir.

Photographer: Hugo Mendelson, Government Press Office, January 5, 1949

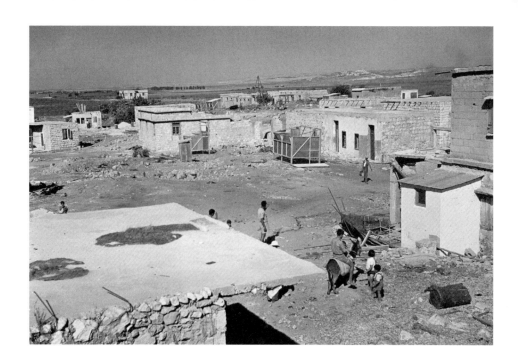

93   **Rantiya/Rinat'ya** From the time the state
of Israel was established until the end of 1949,
approximately 200,000 immigrants had arrived,
and they had to be housed. The hairsplitting
over how to legalize using the "abandoned" or
"emptied" Arab houses was overtaken by the need
to deal with urgent practical issues related to the
immediate settlement of immigrants and their
inclusion in the labor force. The photograph shows
a busy construction site in Rinat'ya, a moshav
whose previous Arab name was Hebraized by
slightly altering its pronunciation. Rubble from the
destruction of most of the Arab village houses is
mixed together with new building materials, allowing
the new immigrants from Morocco to build their
homes with their own hands as well as participate
in the new economic order in which both they and
the state make their living from property that doesn't
belong to them. A few of the buildings were originally
Arab (they were given new concrete roofs). Most
are new, with one or two walls constructed of local
building stones that could still be used after the Arab
houses were demolished.

Photographer: Zoltan Kluger, Government Press Office,
November 1, 1949

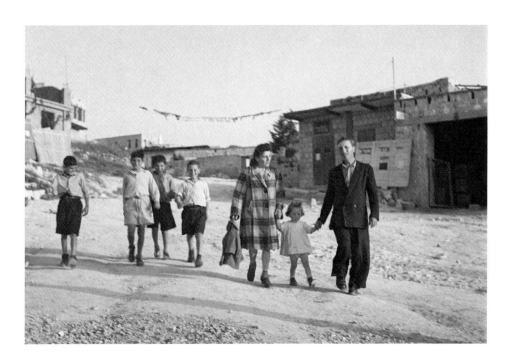

94   **Tarshiha** The official caption describes
the villages in which the immigrants settled as
"abandoned," as if this was a characteristic they
possessed rather than the result of policy. But in the
case of Tarshiha, there's an additional reason why the
description is incorrect – some of Tarshiha's residents
were still living there when the state brought
immigrants from Romania to move into their homes.
Testimony from local residents describes how the
Arab inhabitants were removed from their homes,
gathered together in one area, and forbidden to
leave it while their homes were given to the Jewish
immigrants. The new immigrants benefited not
only from the houses but also from the commercial
infrastructure that included carpentry shops,
ironworking establishments and garages serving the
inhabitants of the entire area from Akko to Safed. The
new workers could now dress up to celebrate May
1st, the workers' holiday, while the Arabs remained
subordinated to military rule that imposed severe
restrictions on their lives. Eventually, when the
immigrants left Tarshiha and sold their houses, Arabs
would be allowed to buy them.

Photographer: Zoltan Kluger, Government Press Office,
May 1, 1949

95   Tarshiha Tarshiha's few remaining Arabs were gathered in a closed area and placed under military rule. Most of their homes were given to Jewish immigrants. When they were allowed to move around in public they could read, in their own language, that they lived in "A socialist society, today, in Israel – Toward peace." In some towns the Arabs were even allowed to carry signs themselves on the workers' holiday demanding equality for *all* workers.

Photographer: Zoltan Kluger, Government Press Office, May 1, 1949

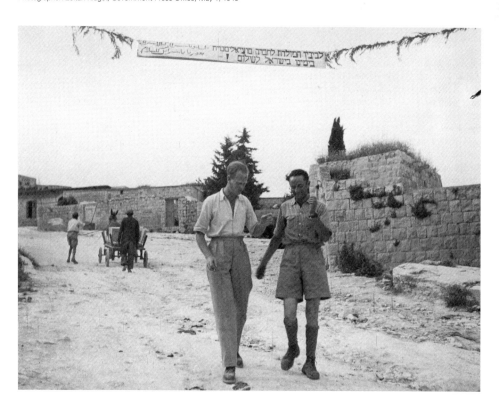

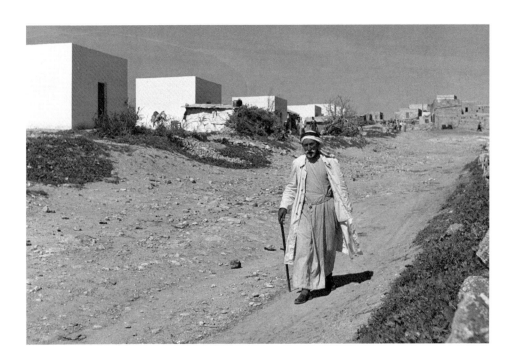

96   **al-Makr** The number of inhabitants in al-Makr, Judayda, Sha'ab, Wadi al-Hamam and 'Akbara even increased because of the presence of internal refugees who found temporary shelter there. The state built new housing units for these refugees, like those shown in the picture, in order to settle them in villages not their own. The refugees wanted to return to their homes. Their return implied a threat – the possibility that the clock might be turned back, if only slightly. To prevent their dream from being realized they were required to sign a document in which they relinquished any future claim to return to their villages. On the left are some of the dozens of houses a private entrepreneur constructed for the state to house refugee families who were permitted to live in them only if they came to an "arrangement" with it. Resettling the internal refugees in villages other than their own was part of a general policy.

Photographer: Fritz Cohen, Government Press Office,
March 10, 1950

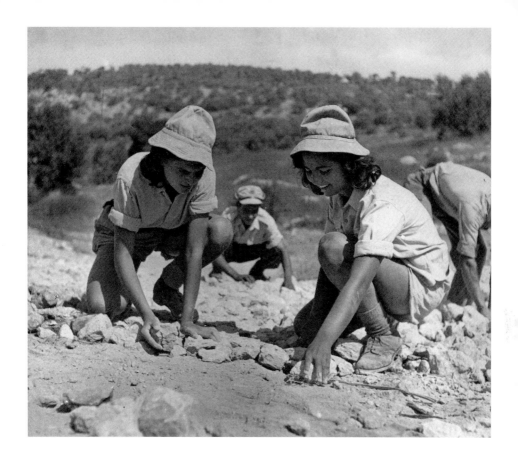

97 **"Abandoned Arab village"** When a village is
completely transformed, and its population replaced
by others, it loses its unique characteristics and its
name and can be more easily represented as an
"abandoned Arab village." The youths were mobilized
to complete the job, to advance the enterprise and
bring about progress. The picture shows young girls,
"Gadna" members, clearing "the rubble of an Arab
village" (created, as it were, by natural forces), so that
immigrants to Israel could be absorbed.

Photographer: Zoltan Kluger, Central Zionist Archive, September 1949

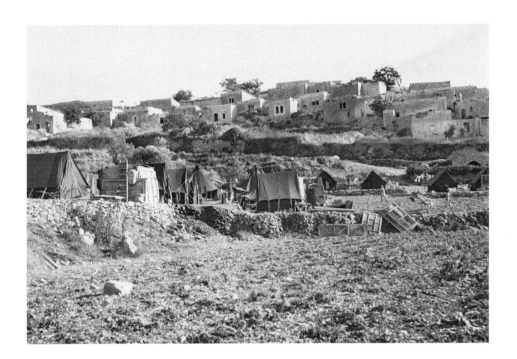

98   **Suhmata** The 1,200 inhabitants expelled from the village left behind 200 homes, a mosque, a church, modern olive presses, schools, two pools, flour mills and a cemetery. Most of the North African Jewish immigrants who arrived in the village were housed at the foot of the hill, where a tent city had been erected for them. Within a year all the village buildings had been demolished, and Tzuriel and Khosen were established on its ruins. Time has come to designate the entire village, with its 200 buildings – walls made of flint, roofed with oak planks covered by a layer of plaster that was refreshed each year – as an historical preservation site. As Israeli preservation methods based on rehabilitating damaged structures aren't appropriate for completely destroyed structures, the Japanese approach should be adopted: preservation not only of buildings as objects, but also the skills – "intangible cultural property" – that were needed to construct it. Since some of Suhmata's former inhabitants are still living, including those who are internal refugees, now may be their last opportunity to teach others these skills, so they can be used to construct a similar village on the nearby hills for themselves, their descendants and others. The 60 years that have passed since those expelled wrote to the state institutions have not blunted at all the validity of their demand and the obligation to grant it: "We hereby request you to give us a place to live, return us to our homes and enable us to work our lands."

Photographer: Zoltan Kluger, Government Press Office, June 1, 1949

CHAPTER 4

Creating a Jewish Political Body and Deporting the Country's Arab Residents

The photographs in this chapter were taken in locations from which Palestinians had been expelled but to which photographers were given access. As such, they provide only a very partial picture of the direct physical violence accompanying the expulsions described in the testimony provided by Jews and Arabs, those expelling and those being expelled. But the fact that the photographs do not capture the direct physical violence carried out in some of the localities does not diminish the fundamental fact of the violence that appears in each of these photographs, that which is involved in the very act of expulsion. To the best of our knowledge, photographs don't exist of most of the localities from which Palestinians were expelled; photographs from places where verbal testimony recounts acts of violence are notably absent. If such photographs were taken, they remain inaccessible to the public. A review of the photographs that do exist should end the decades-long controversy among historians over whether the uprooting from their land of 750,000 Palestinians was planned in advance or the result of widespread local events that show no evidence of prior planning – the sum of which did not constitute a "policy." The photographs show a great deal of activity associated with the expulsions; particularly noticeable is the organization, the order, the discipline and the orchestration of the actions of all those involved.

It isn't a question of spontaneous flight or a natural relocation. People don't abandon their localities of residence, and hundreds of thousands of people don't migrate from one place to another only a few dozen kilometers away, for no reason. Various mechanisms enable this to happen, and they can be discerned even in their absence. So, for example, one can only speculate about what was needed to create an endless column of people along the Ramle–Lod road of those who had just been uprooted from their homes: psychological means, such as threats, intimidation or incentives, and physical means such as rape, beatings, looting or "cleansing" of homes (Photos 103 and 104). Had they not feared that what happened to Palestinians elsewhere in the country would happen to them as well, would the inhabitants of al-Ramle have abandoned their homes of their own free will? Had they not been promised that, unlike those expelled from Lod, who suffered on their long march to Jordan, they would be transported by bus, would those expelled from al-Ramle have formed this line and waited for transportation? Were they not being threatened, wouldn't they have tried to leave the line and return home? The photographs allow the reconstruction of various stages in the operation of the apparatus of expulsion and the identification of various participants

in its final implementation. In the photographs from al-Ramle or al-Tantura, for example, there are traces of how the civilian population was sorted. Men are absent from the picture (al-Tantura, Photo 132), or penned behind fences (al-Ramle, Photo 12), while women stand on the roadside or even move freely on the road (al-Ramle) while the men are still being "dealt with" (Photo 106).

The photographs also show that in some cases people had time to go through their belongings and decide what to take with them, and that the army provided equipment to complete the expulsion – vehicles, water and camouflage netting. The expulsion was the Jewish interpretation of the Partition Plan – an interpretation according to which the establishment of a Jewish state did not simply involve drawing a symbolic or territorial boundary for a state within which Jews could express their national identity, observe national customs and establish autonomous cultural and political institutions. The Jews interpreted the Partition Plan as a way to establish a homogeneous Jewish political entity, and viewed expulsion as a legitimate means to this end. There were localities from which Palestinians fled without having been subjected to violence, but from the moment the state of Israel closed its borders to them and prevented their return, differences in the reasons for their flight and the manner in which they left the country become insignificant in the face of the decision by the government of Israel to prevent their return. That decision, reconfirmed a number of times, transformed them into persons no longer recognized as being part of the political community, as being the "non-governed" of the state.

The photographs show the ways in which the expulsion was carried out, in its various stages (Photos 101, 104, 107, 113, 139, 142). Equally important, however, they testify to the way in which Jewish citizens, in or out of uniform, are constituted as citizens for whom the expulsion of residents of the country has lost any absolute significance as an evil act. It seems that the expulsion is visible to them only in terms of the justification that was attached to it – to enable the establishment of a Jewish homeland for the Jewish people in the land of Israel. The cost – human, civil and political – has been erased.

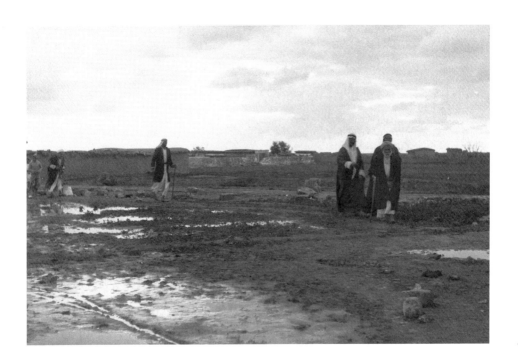

99   **al-Faluja** Most of the people leaving the houses, obeying orders to line up for identification two days after the Egyptian army withdrew, are older men. Most of the women and children had apparently been expelled four days earlier, when many of the residents of al-Faluja and the neighboring village of 'Iraq al-Manshiyya had to leave their homes. One of the elderly men, who appears either in this photograph or in another one taken the same day, greeted the journalist who that day accompanied the Israeli forces entering al-Faluja following the departure of the Egyptian army and hundreds of residents, saying "Markhaba." When the journalist asked why he had stayed, the old man replied that this is his home, and though it's been destroyed he has many Jewish friends and he's sure that nothing will happen to him. After a brief period of military rule, he and the rest of the inhabitants will be evacuated. Kiryat Gat was built on the ruins of the village.

Photographer: David Eldan, Government Press Office,
February 28, 1949

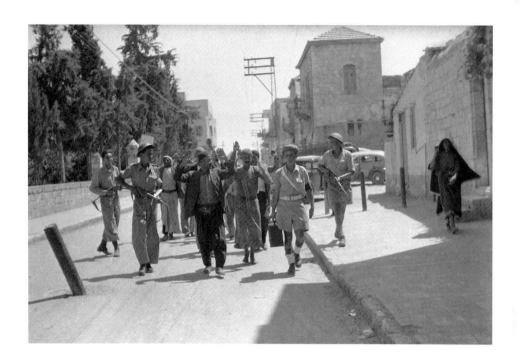

100   **al-Ramle** The fact that the Partition Plan did
not include al-Ramle in the area allotted to the Jewish
state was of no help to its inhabitants when the town
was captured. Nor was what the military commander
of the Ramle–Lod front promised them in the leaflet
that was distributed: "We do not intend to harm people
or property. Anyone trying to resist – will be killed. He
who chooses life – will surrender and save himself and
the members of his family." The men in the photograph,
described in the caption as "being brought," are not yet
refugees; they are prisoners being taken to detention
and then to the prison camps. The first thing the army
did when it captured a village was to separate the men
from the women. The woman walking on the sidewalk
at the right, unguarded by any weapon, will soon
become a refugee. This photograph of her might serve
as additional evidence of the fact that the refugees
were not created by a war; they were the creation of
government policy. After the men are dealt with, it will
be her turn.

Photographer: Beno Rothenberg, Israel State Archive, 1948

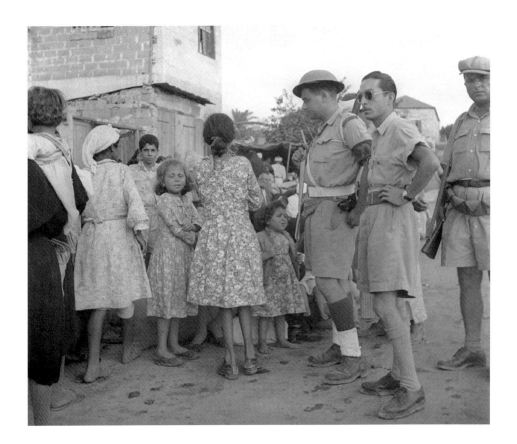

101　**al-Ramle**　The women and children didn't flee the city. Beginning in the afternoon, the soldiers began gathering them by the roadside and they waited for instructions. The soldiers made certain to arrange the expulsion in such a way that people left without having to be physically forced to do so. In order to set the expulsion in motion they arrested the young men, instilled fear in the rest of the population, removed them from their homes to temporary staging areas and provided vehicles to transport them. Here are Ben Gurion's orders to the operation's headquarters: "1. All are free to leave, except those whose departure will be delayed. 2. Warn those who remain that we are not responsible for their protection." The journey awaiting them was quite arduous. 335 refugees (among them many children) died from dehydration on their way to the safety of the refugee camps. Those girls who survived the trek might retain – while recalling the horrors of the expulsion – the memory of their mother's hands with which she very carefully tied the ribbons on the floral print dresses in which she clothed them for the journey, despite the urgings of those telling her to leave her home quickly and join the others by the roadside.

Photographer not identified. IDF and Defense Archive, July 12, 1948

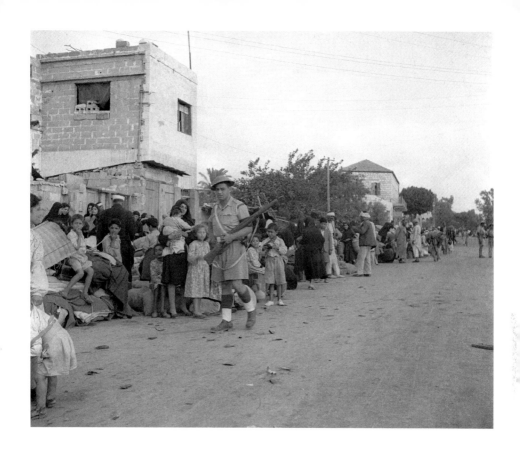

102 **al-Ramle** Each of the expellees who had been forced from his home onto the road could now see that he shared the fate of his neighbors.

Photographer not identified. IDF and Defense Archive, July 12, 1948

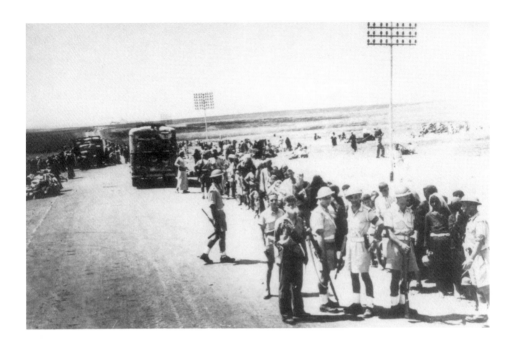

103   **Ramle–Lod Road** Vehicles confiscated from the local population were insufficient to transport all the expellees from the city, and the Operations Branch sent trucks and buses. A short time later the expellees would be used by the Israeli soldiers on the roads as a "human shield" against a counterattack by the Arab Legion. A few condemned the policy – "How easy it is to talk as if it's both possible and permissible to fill the roads with women, children and old people because strategic considerations require us to do so" – but those voices later fell silent for many years. Even today, those who accuse the state of having committed crimes against the Arabs are considered traitors.

Photographer not identified. Palmach Photographic Collection (Yitzhak Sadeh album no. 1, provided by Yoram Sadeh), July 1948

104   **Tabariyya/Tverya** The Arabs wanted to negotiate a ceasefire after the Jews attacked the Arab section of the town, but their requests were turned down. The British, who still ruled the country, declared they were unable to protect the Arab population and proposed instead to assist in its evacuation. King Abdullah, whose diary noted his fear of another massacre like that at Dayr Yasin, also sent trucks, and the evacuation began. This time the Haganah stood by and watched its work being done by others. But it soon began single-mindedly demolishing the old part of the city, and prevented Arabs from returning to their homes. Thus it put an end to the mixed city whose inhabitants lived together as neighbors, and cared about each other even after the Arabs were uprooted from the town.

Photographer not identified. IDF and Defense Archive (Source: Yitzhak Khayyat), 1948

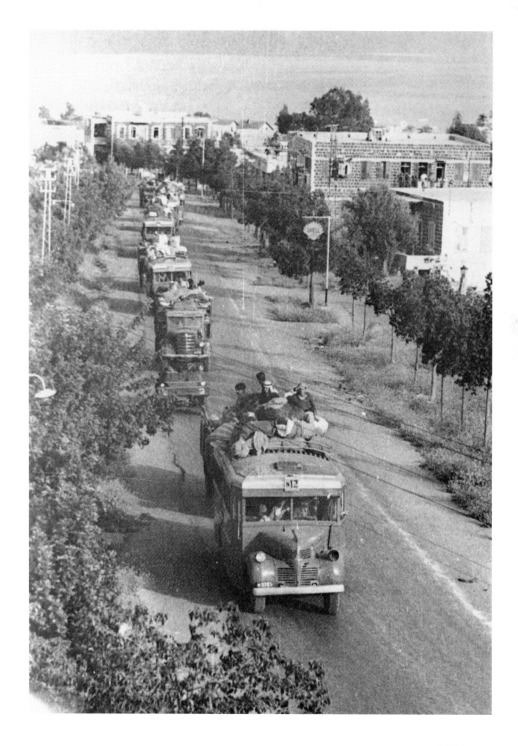

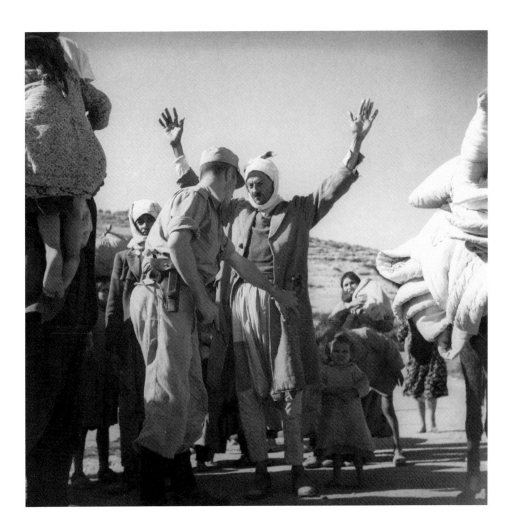

105 **En route from the Galilee to Lebanon** The official caption describes the photograph as showing "Arabs fleeing." The various methods employed to uproot the Arabs make clear that their abandonment of their homes cannot be described as "flight." The expulsion was an organized operation in which the army played a major role. Most of those running it were in uniform, behaving not as combatants on the battlefield but as persons carrying out the political mission of deporting a people. The Palestinian isn't fleeing an armed soldier, but has been ordered to stop and be searched. The women and children wait patiently. Historians searching for a document containing an explicit expulsion order could use the photographic testimonies to the expulsion to convince themselves that the inhabitants aren't fleeing; rather, a systematic effort is underway, operating according to standard procedures.

Photographer not identified. IDF and Defense Archive, October 28, 1948

106   **al-Ramle or al-Lid** These are the sights that
Ministry of Minorities staff must have seen when they
tried to stop the expulsion. Their efforts were met with
hollow promises and fraudulent replies. Soon only
1,000 of the 50,000 Arab inhabitants of the two towns
remained. Ministry staffers not only saw the people
being expelled, but must also have heard their cries of
protest and despair.

Photographer not identified. Palmach Photographic Archive
(Yitzhak Sadeh album no. 1, provided by Yoram Sadeh), July 1948

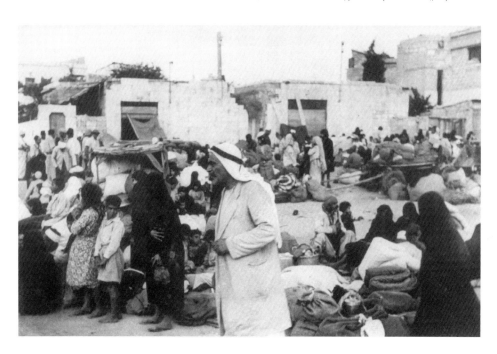

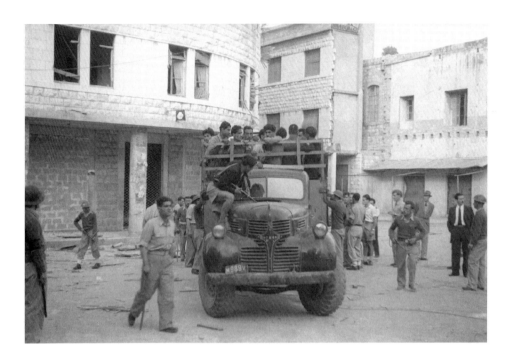

107 **Haifa** On April 20, after some 20,000 Arab residents of Haifa had already been uprooted from the city, the Haganah took over positions in the city center from which the British army had begun to withdraw and began a military operation called "Bi'ur Chametz" (elimination of forbidden food before Passover). The British did not accept responsibility for the safety of the Arabs who remained in the city, and instead offered to escort the refugees to the port, which was still under their control. By afternoon some 6,000 Palestinians had reached the port, and within two days 20,000 Palestinians had left the city. The cynical manner in which the Haganah used the sincere desire of Haifa's Jewish residents that Arabs return to the city to prove that it did not want to expel them is an attempt to blur the clear difference between how the residents felt about their Arab neighbors and the views held by the political leadership, and to create a false picture of a united Jewish side (residents and leadership) versus a united Arab side. We should remember that not only did Haifa's Jews not want the Arabs expelled, in contrast to the policy of the Haganah and the military and political leadership; they also opposed the war undertaken in their name without their having been consulted. The photograph shows Haganah soldiers escorting the expellees to the port, to insure they leave the city.

Photographer: Fred Chesnik, IDF and Defense Archive, April 22, 1948

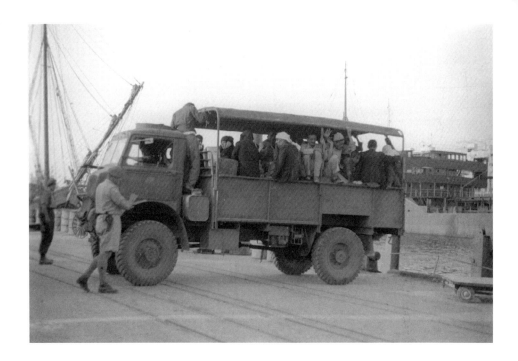

108   **Haifa** The city was still being shelled and total chaos reigned. British police and soldiers awaited the expellees when they reached the port, registering those who had been uprooted. They take no belongings with them, apparently hoping the Jewish leadership will keep the promise their colleagues, the Haifa workers, had made to them: "You have nothing to fear. Don't destroy your homes with your own hands... The gates of Haifa are open to you – return to work, look after your homes and your money, and see to the welfare of your families and your children." (From a proclamation issued by the Haifa Labor Council.)

Photographer: Fred Chesnik, IDF and Defense Archive, April 22, 1948

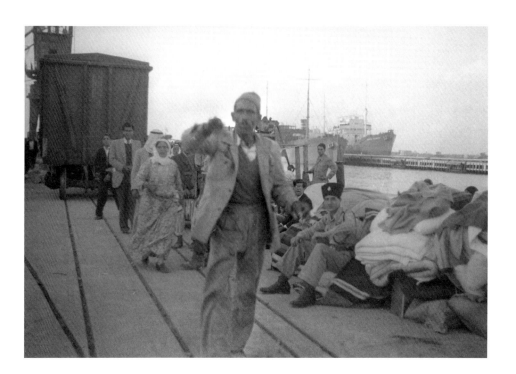

109   **Haifa** The shelling, the detonation of
barrels filled with explosives and, in general, the
implementation of the instructions to "Kill every Arab
you come across … and blow open every locked
door" had the desired result – Haifa's Arabs were
terrified and abandoned the city. The fact that the
Arab leadership had already left the city and that the
British had relinquished their obligation to preserve
order, also contributed to the Arabs' departure. The
British soldier seated next to the pile of blankets and
mattresses doesn't seem concerned by the refugees
dashing around, who realize that no one cares about
the catastrophe that has befallen them, and they'll have
to save themselves.

Photographer: Fred Chesnik, IDF and Defense Archive, April 22, 1948

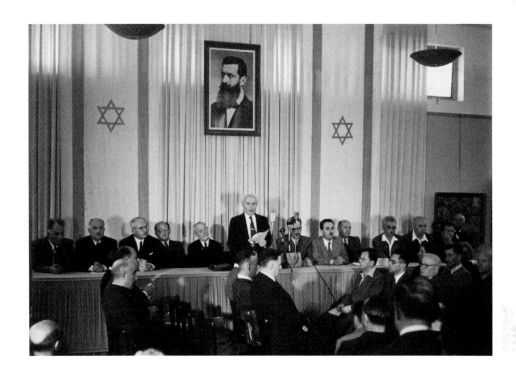

110   **Tel Aviv** The 100 people invited to the ceremony proclaiming the State of Israel were asked "not to reveal the invitation's content or when the Council would convene." The one-sided declaration of the establishment of a Jewish state on contested territories (not even those allocated by the Partition Plan) and the creation of a regime based on members of only one of the ethnic groups over whom it would rule, completed the transformation of the population's demographic structure required to establish a state *not* of all its citizens. The presence of armed members of the Civil Guard at the entrance to the auditorium already symbolizes the violence that will maintain this regime. Those who might have objected to the state's establishment and disrupt the declaration were removed from the area – some were already in refugee camps, some would become refugees in the coming months, and some were already living under military rule. The rest had still to be enlisted to support the new regime. Most of those present in this festive hall had actively participated in creating the new reality in the region and viewed people's lives, Arabs' as well as Jews' (primarily the new immigrants), as clay in the hands of the maker. Facing an auditorium filled mainly with men, Ben Gurion proclaimed the establishment of Israel as a democratic state. The ceremony lasted 32 minutes; in the following months another 500,000 Palestinians will be expelled and those remaining will become a minority.

Photographer: Zoltan Kluger, Government Press Office, May 14, 1948

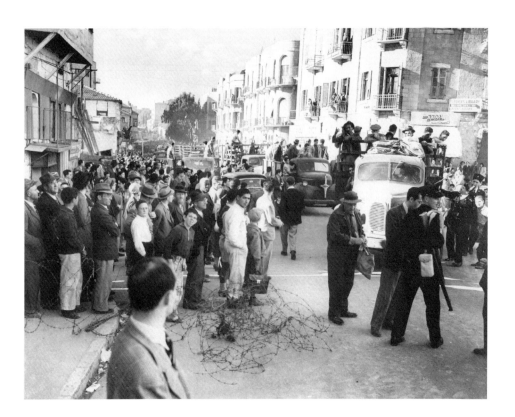

111   al-Quds/Jerusalem From the moment the Partition Plan was announced, the Haganah operated in the city as a supplementary police force, bypassing the British police more and more openly. Haganah fighters stand crowded in the trucks on their way to invade Arab neighborhoods and recover what they'll decide had been stolen from Jewish shops in the commercial center. The Arab demonstration against the Partition Plan had begun as a non-violent march. As soon as it got underway, the Haganah characterized it as a "hostile action." The Haganah believed that the British, by permitting the demonstration, were encouraging those hostile acts. As soon as it learned of the Arab demonstration, the local Haganah headquarters sent a "commanders' reconnaissance patrol" to Princess Mary Street. One of the officers present testified how the political demonstration turned into a series of violent incidents: "While riding on Princess Mary Street they saw an Arab mob coming up Mamila Street. As it drew near, the patrol fired shots into the air. The demonstrators halted, turned around and began fleeing toward Jaffa Gate. A British police unit that was present heard the shots and began chasing those who had fired them. They rushed away, and somehow managed to reach headquarters. At this point the situation began to deteriorate. Shortly after the commanders had returned, we received information that when the mob reached the commercial center it stopped fleeing and, encouraged by the behavior of the police, which took no measures to restrain it, began looting shops and warehouses."

Photographer: Associated Press, December 7, 1947

112 **Haifa** While the expellees, who are being exiled from their land because they are Arabs, crowd together on the ship's deck, proclamations issued by the Emergency Committee ("Va'adat HaMatzav") call upon the Jewish residents (addressed as "Our brothers and sisters in the homeland") to see the Arabs' unjust expulsion as a victory, and the transformation of Haifa into a Jewish city as a reason for celebration: "Haifa has become a Hebrew city, and will remain a Hebrew city." The Arabs were expelled in order to establish a Jewish regime, not in order to establish a state. Failure to distinguish between the "state" and the "regime" has left no room for the voices that from the beginning were raised against the transfer and exile of more than half of the country's political constituency. The dozens of expellees crowding on the deck with mattresses, blankets and suitcases appeared to the photographer to reflect an historic moment that should be documented. A hurried shot, out of focus, but one that could be used to describe the expulsion to succeeding generations as the "terrible price of war" (as another photograph of refugees was captioned in one of the albums portraying the establishment of the state of Israel), making the perversion of history difficult to recognize.

Photographer not identified. IDF and Haganah Historical Archive (deposited by Motilov Dov), 1948

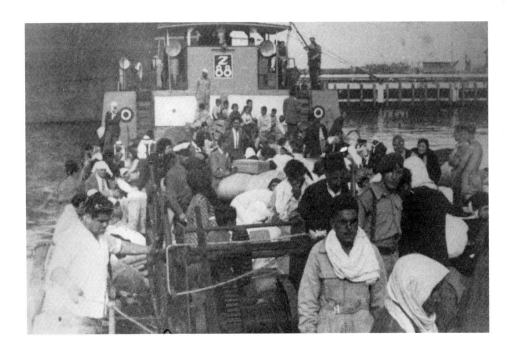

113   **Haifa** The lucky ones found a boat that day to deliver them from the inferno that threatened in the market next to the port where they had gathered to seek shelter, which ceased affording them protection when an officer from the "Carmeli" unit ordered his soldiers to fire from above into the crowd gathered below. The various actions of the Haganah were intended to insure the Arabs wouldn't change their minds, and would continue to leave. Standing crowded together, with very few belongings, most face the open sea; a few dare to look back at the dock where the photographer is standing. The source of the photograph, as well as its quality, suggest that the photographer must have been an amateur, possibly one of the soldiers carrying out the expulsion.

Photographer not identified. Haganah Historical Archive (deposited by Motilov Dov), 1948

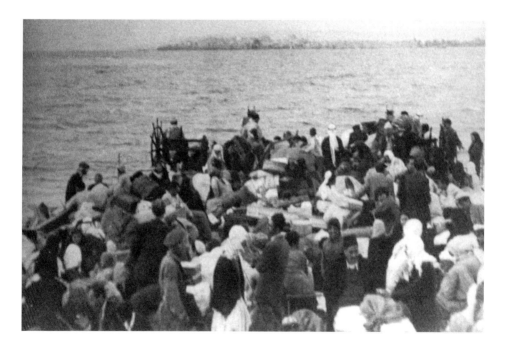

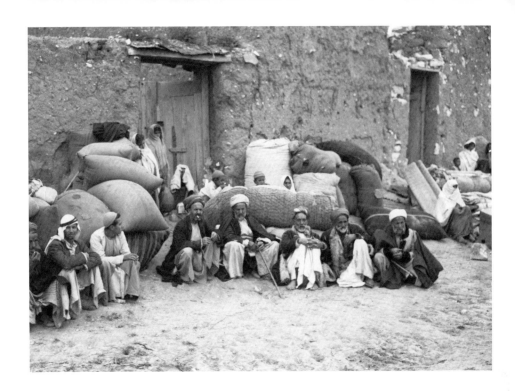

114   'Iraq al-Manshiyya These residents aren't the first to be evacuated from the village. The first group left following heavy aerial bombardments on the 15th and 20th of October. Then, following the ethnic cleansing of the surrounding area, 'Iraq al-Manshiyya and al-Faluja were turned into an isolated Arab "pocket," and the strategic, physical and psychological preparations began in order to take it over militarily and politically as part of the armistice agreement with Egypt. At the end of February, with the implementation of that agreement, the Egyptian army evacuated the "Faluja pocket" along with a few hundred villagers from the two villages who left "willingly." It was clear to all sides that this was the beginning of the end for 'Iraq al-Manshiyya. By this time, any concern for the rights of the villagers had become only an empty promise in an appendix to the armistice agreement. Those who chose to leave their homes could have had reason to believe that Israel would not honor its commitment. Had they remained, they would have been expelled at a later date, an expulsion to which photographers were not invited.

Photographer: Beno Rothenberg, Israel State Archive, no date

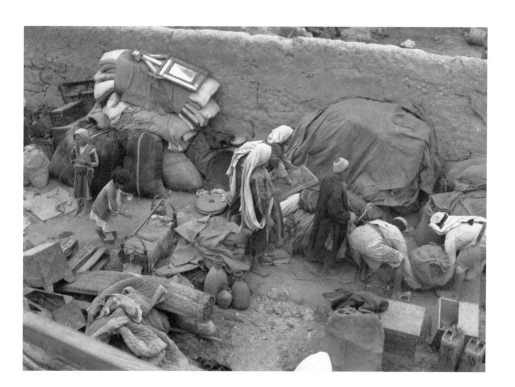

115 **'Iraq al-Manshiyya** The Quakers who were assisting begged them to stay, but the residents were terrified and didn't change their minds. What they had learned about the systematic clearing of the villages captured during the past few months was enough to make them leave. To interpret this decision as flight, or characterize it, opaquely, as "leaving" or "relocation" – as if hundreds of thousands of people decided, out of the blue, to leave their homes without having felt their lives were in immediate danger – and to bequeath this interpretation to succeeding generations without batting an eye, requires a well-oiled propaganda machine that addresses all aspects of life. They were allowed to take all their belongings with them, and they understood the unsubtle hint. These possessions, at least, may help make their new location seem somewhat familiar.

Photographer: Beno Rothenberg, Israel State Archive, no date

116 **'Iraq al-Manshiyya** When the photographer stands at a higher location he can include in one frame the dual drama we witness: a drama in which each and every individual evacuee plays her role, uprooted from her home and transformed into a refugee, as well as the drama of an entire culture in which a village is turned into a ghost town. Soon after the empty shells of its houses echoed with the whistle of the wind, the village was razed to the ground.

Photographer: Beno Rothenberg, Israel State Archive, no date

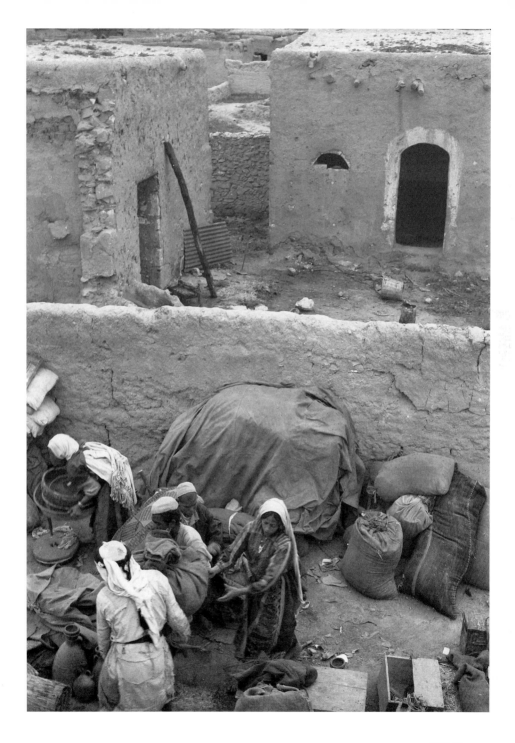

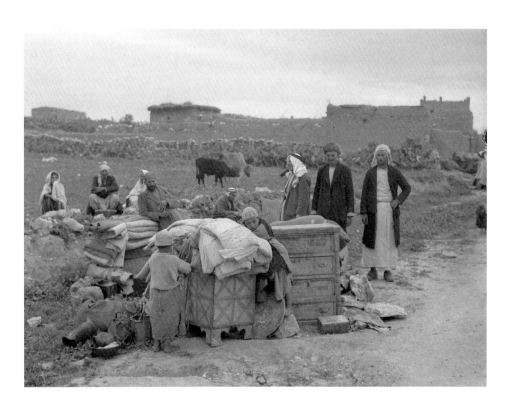

117   **'Iraq al-Manshiyya** They had worked hard
for many hours removing their belongings from the
houses: bureaus, mirrors, boxes, food, baskets, doors,
jars and clothing. Now they're resting, exhausted and
staring into space, gathering strength for the next
stage – loading everything onto trucks. Soon, when
they've found places for themselves in the refugee
camps in Rafah and Khan Yunis they'll understand the
full significance of the events in which they've played
the part of free agents who "chose" to abandon their
homes. With the help of the Quakers they'll organize
demonstrations and demand to be returned home.
After a few more months had passed a similar demand
was no longer being publicly heard in Israel, and for
decades there hasn't been any way of making it heard
again in Hebrew, or of finding the appropriate words to
express it.

Photographer: Beno Rothenberg, Israel State Archive, no date

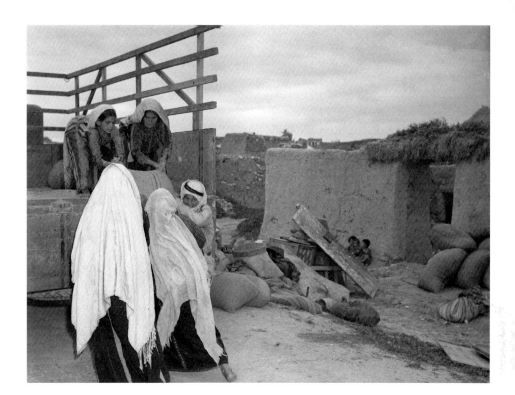

118   **'Iraq al-Manshiyya** The residents also are loading their possessions onto the trucks parked at a distance from the tumult, making sure that the sacks of dry food that saw them through the siege aren't left behind.

Photographer: Beno Rothenberg, Israel State Archive, no date

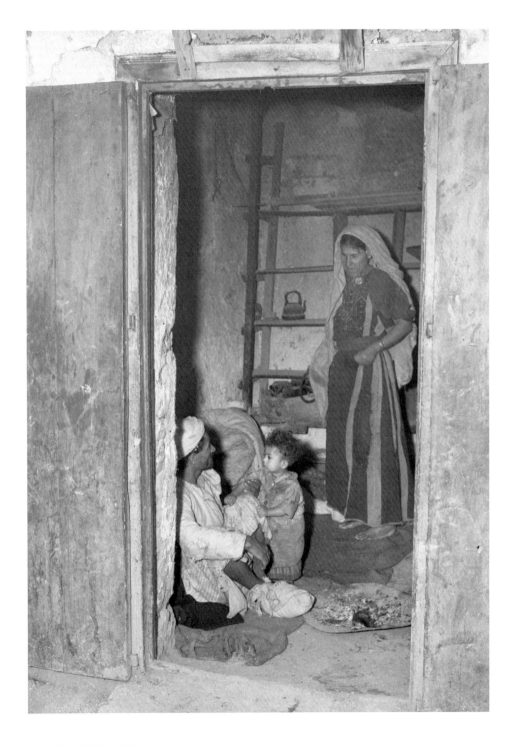

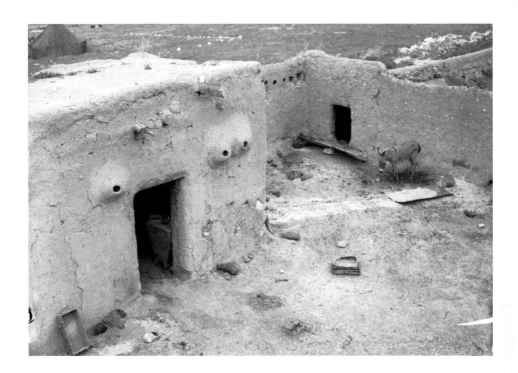

119 **'Iraq al-Manshiyya** The shelves are
emptying, and there's not much left at home to
remove. A kettle, a narghila, some bottles and
blankets. They'll leave behind what remains of the
pita. It won't be long before an armored car backs
into the house constructed of mud bricks and
wipes it off the face of the earth as if it had never
existed. His injured foot prevents him from joining
the others outside; he remains in the house to
look after the baby. In the future they'll remember
that she took her first steps that day. Though she
holds tightly to his shirt, it's apparently not enough
to keep her upright, and without his supporting
hand she probably would have fallen and again
began crawling.

Photographer: Beno Rothenberg, Israel State Archive, no date

120 **'Iraq al-Manshiyya** Will this donkey also find its
way, finally, onto one of the trucks, or will they leave it
behind, so that it too could be the object of a question
asked sadly, painfully, grudgingly, longingly, pityingly,
accusingly, angrily – "Why did you leave the donkey
behind by itself?"

Photographer: Beno Rothenberg, Israel State Archive, no date

121 **'Iraq al-Manshiyya** Everyone's waiting for the decision of the Israeli officer to whom the American observer is appealing on the behalf of the Palestinian. As if his words aren't enough, he leans toward the Israeli soldier, putting himself at eye level. Over his shoulder, another Israeli soldier keeps watching the group, waiting to hear whether new orders will be issued. This appeal, which isn't according to protocol, embarrasses him – he can't grant their wish, but it's also hard for him to reject it out of hand. This business of expulsion isn't pleasant for any of them. They'd prefer that it occurred without anyone's intervention, or that it at least be carried out in accordance with clear orders and instructions. The number of people gathered around indicates that the issue isn't a minor one, though when you consider the thing itself – expelling people from their homes – anything else seems minor. Those not evacuated today will be evacuated tomorrow, and those who aren't evacuated tomorrow will be evacuated a few days later. In a few weeks everyone will have been evacuated and the houses demolished. The Israelis didn't covet the mud houses; they wanted the land on which they stood. They didn't want the land simply as real estate, though that was an important consideration. They wanted it because it belonged to the nation.

Photographer: Beno Rothenberg, Israel State Archive, no date

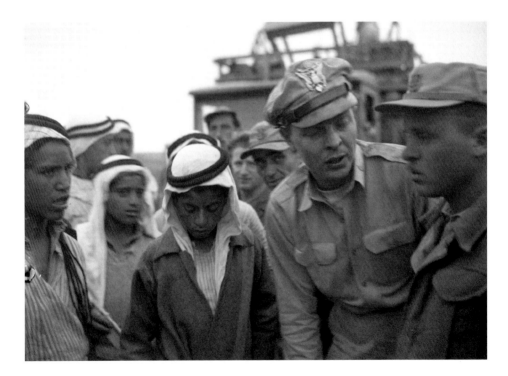

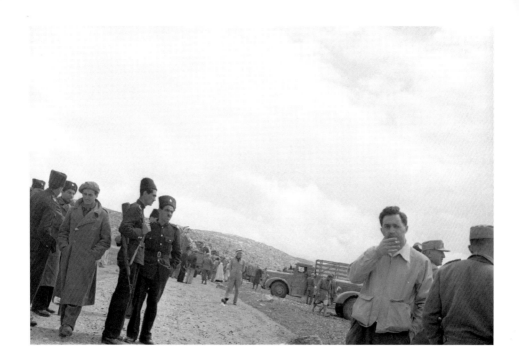

122 **'Iraq al-Manshiyya** The photographer's notes on the contact sheets indicate that the inhabitants are being "evacuated" "to the Jordanian side." If the evacuation occurred at the end of February or the beginning of March, it must have been to Egypt. If it occurred in April, what we see are refugee men and women who were beaten by the soldiers, robbed, the women sexually attacked ("attempted rape," as it was referred to at the time). It seems plausible that these people are the few hundred residents who were evacuated together with the Egyptian army. The permissions, materials and extra time granted to the evacuees to take all their possessions with them, including livestock, and the permission granted the photographer to document the evacuation, are incompatible with the expulsions that will occur a few days later, in violation of the armistice agreements whose resonance the military and political leadership wanted to muffle. If the inhabitants are in fact being deported to "the Jordanian side," we have no way of knowing which expulsion we are seeing. The waves of expulsions continued until the last of the villagers had been thrown off his land.

Photographer: Beno Rothenberg, Israel State Archive, no date

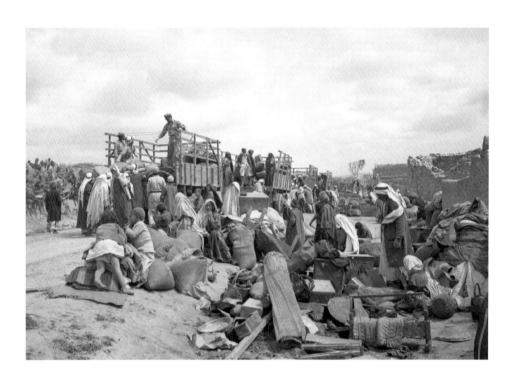

123 **'Iraq al-Manshiyya** Did the evacuation take
so long that the people in uniform, whose only role
was to insure that the decisions were carried out in
the best possible manner, but not actually be involved
themselves in their implementation, had to lend a
hand? One day, when some native-born Israeli is asked
whether there are refugee camps in her country,
she'll answer in surprise, "Here? No, not here." And,
in fact, there aren't any refugee camps "here." Even
those taken over in 1967 were refugee camps located
in Arab countries, in occupied territory. This series of
photographs shows that the people in the pictures
aren't refugees, but citizens turned into refugees by a
mechanism of violence. Interrogating the photographs
allows us to see the deep imprint of the regime's hand
on Palestinian refugeeness.

Photographer: Beno Rothenberg, Israel State Archive, no date

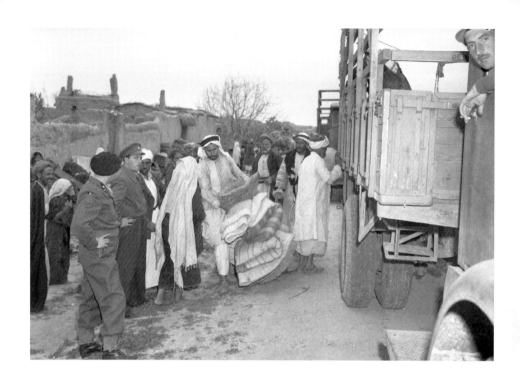

124 'Iraq al-Manshiyya What about the driver?
What was he told? That they got on the truck willingly?

Photographer: Beno Rothenberg, Israel State Archive, no date

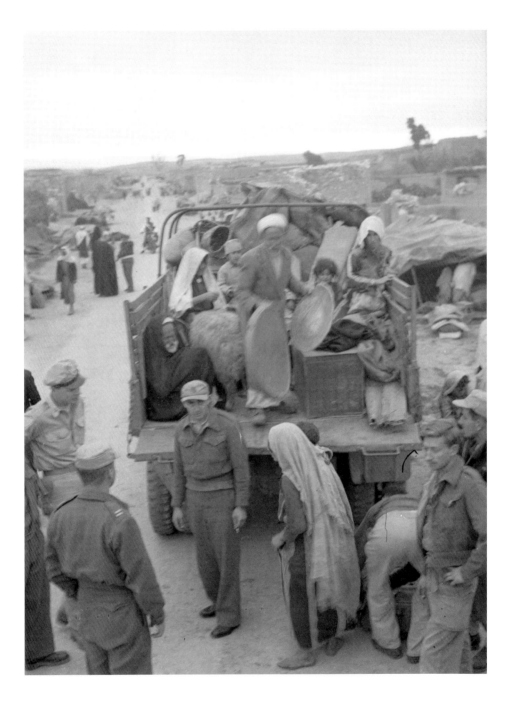

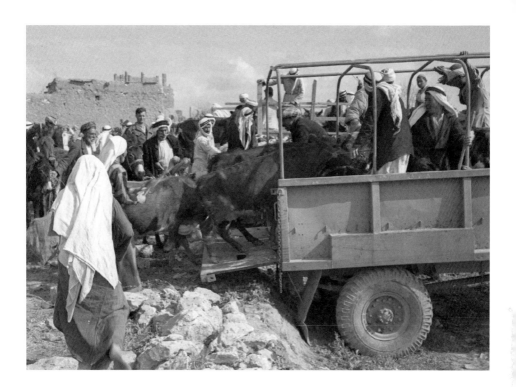

125   **'Iraq al-Manshiyya** They're already on the trucks, ready to go. Is her request to the American UN observer handling their inquiries connected to the fact that the truck hasn't left yet? Holding a baby in her arms, no longer possessing a home where she can meet his needs, you could imagine many things she might ask for even before demanding the return of the home taken from her by force and deceit. The photographer apparently felt that it wouldn't be enough to take a photograph at eye-level, and climbed onto a nearby truck for an overview of the scene.

Photographer: Beno Rothenberg, Israel State Archive, no date

126   **'Iraq al-Manshiyya** Even though they had been permitted to take all their possessions with them, including their cattle and horses, when they had unloaded it all and put everything "in its place," they wanted to go home. They still do.

Photographer: Beno Rothenberg, Israel State Archive, no date

127 **'Iraq al-Manshiyya** The expulsion of the inhabitants of 'Iraq al-Manshiyya, like that of hundreds of thousands of Palestinians from other locations, is an act of state. Israel carried out this expulsion before the state had officially been recognized by the United Nations, but as this photograph shows, Israel already is one of the United Nations. The UN observers, each of whom comes from a country whose establishment was also accompanied by expulsions and ethnic cleansing, pose for a group picture together with the Israeli officers, who are at this very moment completing the expulsion and ethnic cleansing which created their own Jewish nation state. In less than two months the UN would consider Israel's application for membership. The minutes of the meeting of May 5, 1949, record a discussion of the deportations Israel carried out and its occupation of areas that had been allotted to the Arabs. But the main concern reflected in those minutes is the need to stabilize the region. The UN's recognition of Israel – implying its recognition that Israel's actions were those carried out by a state – is presented as a first step toward regional stabilization. Six days later, on May 11, 1949, despite the expulsion of some 700,000 Arabs and Israel's refusal to recognize their right to return immediately, the UN recognized Israel as a country "seeking peace." UN representatives had already addressed the needs of evacuees when they were trapped in what was known as "the Faluja pocket." But addressing their needs is possible only when doing so does not undermine the compact among nation states that leaves unprotected the persons they deport. And so, after more than 60 years, no one can force Israel to repatriate the refugees it created.

Photographer: Beno Rothenberg, Israel State Archive, no date

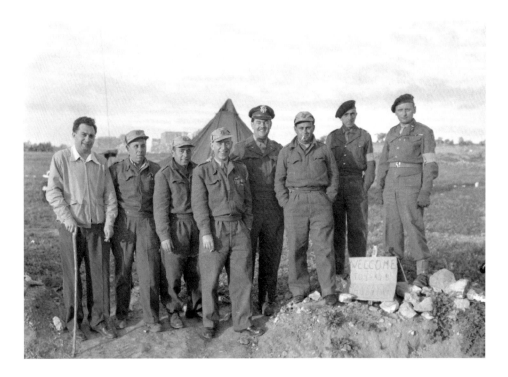

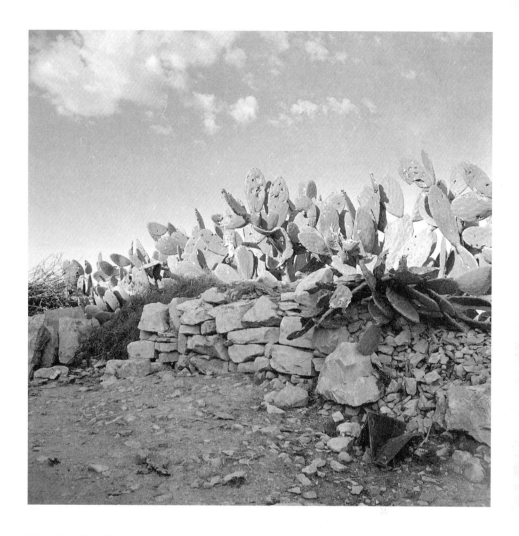

128 **Dayr Yasin** The people carrying out the massacre went from house to house. First, grenades were thrown into the buildings. Those not killed instantly were slaughtered in horrible ways, and women were raped. Those who fled the houses were slaughtered outside. A total of 110 people. A few dozen of the survivors – men, women and children – who had been taken prisoner were trucked in a "victory march" through Jerusalem's Jewish Quarter and then returned to the village. About 20 were then shot to death. Some of those fatal shots pierced the prickly pear hedges.

Photographer: Associated Press, April 1948

129   **Dayr Yasin/Giv'at Sha'ul B** The memory of the massacre threatens to attach itself forever to the name of this place. That's how the few people felt who, one year later, protested the repopulation of the village and asked that it be delayed until conditions were ripe for turning it into a memorial shared by all. Resettlement of other villages by Jews was no less criminal, but their names had not been associated with massacres, even though, according to the official historiography, these had occurred in at least 20 locations. Dressed festively, with many speeches, songs, declamations, and in the presence of government ministers and rabbis, they announced the establishment of "Giv'at Sha'ul B" on the lands of the village. And the children? They'll learn to love their country, and the ruins of the village will be the landscape of their childhood.

Photographer: Yehuda Eisenstark, IDF and Defense Archive, June 1949

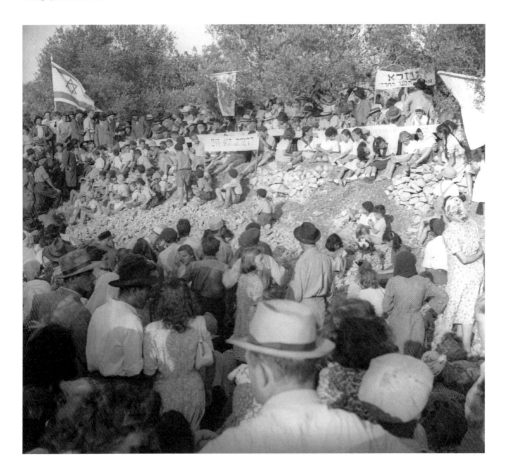

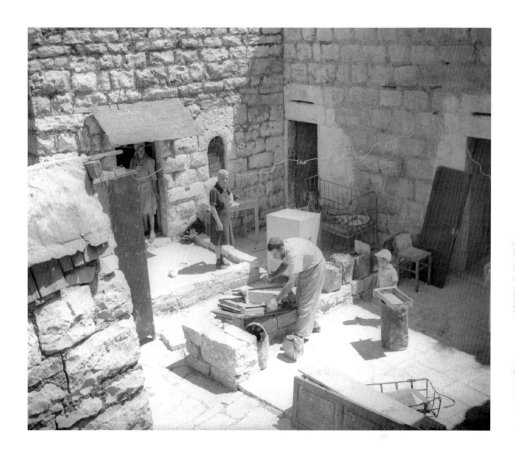

130   **DayrYasin/Giv'at Sha'ul B** This handsome
house belonged to a Palestinian family. They, along with
90 other families who lived here before the massacre,
signed a "good neighbor" agreement with the Jewish
families who lived in nearby Giv'at Shaul, which was
established in 1931. The Haganah was informed of
this civil initiative, and approved the agreement. Both
sides adhered to it, and evidence of the villagers'
commitment can be found in testimony that they
prevented Arab forces from taking up positions in
the village as a base for attacks. But repressive state
mechanisms, including those of a state-in-formation,
are indifferent to civilian agreements, and certainly to
those that threaten to stand in the way of grandiose

plans of state and nation building. The state
wanted to settle Dayr Yasin come what may.
Here a Jewish family makes its home in a house
where a massacre occurred one year earlier, and
whose inhabitants were expelled. The new state
had no place for agreements among citizens;
all relationships between Jews and Arabs were
nationalized and administered from then on
almost entirely by the state, orchestrated and
bounded by the limited framework of possibilities
that it had created.

Photographer: Yehuda Eisenstark, IDF and Defense Archive,
June 1949

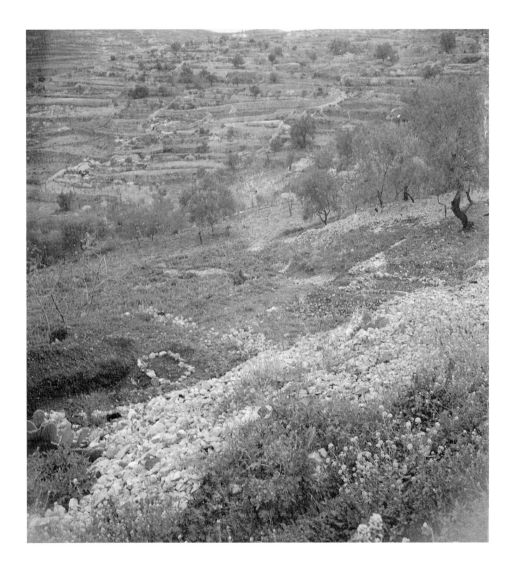

131　**Dayr Yasin** Testimony about the massacre – from survivors, perpetrators and witnesses (who entered the village immediately after it had occurred) – is horrifying. Disfigured and dismembered corpses were scattered in the houses and the streets, and there was an overwhelming stench of gunpowder and of death. But less familiar testimony about other massacres, which did not come to public attention or lead to protests, is equally horrifying. Those who carried out the other massacres, but were the first to be shocked by this one, didn't hesitate to use it in order to expel Arabs from other villages. We know of Haganah Radio broadcasts repeating the following warning to make Arabs leave their villages: "Remember Dayr Yasin." Three days after the massacre a group of youths, Gadna members, were taken to the village to dig two mass graves. One, for women, is indicated in the photograph by a circle of stones. The other, for men, is marked by stones arranged in a square.

Photographer: Associated Press, April 1948

132   al-Tantura Many women and children can be seen in the foreground, and a number of soldiers in the background maintain order. The official caption indicates when the photograph was taken – "after the place was captured." An examination of the photograph shows that "after" doesn't mean immediately after, but refers, rather, to an unspecified time – "before" the place was captured and was still Arab; "after" it was captured and was losing its Arab character. Sorting the population, the results of which are visible in the photograph, was usually a crucial moment in this transformation. The men are already gone – they've been taken to prison camps, and now the main effort is devoted to dealing with women, children and the elderly. The village was captured on May 22–23, and the photograph was apparently taken a few days later, after they had finished separating the men from the women and children. The people in the photograph didn't remain long in the village. We see them at the beginning of a painful journey which not all of them survived.

Photographer not identified. IDF and Defense Archive, May 1948

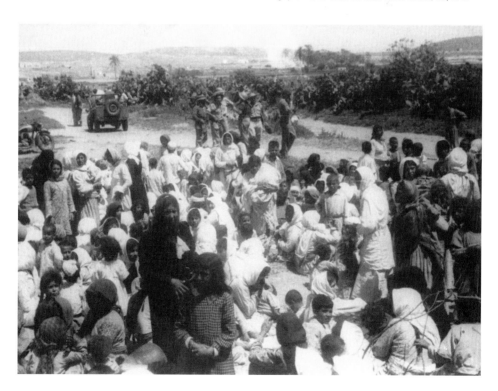

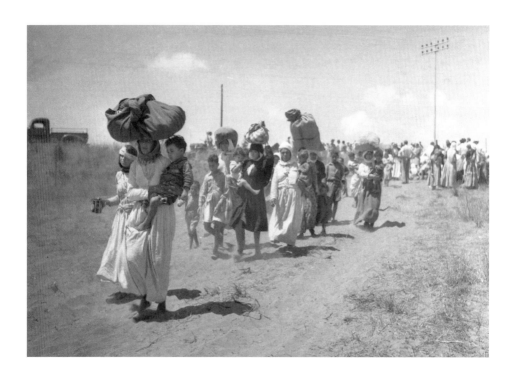

133　**Deporting the women of al-Tantura**　The photographer wrote on the contact sheet, "Arab women from Tantura going to Jordan." This caption, in addition to what we learn from it about the limits of Zionist discourse at that time – the use of the neutral verb "to go" and the attribution of the act to the expellees as if they were "going" on their own initiative – shows how the Arabs were severed and exiled from their home in a manner designed to deny them "native" status. The women deportees in the photograph aren't leaving from al-Tantura but from Fureidis, where they had been held for the last couple of months after being uprooted from al-Tantura, even if most of them came from al-Tantura and eventually ended up in Trans-Jordan. Nor was the photograph taken in al-Tantura, which was why the photographer couldn't simply write "Tantura" on the contact sheet, but only what the photograph in fact documents – the uprooting of al-Tantura's residents from their homes. Tantura became the name each of them bore on her back, along with her children and her belongings.

Photographer: Beno Rothenberg, Israel State Archive, June 18, 1948

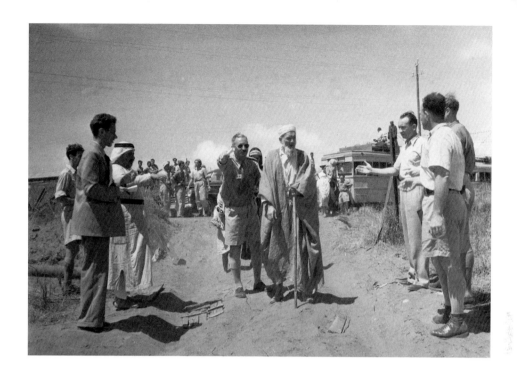

134 **Deporting the women of al-Tantura** The
photographer used the feminine form in his caption,
but not because there were no men among the people
being expelled – in Hebrew, certainly at that time, the
presence of even one male among hundreds of women
would require the masculine form. He did so because
it was so obvious they had been separated from men
"of military age." The men were treated differently.
Historians still argue about how many were massacred.
Most were moved from place to place in the village –
blindfolded, their hands tied – until they were sent to
prison camps. The photograph shows an elderly villager
walking along a path. His mouth is open in amazement
or dismay. Or perhaps this is the moment he's telling
the people watching his expulsion exactly what he
thinks about it. They're not indifferent to his elegant
appearance; three hands point from different directions
to show him the way.

Photographer: Beno Rothenberg, Israel State Archive, June 18, 1948

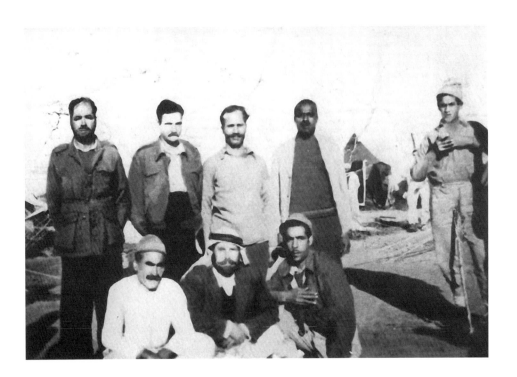

135 **Detention pen for prisoners,** apparently in
the village of Umm Khaled or Ijlil, where most of the
men from al-Tantura were sent. Seven Arab deportees
from al-Tantura stand for a photograph, apparently
at the initiative of the soldier on the right. Was the
photographer a Jew immortalizing the image of a
soldier together with seven prisoners? Was it someone
from the Red Cross, using a photograph to mediate
between the prisoners and their families? Was it an
Arab kidding around, taking a picture of the Israeli
soldier as a souvenir? Each of the people in the picture
could have wanted such a photograph, but it isn't clear
whose idea it was, who has the negative, who saw it
being developed and printed. We can only hope some
day to discover additional photographs taken in that
camp, and with them additional testimony about what
went on there.

Photographer and date not specified. From *Palestine Remembered*
web site

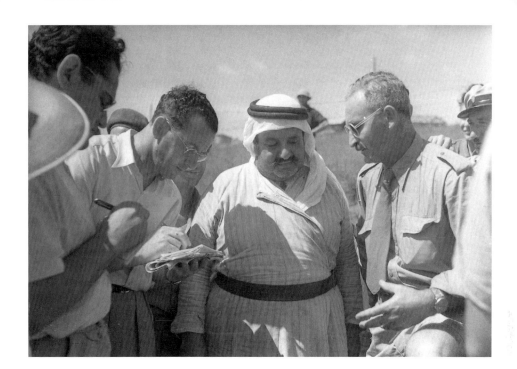

136   Deporting the women of al-Tantura In this "model deportation" which many journalists and photographers have been invited to cover, the women being expelled from al-Tantura, who've been held in Fureidis for a month, are now being deported to Tulkarm. The mukhtar of Fureidis, in the center of the picture, is expected by the Israeli soldiers to collaborate in presenting the deportation as an expression of the will of the deportees and to insure that they actually leave the village. The journalists act as military correspondents, and receive most of their information from the military without questioning it, serving as mouthpieces for the claim that this deportation was conducted legitimately, according to the stipulations of the Geneva Convention, and that those who left "went voluntarily." They reported on the women's distress and their "reluctance" to leave, but explain the women's apprehension as caused by "what they've heard about harsh treatment of the refugees in the Arab countries." Their reports also express amazement that the women don't seem to be looking forward to reaching Tulkarm, even though their husbands await them there. This accusation is both arrogant and dishonest, since it was well known, and also reported in the press, that men of military age, and those physically able to work, were detained in prison camps.

Photographer: Beno Rothenberg, Israel State Archive, June 18, 1948

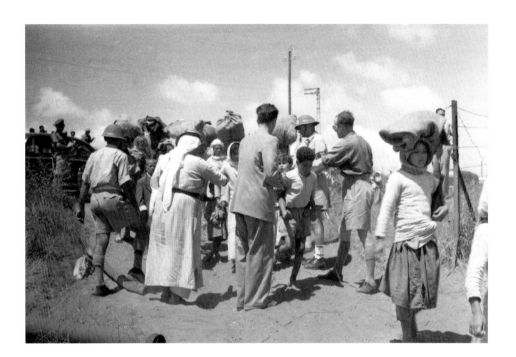

137   Deporting the women of al-Tantura So many
officials count the deportees one by one, check their
names against lists, touch them lightly on the shoulder
as if they were most valued citizens – only to make
them unwelcome, sentence them to homelessness,
provide them no place to live, destroy their community,
turn them into stateless persons – refugees knocking
at others' doors. So many people observed these
expulsions – the many bus drivers who transported
them, the ladies of Kfar Yona who filled the women's
water bottles – without realizing they were seeing
people being deported. Did they not recognize the
dissonance between what they saw and how they
conceptualized it to themselves because of the
success of the "Office of Propaganda and Psychological
Warfare," which had been shown the way by the Israeli
press and public?

Photographer: Beno Rothenberg, Israel State Archive, June 18, 1948

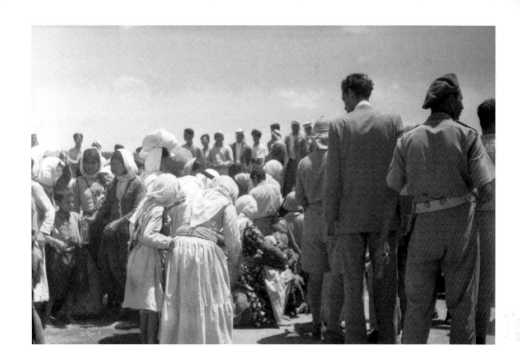

138   **Deporting the women of al-Tantura** Of 2,000
female refugees, most of them from al-Tantura, who
were held in Fureidis for about a month, only 1,004
eventually signed a declaration that they were leaving
voluntarily for Tulkarm. The army hoped 1,600 women
and children would leave, but at the moment of truth,
when they had to sign, 600 of them decided to risk
remaining under Israeli rule, despite knowing very
well they'd remain unprotected here. Expelling the
Palestinian women from their homes was completed
in broad daylight, under the eyes of officials from
international organizations and journalists, to show
the entire world – including Metro-Goldwyn-Mayer,
which was filming a newsreel – how faithfully the
relevant Israeli agencies granted the women's request
to be taken to Tulkarm. Perhaps those gathered here
in the field who aren't marching in the column of the
uprooted, sitting amid the official tumult, are those who
chose to remain, and no one here is publicly trying to
pressure them to leave.

Photographer: Beno Rothenberg, Israel State Archive, June 18, 1948

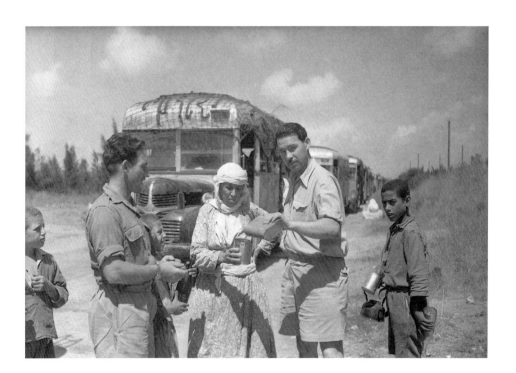

139   **Deporting the women of al-Tantura** The long
column of buses carrying the women who had been
expelled from al-Tantura drove by day about 30 km
from Fureidis to Tulkarm. You could see the expellees
through the windows of the buses. Even those who
would one day deny there had ever been an organized,
mass expulsion didn't think at the time they had
anything to hide. Only the violent acts of the machinery
of expulsion were conducted out of the view of
photographers and journalists. They were invited only
later to observe humanitarian moments such as this,
when those carrying out the expulsion could boast of
their humanity as they quenched the refugees' thirst.
The limited interest shown by the free press in Israel in
the men and women being expelled ended here. Even
stories that were definitely newsworthy, like those
heard in shortwave broadcasts from Syria or Jordan
from refugees hoping to inform relatives who had not
been expelled that they were still alive, were of no
interest to the Israeli press. That most of the country's
Palestinian inhabitants were made refugees was
quickly accepted as a fact, a reality, joining the other
facts about whose creation no questions were asked.

Photographer: Beno Rothenberg, Israel State Archive, June 18, 1948

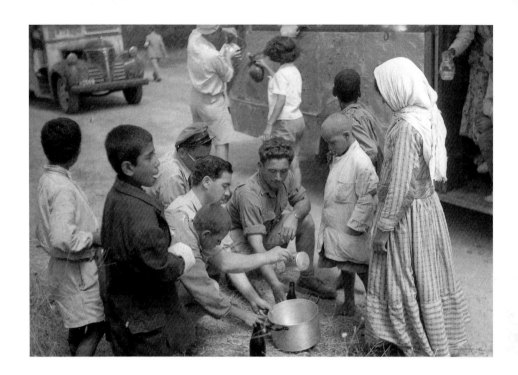

140   **Deporting the women of al-Tantura** Dressed
in shorts and a white shirt, the Jewish woman in the
background, who apparently lives in Kfar Yona, fills the
clay pitcher in her hand from the jerrican held by the
soldier. The newspapers have already reported how
generously they behaved to the expelled women.
Now she herself will be able to give some water to a
refugee. Soldiers stand helping children who've come
carrying empty bottles. From here the expellees will
walk another few hundred meters and be transferred to
the custody of Iraqi officers on the outskirts of Tulkarm.
Referring to the jerricans filled with water that the
Iraqis had readied for the refugees, the Israeli journalist
covering the expulsion would proudly report that "the
refugees didn't need that water because their bottles
were full." We'd expelled them and also slaked their
thirst.

Photographer: Beno Rothenberg, Israel State Archive, June 18, 1948

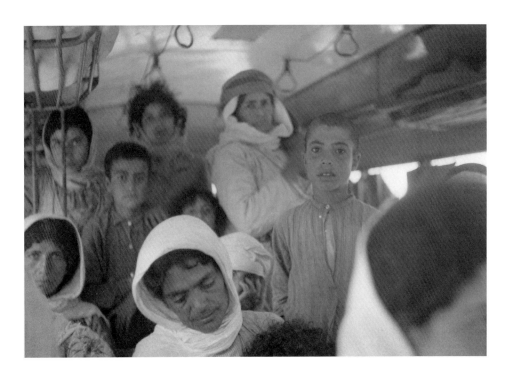

141 **Deporting the women of al-Tantura** Whoever
looks at this photograph for a while (without being
influenced by the extensive propaganda effort to
present the expulsion as a voluntary transfer) will not
easily erase from her consciousness the expression
in the eyes of these women. Bleary-eyed, hollow
looks, pained, angry, frightened, enraged, screaming,
weary, exhausted, staring, blank, unbelieving, scornful,
dubious, horrified at what they've seen with their own
eyes. One day sometime in the future, when she sees
people being expelled, she won't imagine they're being
transferred voluntarily.

Photographer: Beno Rothenberg, Israel State Archive, June 18, 1948

142 **Deporting the women of al-Tantura** Carrying
sacks on their heads, children in their arms or holding
their hands, walking through a familiar landscape on
an unidentified path, neither here nor there, no longer
able to see the home they were uprooted from, not yet
part of the nightmare in the camp they're being sent to,
only they and their possessions moving slowly toward
the horizon, embodying the image of the refugee. The
refugee who has come into existence on his own, the
refugee as an adjective rather than as the product of a
mechanism, of a process.

Photographer: Beno Rothenberg, Israel State Archive, June 18, 1948

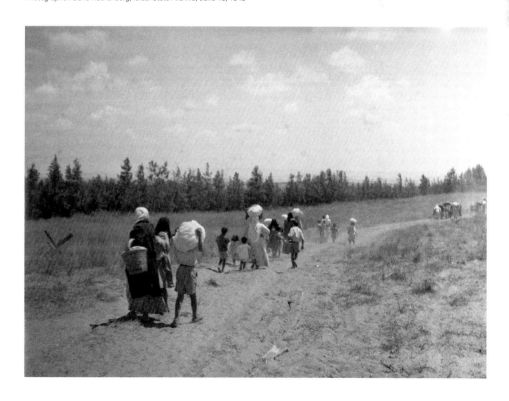

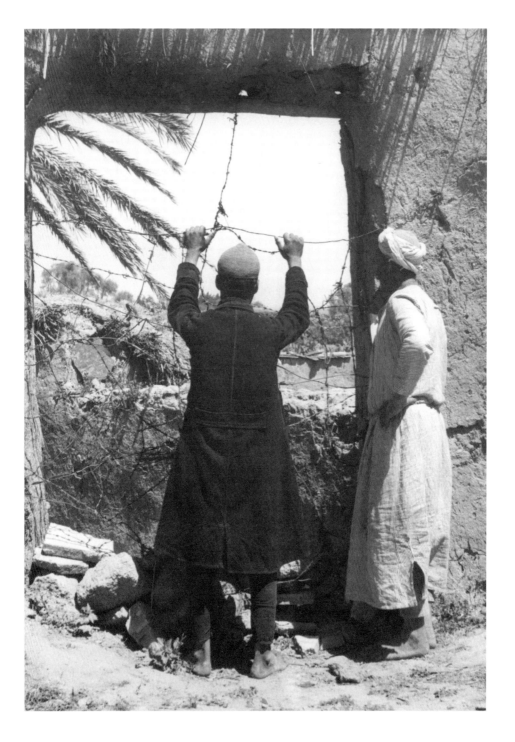

143   Gaza From the refugee camp in Gaza they look at the homes in Beit Hanoun from which they were expelled. Soon they'll be among the few allowed to return to what remains of them. They'll now be under Egyptian rule, because the armistice agreement placed Beit Hanoun under Egyptian control.

Photographer not identified. AFSC Archive, end of 1948

CHAPTER 5

Borders, Strategies of Uprooting, and Preventing Return

During the period prior to the adoption of the Partition Plan, the Palestinians refused to cooperate with those involved in its preparation or to discuss its details because of their objection in principle to dividing the country. Although many Palestinians criticized Jewish immigration to Palestine, and particularly the fact that Jews were taking over land in Palestine, and in certain cases various forms of opposition arose, the Palestinians were relatively tolerant of the Jewish presence. Evidence for that can be found in the many areas of life in which Jews and Arabs cooperated. The Partition Plan was not designed to address the existing situation in a given region, but rather the national aspirations of representatives of one national group. The Partition Plan was not a solution to the problem – it was itself the problem because it resulted in the clear and radical division of a country's population along national lines for the first time. Not only was this division fortified by the violence attending its creation and by a political declaration; henceforth, borders and fences were required to preserve for the future the achievements of the Jewish national movement that had been imposed on the Palestinians. The destruction and rebuilding by the Jews was intended to extend their hold on the land, and turned the Palestinians into homeless, exiled refugees and internal displaced persons. Those who remained inside the new country's borders were not allowed to return to their homes, which were either demolished or survived as isolated ruins whose surroundings had been wiped clean. Sometimes, when the hand-carved building stones were particularly impressive, they were used as decorative elements in the construction of public buildings for the Jewish community (Photos 155 and 156).

The new borders established by the extension of military control isolated the new state from its surroundings, separated it from those people who had been expelled from its territory and prevented them from returning home. Henceforth, every Palestinian expelled from their land who sought to return became an "infiltrator," a person threatening to invade a territory that does not belong to them. The movement of those who remained was restricted to an area whose boundaries gradually became more clearly defined; some were placed in ghettos and most subordinated to military government and needed passes in order to travel beyond their "pale of settlement." But the borders that now divided Palestine and separated the Israeli portion from the surrounding region had also been imposed on the Jewish population whose members had been accustomed to travel between Beirut and Nablus or Haifa and Amman to study, for commerce, entertainment and vacations.

This chapter portrays a variety of relationships between representatives of the new regime and the Arab inhabitants of the country, from expulsion (Zahleh, Lebanon, Photo 163), through the initial stages of the refugee condition when there is still hope of return ("on the roads" or "in the fields"), to discussions with those who remained on practical matters involving travel, housing, provisions, etc. Conversations and gestures have not yet been institutionalized – sometimes they are visible on the street, where women (in al-Nasirah, Photo 148) assertively demand what they view as a basic right that has been denied them – freedom of movement. Sometimes the head of the locality (Iqrit) is still important enough to host the officers at home and try to obtain commitments from them (that still remain unfulfilled) (Photo 151). The interactions in some of the photographs have "expulsion-lite" – mutually agreed upon – as their goal (al-Majdal, Photo 165), and sometimes all we can see are official gestures – presenting ID cards and travel documents (one of the roads in the "Triangle") (Photo 150).

The photograph is available for public viewing at the Meitar Collection, Tel Aviv. Permission to reprint the photograph to which the caption below refers was denied.

The empty frame represents not only the unavailable photograph, but also a civil claim of the right to quote photographs to which historical archives have denied public access.

In the center of the photograph, taken in an open area, stand a Palestinian man with a donkey carrying a Palestinian boy. Around them are armed soldiers in uniform.

144   **Negev**   The official caption referring to "The Golani Brigade in action against infiltrators," hides the fact that we're actually looking at an expellee and his son who have been deported from their land and are now prevented from returning. Longing, memories, family, relatives, home, possessions, lands, crops, livestock – they've left so much behind, and any of these could have been why they tried to return and given them the strength to overcome their fears of all that lay in wait for them as "infiltrators." Despite the horror stories they heard in the camps about violence, shootings and rape, they were determined, again and again, to make the long, exhausting and dangerous journey home, hoping only to taste a bit of the place from which they had been expelled, sometimes to gather produce or collect livestock they'd left behind on their land, sometimes just to find out what happened to their relatives, obtain one more scrap of information about those they've lost track of. They must have ridden the donkey, and wanted to take the black sheep back with them to where they now lived. Perhaps it can ease slightly the distress of hunger in the camp where they live, in Gaza or in Hebron. The term "infiltrators" was designed to be threatening, and this photograph could also have accompanied straightforward newspaper reports about "infiltrators" who had been shot to death because "there was no other choice." We can only hope that when the photographer left, the soldiers didn't view them only as "infiltrators."

Photographer: Beno Rothenberg, August 1950

145   **'Irndal** The borders established by the
armistice agreement with Jordan were drawn
on maps with a scale of 1:250,000. When these
borders were redrawn on more detailed maps,
and surveying teams went out to determine their
actual location on the ground, there were many
disagreements and conflicting interpretations. The
border in the Arava was to have been 182 km long.
Discussions between a Jordanian royal delegation
and the Prime Minister of Israel led to an agreement
on a route that met the needs of the statesmen on
both sides. The local Palestinian population was not
a party to the agreement. The Bedouin who, upon
the establishment of the state, were systematically
deprived of rights, including rights to territory, have a
role in this controversy as witnesses on behalf of one
side or another: "Arabs in 'Irndal testifying to whom
they'll pay taxes, which determined the location of the
border." The border that was drawn through the Arava
satisfied the generals on both sides but was harmful
to the Bedouin who were accustomed to travel freely
in the area.

Photographer not identified. Palmach Archive, no date

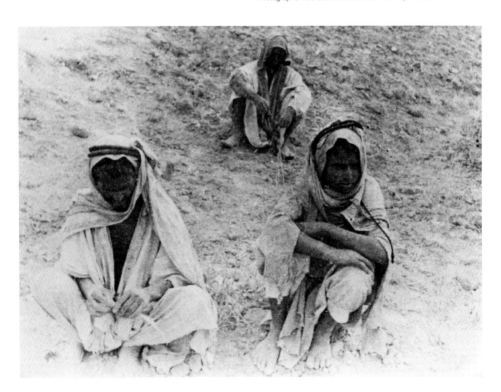

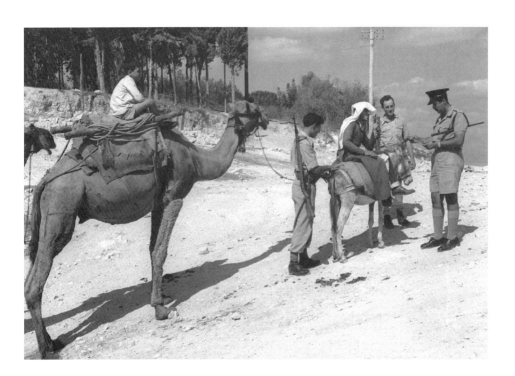

146 **al-Nasirah** Even before the military
government invented repressive procedures of its
own, it could implement regulations inherited from the
British Mandate to prohibit Arabs access to various
places, impose a curfew on them and declare their
neighborhoods to be closed areas requiring a permit
to enter or leave. The travel permits given to Arabs
so they could enter and leave their ghettos were in
Hebrew, a language most did not yet know when
military government was imposed. Thus was the Arab
distanced from the imaginary dialogue that went on
over his head between the soldier who stopped him
and the one who issued the permit. If all went well,
the soldier graciously waved him through without his
having taken part in this conversation.

Photographer: Teddy Brauner, Government Press Office, July 1948

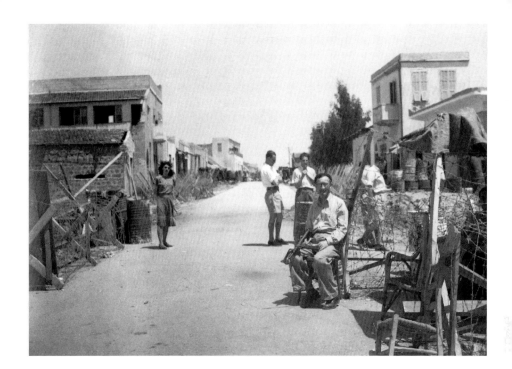

147   **Salama** Seated on a chair taken from one of
the houses, next to an improvised gate made of a few
wooden boards and wire, an armed guard protects the
village. It had been declared a "closed military area" in
order to prevent looting and unauthorized expropriation
of buildings until preparations for resettlement of
Jews (immigrants from Yemen and some of the 5,000
Jewish displaced persons who left their homes during
the fighting in Yafa and Salama) had been completed,
and to prevent the return of the Arab residents of the
village, who will be defined as "infiltrators" if they dare
to come back.

Photographer: Beno Rothenberg, Israel State Archive, probably late
April/early May 1948

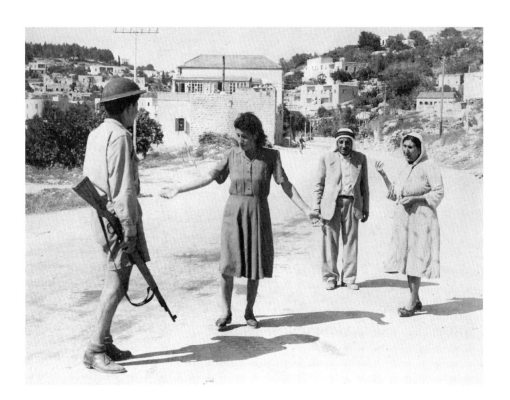

148   **al-Nasirah** The city had been captured the day
before the photo was taken. Men "of military age"
were gathered in one place and asked to turn over their
weapons. Women, children and the elderly remained
in their homes under curfew. The elderly man seems
hesitant. He stands shrunken in his suit while the two
women openly and vigorously gesture to the soldier.
They're telling him they don't understand the curfew.
It's not that they don't know what the word means;
they don't understand how it's possible to forbid people
to move around freely from place to place in the area
where they live. They're fearlessly demanding their
civil rights even though the soldier with whom they're
negotiating, and another soldier on the other side,
are both armed, and despite the news that men and
women elsewhere who talked back to soldiers had
been shot. Was it the presence of the photographer
that allowed them to act this way? From now on, their
movements will be more restricted.

Photographer: Associated Press, July 17, 1948

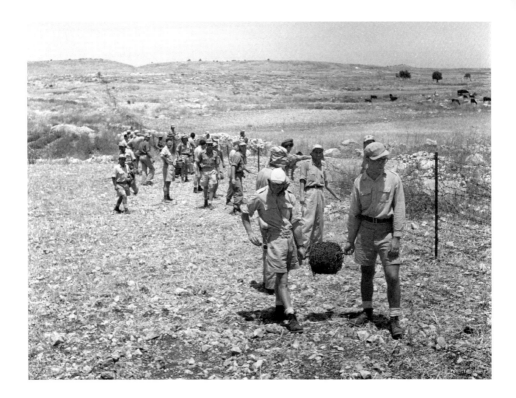

149   Between Jordan and one of the villages in the "Triangle" The armistice agreement with Jordan defined a border 624 km long passing through 73 localities, disrupting the lives of almost 100,000 people who were trapped along the boundary and cut off from their lands and places that had until then been part of their lives. The border helped make permanent the expulsion of thousands of internal refugees who found temporary haven in the Triangle. Complaints by Jordan's Arab Legion about expulsions carried out after the armistice agreement went into effect led to an investigation by the committee dealing with implementation of the agreements. Israel pressured the Arab municipal councils to tell the committee that they decided the expellees should leave because they were unable to shoulder the burden of providing for them. No country was willing to meet their needs. The planned expulsion was completed successfully in five weeks: "This action clearly proved that fair and aggressive rule in the villages allows us to fulfill our missions and strengthen Israeli authority" (in the words of the military governor). The committee investigating the expulsion decided that Israel was required to take back only 36 of the thousands of refugees who had been expelled. The Jordanian soldier and the villagers grazing their cows in the meadow on the other side of the fence observe how it separates them from the area which they had used until then for agriculture, commerce, services and leisure.

Photographer: Frank, IDF and Defense Archive, June 10, 1949

150   **A road in the "Triangle"** First he had to lobby the Military Governor for a permit to leave his village. Then, when he was already on the road, he was stopped at a roadblock and was at the mercy of the soldiers examining whether his permits were in order. In addition to stealing his house, his property, his land, his job, his status, his affiliations, his society, his freedom of movement, the new state would now steal his time. Anything he once did would now take much longer, assuming he was even lucky enough to be allowed to do it.

Photographer not identified. IDF and Defense Archive, May 11, 1949

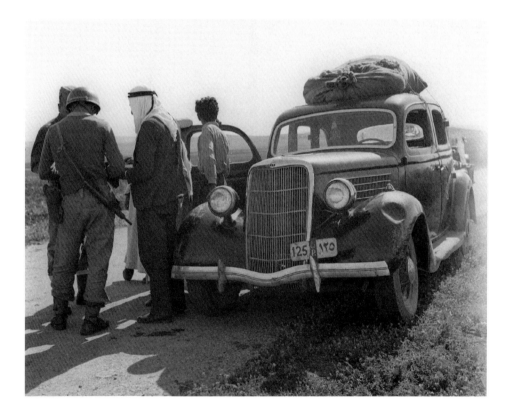

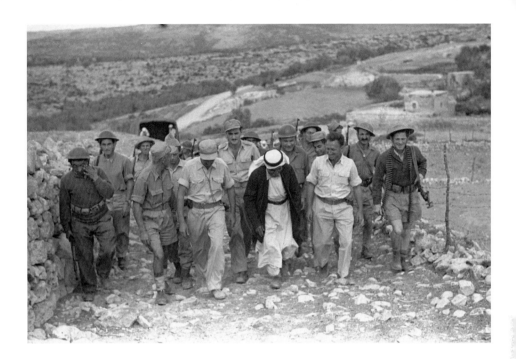

151   Iqrit The day after the village surrendered, the mukhtar invited the soldiers to lunch at his home. The excitement of victors admired for their achievements can be read in the faces of the Israeli soldiers – accompanied by the mukhtar who surrendered without a fight. We can imagine them seated around the table at his home. He gained their respect for the decision that prevented unnecessary bloodshed, and together they agree on the nature of their common future. To see this requires transcending what is possible within the limits of the nation-state in which the story of Iqrit and Bir'im could serve as a parable. The nation-state's leaders sought to surround it with various types of "security regions" and "sterile areas" to "protect" their ethnic group against invasion by external enemies, possibly assisted by internal enemies on the home front. Thus, a few days after the fall of Iqrit and Bir'im, a military-political decision was made to "cleanse" of Arabs a strip along the country's borders. The inhabitants of Iqrit and Bir'im were evacuated from their homes deceitfully, and promised they would be able to return in a few days. The evacuation was carried out under the "laws of war" permitting residents to be temporarily evacuated. The residents of both villages, who today live only a few kilometers away, have not yet been allowed to return, even though there are no Jewish localities on the villages' lands. The Bar'am National Park stands on part of Kufr Bir'im's lands, and localities in the area use some of the villages' agricultural land.

Photographer not identified. Government Press Office, November 1, 1948

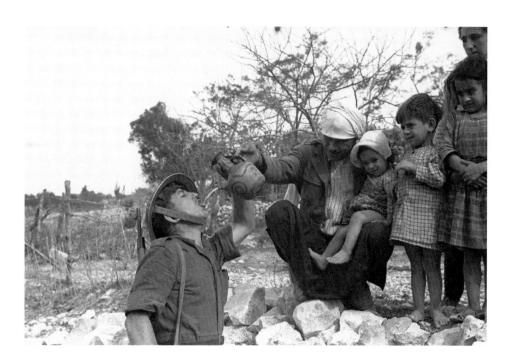

152   **Iqrit** They have heard what happened to the
residents of other villages, and are trying as hard as
they can to behave politely and nicely to the soldiers,
so the same thing won't happen to them. The children
stand reserved, suspiciously watching this man whom
their parents are devoting so much attention to. Two
days later they had already been asked to leave their
homes and move to Rame, to live in houses left behind
by the inhabitants who had been expelled.

Photographer not identified. Government Press Office,
November 3, 1948

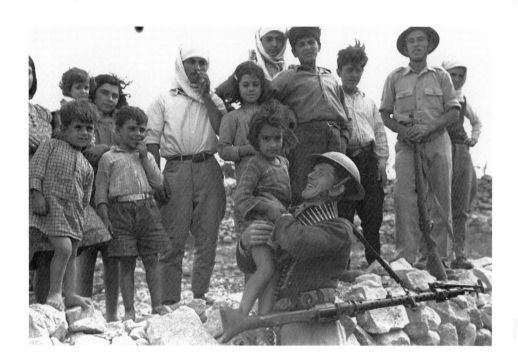

153 **Iqrit** Boys and girls who haven't been hearing since they were infants the song about their uncle the soldier who keeps them safe are uncomfortable being held by a strange soldier wearing a scary necklace of live ammunition, a gun as long as they are tall hanging from his shoulder. The Government Press Office wants a photo like this, so it can point out the nice soldier holding a little girl in his arms and ignore her distant expression and the fact that she's not enjoying the occasion at all.

Photographer not identified. Government Press Office,
November 1, 1948

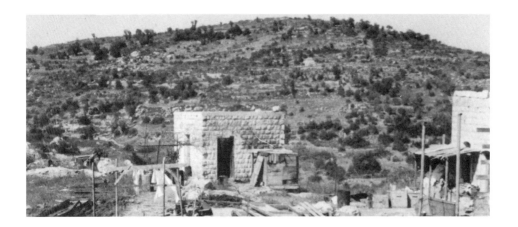

154 **Kufr Bir'im** The village's residents were
expelled from their homes, and most fled to the
wadis. They were promised they'd be able to return.
They received similar promises from the Supreme
Court, which heard their case, and its decision/
promise was not carried out either. While members
of the HaShomer HaTza'ir settlement group lived in
their houses, used their possessions and hung their
white garments on the clotheslines, the expelled
residents of Kufr Bir'im slept outdoors, unprotected
from the cold.

Photographer not identified. The photograph was given to Nahida
Zahra, a member of the second generation of those uprooted
from Kufr Bir'im, by a member of Kibbutz Bar'am (scanned with
the compliments of Meron Farah, who is also one of those
dispossessed from Kufr Bir'im), 1948

155 **Sar'a** Members of the settlement group work
energetically; soon they'll see the fruits of their labor,
and they'll erect another new temporary structure on
the site in response to the slogan on the sign, "Arise,
go up and inherit." To make sure it stands level on the
slope of the hill, and remains stable, they're laying
courses of stones instead of a foundation. That's an
additional way to conserve materials and remove
some of the many dressed stones scattered on village
land, the remains of homes belonging to the expelled
villagers. As time passed, the presence of those stones
became troublesome, and even seemed to indicate the
possibility that those who were expelled might return
– a vision, as it were, of stones coming together to re-
erect the Arab homes. Burying these stones beneath
the structure gave the hillside a new look, one in which
the new springs from the old.

Photographer not identified. Palmach Archive (Album of the
Har'el Brigade, Sixth Battalion), December 7, 1948

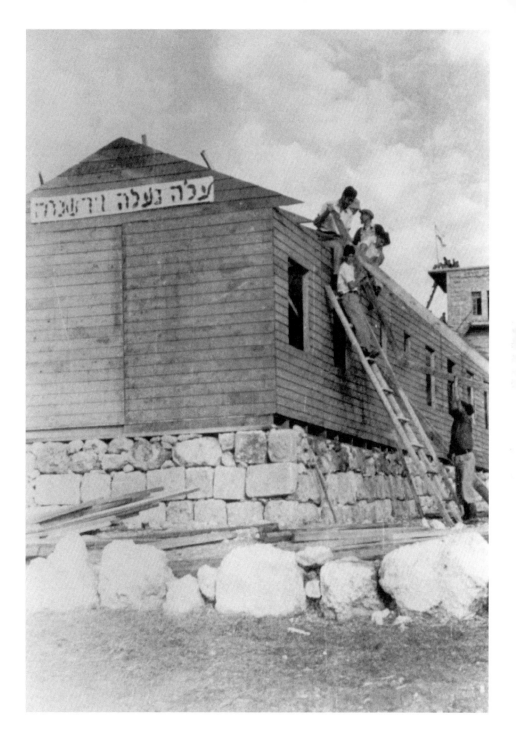

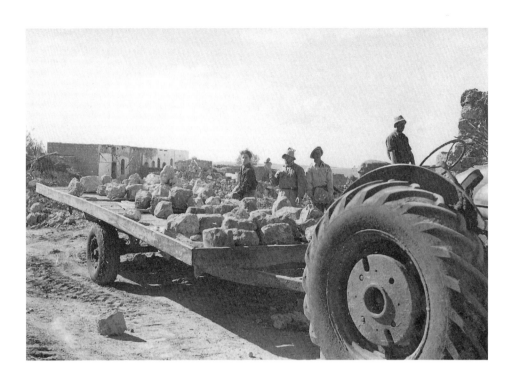

156   **Qaqun** Members of Kibbutz HaMa'apil loaded
these dressed stones from the nearby village of Qaqun
onto a wagon attached to their tractor and took them
to the kibbutz for reuse in construction. Other than the
village school that remained intact, and which today
serves Israeli children, most of the village buildings
were demolished and its residents expelled. Dressed
stones in good condition that had been removed
from the destroyed Arab villages provided high quality
building material to the nearby kibbutzim and, what
was more important, insured that those expelled from
the villages would not "infiltrate" and use those stones
to rebuild their homes. These stones, among the last
remnants of what once was the village of Qaqun, are
easy to identify. The monument that will be erected
one day to commemorate the village that no longer
exists could be placed where the stones now lie.

Photographer not identified. Courtesy of Bitmunah Lab, 1948

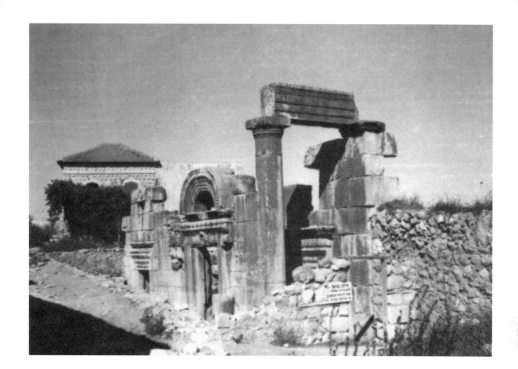

157   **Kufr Bir'im** This ancient synagogue is better
preserved than others dating from the Talmudic period.
In the years preceding the capture of Bir'im, the
residents of the Arab village were the ones directly
responsible for preserving the synagogue. When
the village was captured, a sign was placed on the
structure: "State of Israel – Property of the Department
of Antiquities. Removing stones or other antiquities
is prohibited." The rest of the village's buildings
were erased from the face of the earth by the same
state, with the approval of the same Department of
Antiquities. Today the synagogue stands in the Bar'am
National Park as the sole remnant of the Talmudic
period. No later cultures are mentioned.

Photographer not identified. The photograph was given to Nahida
Zahra, a member of the second generation of those disposed from
Kufr Bir'im, by a member of Kibbutz Bar'am (scanned with the
compliments of Meron Farah, who is also one of those dispossessed
from Kufr Bir'im), 1948

158 **On the roads** This picture provides a rare view of the first days that expellees from villages spent on their journey into exile, before they became "tenants" in an organized refugee camp where their basic needs were met more or less consistently. Here they improvise a camp beneath trees, weary from the journey, regaining their strength in the open air, in the chilly night, without shelter or hot food, sustained by what little dry food they brought with them. Many children who certainly aren't able to make the journey alone need help from the adults, who also find it difficult to walk from their homes in the neighborhoods around Jerusalem from which they were expelled to the refugee camps that will be built for them on the West Bank or in Jordan about 100 km from where they had lived. Israel physically erased the villages from which they came, and also tried to erase their villages from their identity as refugees, as well as its responsibility for turning them into refugees. But that was a battle they were determined not to lose, and even today each insists on a dual identity which has one permanent component: the village – al-Maliha, Ayn Karim, 'Aqir, Bayt It'ab, Bayt Naqquba, Dayr Yasin, Kasla, Sataf, Sufla, Dayr Raf'at, Dayr Am'ar or any other village – and one that is temporary, the refugee camp: Balata, Daheisheh, Jenin.

Photographer: Ali Zaarour, with the compliments of Zaki Zaarour, 1948

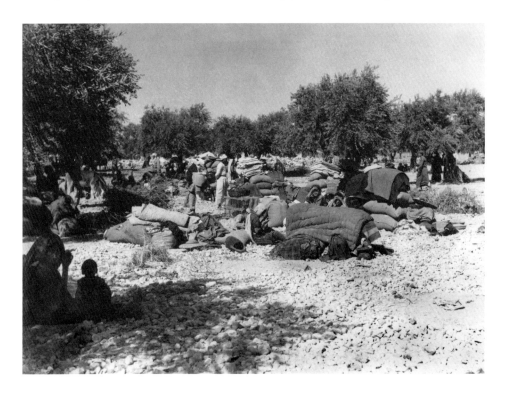

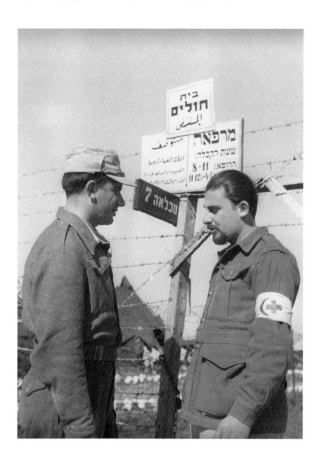

159 **Ijlil** The camp became the new living environment for all Palestinians, without exception. Place of origin vanished, and the temporary camp became permanent. The textures of camp life replaced those of the Palestinian village and town. There were improvised, temporary camps as way-stations, permanent UNRWA refugee camps both outside and inside Israel (until the latter were dismantled in 1952), shelters in mosques and monasteries, detention camps and prison camps, ghettos in mixed cities in Israel and military government in most of the other places they lived. In all these spaces they were transformed from free individuals meeting their own needs and those of their families and communities into people at the mercy of others, objects of humanitarian intervention. Sometimes these others, such as UNRWA, provided assistance, supplies and services; sometimes they were soldiers and jailers who administered their lives down to the smallest detail, as well as providing some aid and welfare services; and sometimes they were inspectors and professionals who drafted reports about them, such as Red Cross personnel who visited the prisoner of war camps every two weeks. While a few of the camps were eventually shut down – primarily detention camps and shelters in Israel – those who were in them no longer had anywhere to *return* to, because the place from which they had been expelled no longer existed. Those expelled from al-Tantura, for example, were held in this detention camp for almost a year, and when released it was suggested – essentially, they were compelled – that they join their families, who had been deported to the other side of the Jordan River. Thus, most of the Palestinians released from the camps usually went to places other than those from which they had come originally – in most cases, to other camps.

Photographer not identified. IDF and Defense Archive, 1949

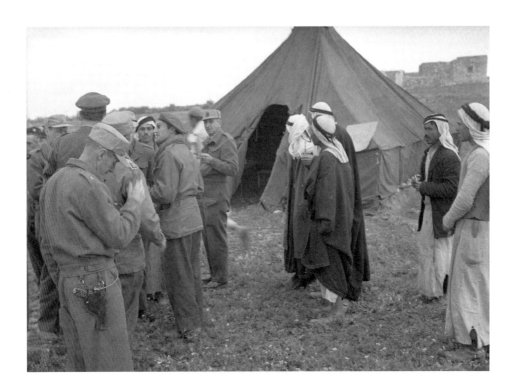

160 **'Iraq al-Manshiyya** Army tents, like this one
from which their evacuation from 'Iraq al-Manshiyya is
being organized, will continue to dot these roads and
other locations for a few years, until Israel manages
to stop attempts by expellees to return from refugee
camps to their homes. Here they're still negotiating
some details with the Israeli soldiers and the UN
observers, but in a few hours they'll no longer be part
of the discussion and will observe it with longing from
a distance.

Photographer: Beno Rothenberg, Israel State Archive, no date

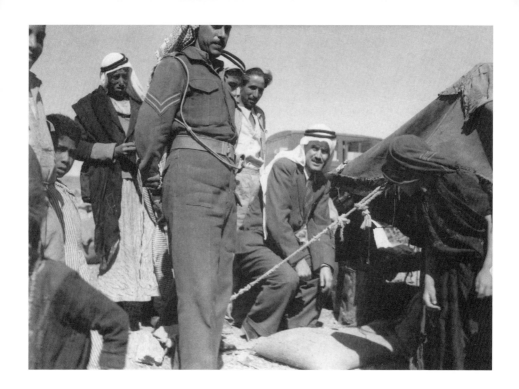

161 al-Quds region The photographer's son remembers that in the center of the photo you can see "UN representatives providing food to refugees in the Jerusalem area." And, in fact, there's a large sack of wheat in the center of the photograph, the kind which the UN had already supplied to the refugees during the siege of Jerusalem, even before they reached the refugee camps. Some of those in the picture are leaning toward the sack, looking at it and at the tent in front of which its lying, or from which it was pulled. Even if the sack is very big, and its contents sufficient to sustain the refugees crowded around it, this is food intended for them later, when they arrive in a place where they'll be able to bake and cook. Until then, reports tell of refugees out in the open near Jerusalem, with only meager amounts to eat,

suffering from malnutrition. Nevertheless, the situation of the expellees who remained near Jerusalem was apparently better than that of those who made their way to the West Bank and to Gaza. The "veterans" expelled from Yafa just before the state of Israel was established, who reached Trans-Jordan, found shelter in monasteries and schools, while those who came later, from al-Ramle or al-Lid, for example, were unable to find a place in public buildings and most of them slept outdoors. Each of the expellees received a small daily bread ration. Those with more money obtained slightly more. Only later did relief organizations take it upon themselves to organize systematic assistance to the refugees.

Photographer: Ali Zaarour, with the compliments of Zaki Zaarour, 1948

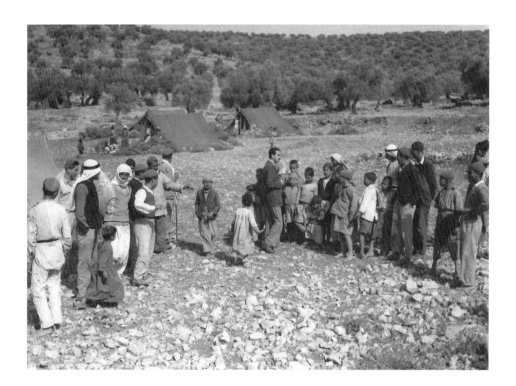

162 **On the way to Jordan** They understand they're
going to be away from home for a long time. Education
is one of the first things they organize. The teacher
wearing a suit gathered the children around him.
The fathers stand at the end of the row, opposite the
children, listening as they demonstrate their knowledge
to the teacher, who's apparently trying to find out what
they know and planning future lessons. Mothers with
younger children are in tents farther away. One of the
girls, already holding a brother in her arms, apparently
refuses to remain where they've put her with the
mothers, and approaches the circle of pupils with a
curious expression on her face.

Photographer: Ali Zaarour, with the compliments of Zaki Zaarour,
1948

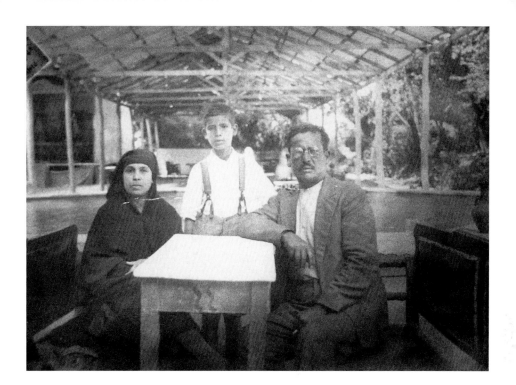

163   **Zahleh, Lebanon** A few days after Abdel Hay
al'Khatib, a fisherman from Haifa, had been expelled
to Lebanon together with his family, he wanted a
photograph of himself and his daughter, Jamila al-
Khatib [today she's Umm Faisal Zablawi], as a souvenir.
Because of his love of photography, he wanted to be
sure they'd have souvenir photos of this brief Lebanese
exile, from which they expected to return to Haifa
in two weeks. Israel never allowed them or other
expellees to return to their homes, and from Zahleh
they continued to the Nirab refugee camp in Syria.

Photographer not identified [the photograph and the information
were provided by Umm Faisal], April 1948

The photograph is available for public viewing at the Meitar Collection, Tel Aviv. Permission to reprint the photograph to which the caption below refers was denied.

The empty frame represents not only the unavailable photograph, but also a civil claim of the right to quote photographs to which historical archives have denied public access.

A long line of trucks piled with mattresses, blankets and other items crosses the photograph. The roadside is almost empty of people, the loaded trucks ready to drive away. Only four Palestinians still walk alongside. A Palestinian woman in the rear sits motionless by the road.

164   **al-Majdal/Migdal-Ashqelon** About 2,500 Arabs still lived in Migdal-Ashqelon until the beginning of 1950. Most of them were already displaced persons who had been uprooted from their homes and gathered into the ghetto the state established for them on the outskirts of the town. Their freedom of movement was limited, and they were allowed to leave the ghetto primarily to work. Depending on how much freedom of movement each had been granted they'd seen or heard how their homes had been given to Jewish families who were moving into them. About ten months elapsed from the day Moshe Dayan decided they were unwelcome in the town until the expulsion of all Arabs had been completed. The main argument was, as always, that they provided "a haven for infiltrators." The success of the project, which depended on the cooperation of more than a few Israelis – truck drivers, government ministers who were familiar with the decision, journalists adhering to the official line – would not have been possible had those involved not been convinced that it was "for the refugees' own good" – they were treated as refugees even before being expelled. It wasn't enough that the Israeli Jews accept the separation of the "refugees" from family members who had already been expelled to Gaza, or their life in the ghetto, as a fact not subject to appeal. Israel also tried to convince the Palestinians themselves that their evacuation to refugee camps in Gaza was a rescue. The procedures were similar to those the army and the state had previously employed elsewhere, but this time a few months of systematic effort were invested, including a "campaign of whispers," lies and deception, daily violence and abuse, and a slightly more favorable currency exchange rate. Is that woman seated by the roadside, when most of the others are already on the trucks on their way to the refugee camps in Gaza, unwilling to go even though she's signed the papers confirming she's being evacuated voluntarily?

Photographer: Beno Rothenberg, October 12, 1950

The photograph is available for public viewing at the Meitar Collection, Tel Aviv. Permission to reprint the photograph to which the caption below refers was denied.

The empty frame represents not only the unavailable photograph, but also a civil claim of the right to quote photographs to which historical archives have denied public access.

A smiling Palestinian man dressed in a jalabiyah stands in the center of the photograph wearing a kaffiyah and holding sacks of money. Behind him are a table and two chairs serving as an improvised office on the road. Two men, a Jew and a Palestinian, sit at the table, preparing documents for the last of the Palestinians being expelled from Migdal.

165   **al-Majdal/Migdal-Ashqelon** Here's a photo of someone who's been "evacuated voluntarily." He's holding bundles of Jordanian money that he received in exchange for his Israeli pounds. If until now he was unemployed, he's just received 50 Jordanian pounds as a stimulus grant to encourage him to "leave voluntarily." That could have been a pleasant surprise on a long journey of dispossession in the course of which he was robbed of everything he owned. If he'd worked and earned money, and had cash that the clerks at the improvised table behind him could exchange for him, he now received three times its value. The unemployed Palestinian, as well as the one who had just been fired without receiving severance pay, had to sign documents declaring he was leaving al-Majdal of his own free will, relinquishing any future claims, including the right to return. He wouldn't have been able to change very much money, since it didn't include the value of his house already expropriated by the state without paying him for it. The cash he had came from what property he'd been allowed to sell to the Jewish immigrants, and what he'd been

able to save from his laborer's pay. His job, like that of the other Palestinians in al-Majdal employed by the Custodian of Absentee Property, removing "abandoned" property or working "abandoned" fields, was gradually abolished. Perhaps the Custodian's office no longer needed workers, or perhaps it was necessary to reduce unemployment among the Jewish immigrants, or perhaps this was part of the preparations to expel him. In any case, many found themselves without work during these final months. A few weeks after all the inhabitants of al-Majdal had been expelled to Egypt, the OC Southern Command and officers in charge of the operation gathered in an Ashqelon café to celebrate the closing of the al-Majdal ghetto which they had created two years earlier. The military government came to an end and the town became a Jewish town. When, exactly, was this Arab expelled, the one shown sitting at the table, helping the government clerks reach the moment everyone was waiting for, when al-Majdal would be empty of Arabs?

Photographer: Beno Rothenberg, October 12, 1950

The photograph is available for public viewing at the Meitar Collection, Tel Aviv. Permission to reprint the photograph to which the caption below refers was denied.

The empty frame represents not only the unavailable photograph, but also a civil claim of the right to quote photographs to which historical archives have denied public access.

Elsewhere in town, at a counter improvised in an open doorway, two Palestinian men being paid for agreeing to leave the city meet with two officials wearing ties – Jews, apparently – who are counting the banknotes the Palestinians will soon receive as part of this transaction.

166   **al-Majdal/Migdal-Ashqelon** Perhaps his sunglasses protect him from the sights of the expulsion, and his necktie blurs somewhat the fact that he's also contributing to it.

Photographer: Beno Rothenberg, October 12, 1950

167   al-Nasirah/Nazareth Life in the Silesian Monastery became communal due to the extreme crowding in the rooms where hundreds of uprooted from the village of 'Illut were housed. They came together daily in the central hall to share their experiences, make plans for the future and try to improve their current situation and create an organized educational framework for the children. The fortunate ones among the uprooted managed to reach monasteries like this one in al-Nasirah, whose personnel not only took care of their needs but also created, with the help of volunteers from abroad, a supportive and encouraging environment, and endeavored to rehabilitate them socially and politically as full citizens. After they had been in the monastery for nine months, the head of the monastery led an organized procession of internal displaced persons to the office of the military governor to demand he allow them to return to their village. They persisted in this demand despite the fact that some of the village lands had been distributed to neighboring localities, some of the village buildings had been destroyed, and people uprooted from the adjacent village of Saffurya had been housed in some of the others. Israel's general policy was to prohibit the return of internal displaced persons to their villages. At best, when pressure was not put on them to leave the country, the Committee for Transferring Arabs relocated them to other villages in which they could try to be integrated. Surprisingly, and unusually, the demand by 'Illut's uprooted was met, and they received permission to return to their village.

Photographer not identified. The Monastery and School of "Jesus Adolescent" (Don Bosco), Nazareth, January 1949

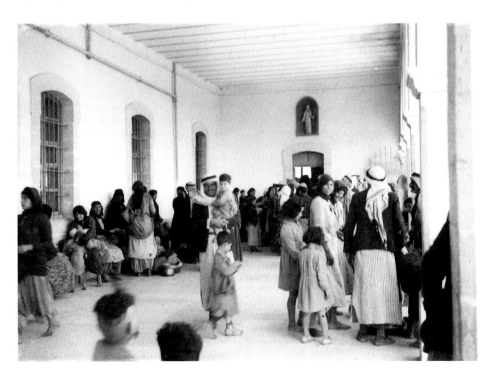

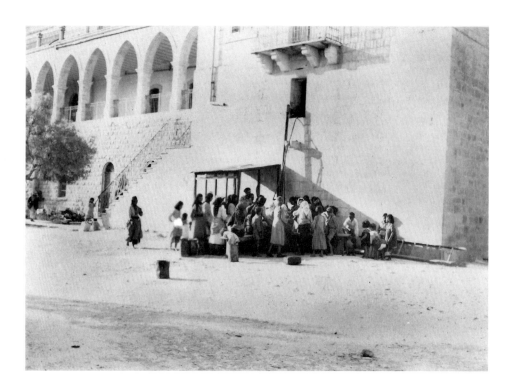

168   al-Nasirah/Nazareth Providing for the
refugees' needs was quickly organized into a
routine that allowed their life in the monastery to
go beyond dependency. Children played in the front
courtyard and women gathered under the canopy
near the location where UNICEF representatives
distributed water, as they had at the village well,
enjoying each other's company. They could also
meet acquaintances from neighboring villages
who came to the monastery to obtain some of the
services and assistance they needed to rebuild
their lives in the places where they found refuge.
But however pleasant life in the monastery may
have been, the proximity of their village, which
was only 1 km away, gave them no rest, and was a
constant topic of conversation when they gathered
around the "well," until they formulated their plan
for a political march. Although they knew the village
was not the same as it had been when they were
uprooted, this did not weaken their desire to return
home.

Photographer not identified. The Monastery and School of
"Jesus Adolescent" (Don Bosco), Nazareth, January 1949

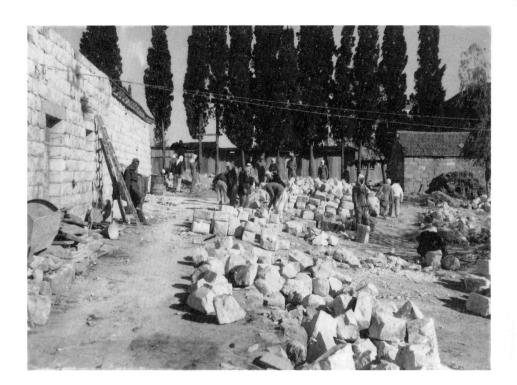

169 **al-Nasirah/Nazareth** Shortly after arriving at
the Silesian Monastery, the uprooted people began
restoring the building's foundations and its retaining
walls. To do so they needed stones that matched
the original ones. Tens of thousands of such stones,
scattered among the ruins of the destroyed villages,
had been loaded onto tractors by members of nearby
kibbutzim who used them for construction. Dayr
Yasin's renowned stonemasons had been massacred
or expelled, and their enterprise destroyed. These
uprooted people were now trying to learn the
stonemason's skills and produce the building material
they needed. They established a small stoneworking
operation at the foot of the hill to prepare the stones
required to rebuild the wall of the south court. In July
1950, in the presence of the Belgian Consul, the wall
they built was dedicated.

Photographer not identified. The Monastery and School of
"Jesus Adolescent" (Don Bosco), Nazareth, January 1949

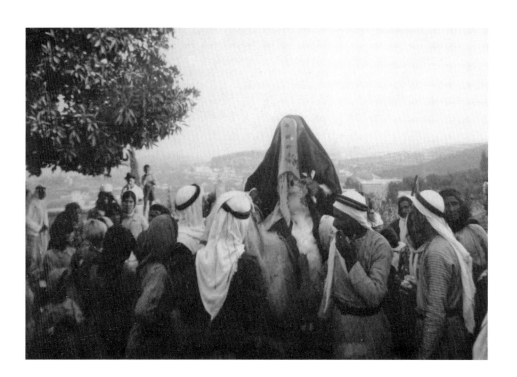

170   **al-Nasirah/Nazareth** Perhaps, when the
wedding was over, those who were celebrating
expressed, either in whispers or aloud, their hope that
the next wedding would take place in a rebuilt 'Illut.

Photographer not identified. The Monastery and School of
"Jesus Adolescent" (Don Bosco), Nazareth, January 1949

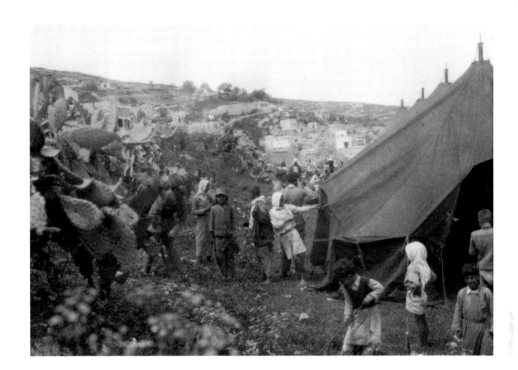

171   al-Nasirah/Nazareth While they were trying
to rebuild their lives, some of their homes had already
been turned over to people other than those who had
been uprooted. Other homes had been demolished.
When they were allowed to return, they weren't
exactly "returning" to something that was familiar.
Not all of them still had homes, their possessions had
disappeared forever, and expellees from Saffurya had
been housed in the school which had been the center
of communal life. None of those returning to 'Illut even
considered evicting them. The landscape was still the
one they remembered – the hills, the prickly pears,
the houses on the slope of the hill, the gentle breeze.
They are tightening the ropes of the tent that will serve
as a temporary school, trying to turn the event into a
celebration of returning to their land.

Photographer not identified. The Monastery and School of
"Jesus Adolescent" (Don Bosco), Nazareth, April 10, 1950

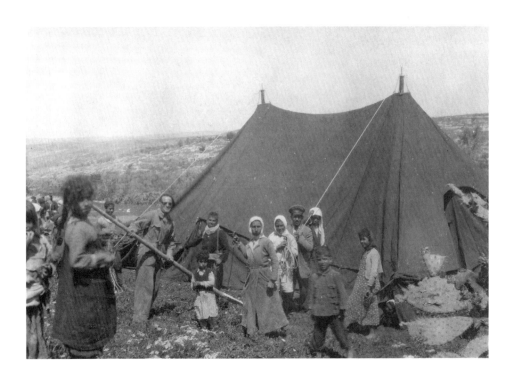

172   **al-Nasirah/Nazareth** Even if the
young people will miss the monastery's stone
walls on cold nights, the adults will be there
to tell them that soon, when their house in
'Illut is rebuilt, nothing will compare to it. The
dedicated people from the monastery were
the ones who provided them with tents during
the transition period, and helped in the effort to
create a decent shelter until they could move
back into their homes.

Photographer not identified. The Monastery and School of
"Jesus Adolescent" (Don Bosco), Nazareth, April 10, 1950

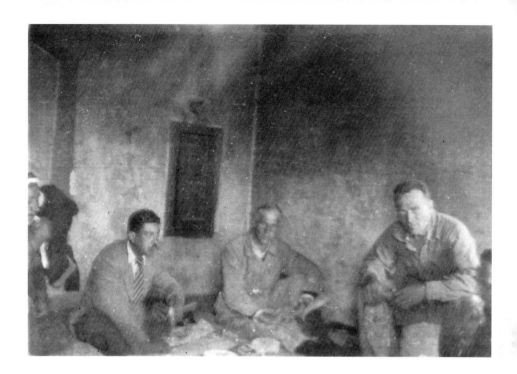

173   al-Nasirah/Nazareth Some lived in tents for a while, and some returned to the houses. During the day, they worked alongside the people from the monastery rebuilding the village and erecting temporary tents to meet some of the urgent needs. At the end of the work day, some would gather for coffee with their guests in one of the village houses. Returning to the village must have brought back memories. They had to deal not only with the memory of the expulsion and with the threat that their permit to return was valid only for one year, but also with the memory of the massacre. Members of the Haganah used intelligence they had prepared about the families in the village and relationships among them, and forced one of the residents to accompany them to the village and point out those persons who appeared on lists that had been drawn up in advance. Out of "consideration" for the informer, they covered his head so his compatriots would not be able to identify him. Fourteen Palestinians on the list were identified; they had worked in the oil refineries or had participated in the Arab Revolt. They were taken from the circle and shot in the presence of the others.

Photographer not identified. The Monastery and School of "Jesus Adolescent" (Don Bosco), Nazareth, April 10, 1950

CHAPTER 6

Looting, Monopolizing and Expropriation

Hundreds of thousands of people expelled from their homes leave behind a tremendous amount of property. The borders are closed to most of them, and the few remaining in the country are concentrated in particular areas which they may leave only with a special permit. Those responsible for their expulsion may now decide how to proceed, and administer in an orderly manner the property that fell into their hands, without unnecessary interference. First they prohibit looting – they don't allow people to do whatever they want or individuals to take anything they can lay their hands on. The new state wants to maintain order, and so appoints a Custodian of "Absentee Property." Even when they're decorating the Prime Minister's Office and looking for appropriate carpets, the secretary coordinates with the Custodian's office the transfer of rugs from "abandoned homes," which are duly recorded in the books (Photo 196). Henceforth, ministers and heads of state will walk on them. The shops in the photos are marked appropriately ("Jewish store," Jerusalem, Photo 174); some have already been allocated to "important" functions (such as the "Demobilized Soldiers' Cooperative," Photo 176); other shops fill with Jewish products (al-Nasirah, Photo 177).

The considerable amount of property left behind provides employment for many. Rubble must be removed, homes emptied, abandoned homes guarded, Arabs kept behind the fences erected to restrict their movement, entries to abandoned shops blocked with sandbags, signs replaced, languages changed, agricultural produce gathered, the land cultivated. All are busy and no one has time to waste asking "inconvenient" questions or wonder about them, while those who were dispossessed and whose property was plundered are no longer around to protest.

Though all were dispossessed and most expelled, enough Arabs remained in the country to "spoil" the Jewish celebration. Now new forms of exchange began to develop and, slowly, also new, measured forms of cooperation. But wherever they existed they occurred in a single, unified context – the invariable subordination of Arabs to Jews, according to the Jews' rules.

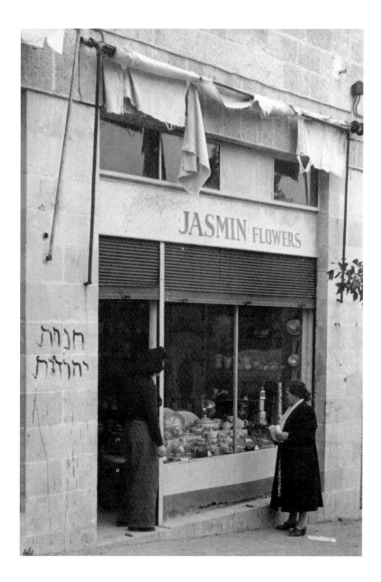

174   al-Quds/Jerusalem A few days after this part of Jerusalem had been captured, the words "Jewish shop" were written on stores belonging to Arabs. The original shop sign still hangs above the store window as a reminder that until a few days ago it had been an Arab florist shop. Now a pleasant salesgirl speaking Hebrew stands at the store's entrance, her customer inspecting the kitchen utensils on display. In one of the countless official documents produced by the office of the Custodian of Absentee Property on which "abandoned property" was recorded, he complained that although tens of thousands of buildings had been abandoned, many kinds of articles that were easily looted never arrived at his warehouse because they were small enough, or light enough, to be carried off by hand. The Custodian noted in particular that kitchen utensils were among the missing items.

Photographer: Fred Chesnik, IDF and Defense Archive, no date

175 Yafa/Jaffa After Yafa had been struck by the man-made earthquake, representatives of the state imposed a centralized administration on the city. They concentrated the Arabs in Ajami and collected the "absentee property" in warehouses. Only later did they distribute the homes and businesses to the new immigrants, using detailed registers, according to criteria and procedures established by various committees. The chaos in the city was great, the immediate needs of the local population, both Jews and Arabs, were many, and some of the residents acted for a while (sometimes in cooperation with other government departments focused more on welfare issues, like the Absorption Department) as a force supplementing, and sometimes opposing, the centralizing state efforts. The state turned Ajami into a ghetto for Arab displaced persons. Jews also invaded Ajami, its houses and its shops, and the reality was often one in which Jewish immigrants from Bulgaria and displaced Arabs attempted together to survive. Even if the photographer played a role in creating this idyllic scene, the ease with which the Arab and the Jew sit on chairs outside the shop seems to indicate they're

used to doing so rather than being something unusual. Even if the immigrant received the business which, until recently, was a hairdresser's owned by Arabs, the Arab seated there doesn't necessarily view him – the uprooted immigrant – as the one who dispossessed him. They do not see each other solely through the national lens which the state uses to define the relationship between them. Nor did the Jew who received the shop participate in the frenzied erasure of the Arab past, or see the Arab letters ("Salon Mira") on the shop window as a threat to the purity of Hebrew (which, in any case, he doesn't know yet). They're polite to each other, joking like old acquaintances, having a pleasant time together. It won't be long before the differences between them, based on their origins, will find expression: better jobs and housing will be found for most of the Jewish immigrants outside of Yafa, and the separation between Jews and Arabs, overseen by the state, will deepen. The street name will be changed from al-Halwa ("the beautiful") Street, to Jafet Street.

Photographer: Zoltan Kluger, Government Press Office, October 1, 1949

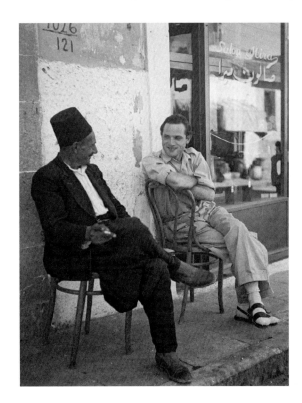

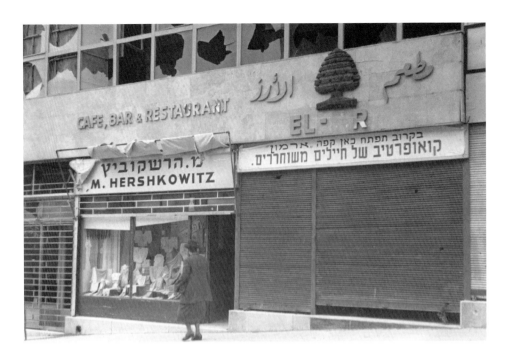

176 **al-Quds/Jerusalem** When the state
succumbed to looting's "evil impulse," and distributed
property, established criteria, kept registers and drew
up lists, looting received a new name – "Administration
of Abandoned Property." The army headed the list
of beneficiaries, and carpentry shops, ironmongers,
smithys and metalworking establishments all came
"naturally" into the army's possession. But when
a particular military unit took what was "theirs"
without going through the Custodian, its commander
was censured and there was sometimes a mini-
investigation. When the army "justifiably" obtained
property allocated to it by the Custodian, the fact could
be publicized, as in the case of this café which will
open as a "Demobilized Soldiers' Cooperative." It's
likely that before it opens the unnecessary Arab sign
("Cedars Restaurant"), which might raise unnecessary
questions, will be removed.

Photographer: Fred Chesnik, IDF and Defense Archive, no date

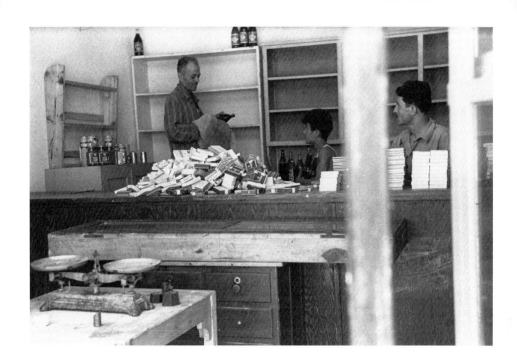

177 **al-Nasirah/Nazareth** The staff of the
Government Press Office was very proud that year
of everything that became Jewish, and it's possible
to find references in its archives to various aspects
of the looting, such as the Jewish cooperatives that
came to dominate commercial markets. Until the war,
the manufacture of tobacco and cigarettes was one of
Haifa's largest industries. The Arab Karaman, Dik and
Salti cigarette factory in Haifa, with 1,200 employees,
did not reopen after the war, and Jewish tobacco
manufacturers could flood the market with their own
products. The official caption reads, "A shop in Nazareth
fills up with Jewish products." A pack of "Atid" (Hebrew
for "future") cigarettes is clearly visible.

Photographer not identified. Government Press Office,
December 1, 1948

178   Yafa/Jaffa Immediately after Yafa was captured, the street names were replaced by numbers until appropriate new names could be selected. This step was unnecessary where the British Mandatory authorities had already numbered the streets. After Yafa was captured, the printing shops on this street, that had printed the Arabic newspapers *Filastin* and *al-Difā'* ("Defense"), were closed, and it was not included in the area allocated to Arabs. Only after the Jews became a majority in the city were Arabs permitted to leave the ghetto. Neighborhoods housing Jewish immigrants who weren't trying immediately to become "sabras" preserved some of the cosmopolitan syntax of Arab urbanism that made possible contacts such as that shown in the photograph, which transcended commercial relationships.

Photographer: Zoltan Kluger, Government Press Office, October 1, 1949

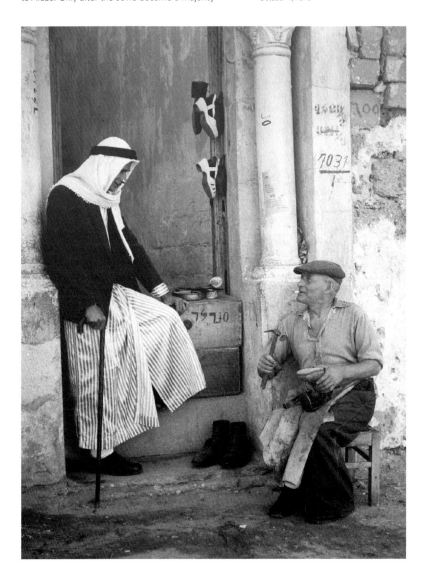

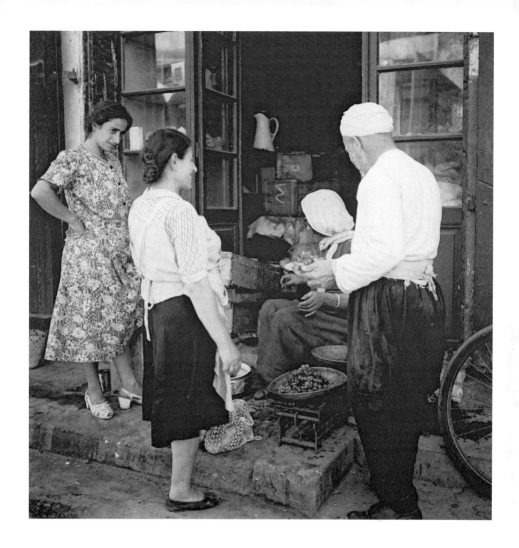

179   **Yafa/Jaffa**   The Ajami ghetto is located on
the edge of the city, the center of which gradually
became a "Hebrew town" whose narrow conception of
"modernity" led it to erase traces of its predecessors.
In the midst of the chaotic conditions in the city, Arabs
also sometimes managed to find a small shop or corner
where they could engage in petty commerce. The
photographer didn't overlook such examples, and added
this scene to the series of photos of co-existence that
he took in Yafa.

Photographer: Zoltan Kluger, Government Press Office,
October 1, 1949

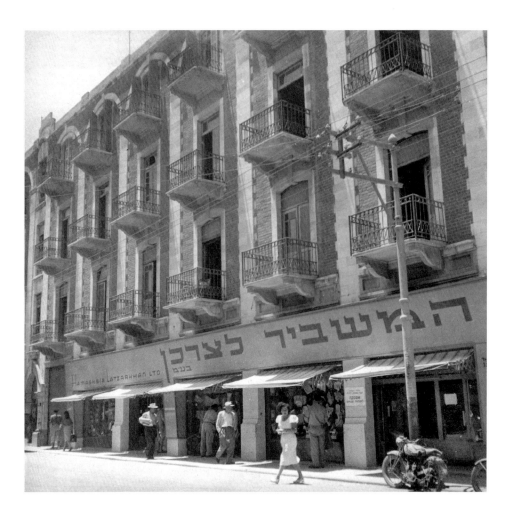

180   **Yafa/Jaffa** One year after Yafa was captured and transformed into a "Hebrew city," many talked proudly about the "optical paradox" of its streets: modern, western commercial buildings with large show windows and advertising signs at street level, and above them richly ornamented upper stories displaying oriental motifs. That paradox, however, was deceptive. This magnificent apartment building on Negib Bustros Street was built by a Lebanese entrepreneur who designed spacious shops on the ground floor with large windows looking out onto the street. The building was a commercial and shopping center for the Palestinian bourgeoisie of Yafa and elsewhere in the country. There were lawyers' offices on the upper floors, including those of Jews, whose employees wore expensive suits, and the shops sold jewelry, perfume, suits and carpets from all over the world. For years talk of this "optical paradox" didn't allow the real paradox to appear: free citizens alongside others subordinated to military rule. Had that paradox, essentially civil in nature, been visible, those who enjoyed the combination of a free, open market and a public space open to all without restriction would have had to object to the subordination of Arab citizens to military rule. The sign on one of the columns proclaiming a "Commissary for families of the mobilized" isn't understood to be part of the paradox, but part of the natural order.

Photographer: Zoltan Kluger, IDF and Defense Archive, July 1949

181 **Yafa/Jaffa** The sign reads "Jaffa Office/ Breaking-in is forbidden/ Violators will be severely punished." What might be inside? Carpets, pianos, vases, mattresses, furniture, phonographs, tea tables, shelves, breakfronts, mirrors, clothes racks, round chairs, upholstered chairs, clocks, a complete dental clinic, small medical tables, samovars, bed tables, dressers, small square tables, upholstered sofas, overstuffed leather chairs, upholstered armchairs, fans, plant stands, ovens, refrigerators, piano benches, standing lamps, small glass-topped tables, shoes… Did we miss anything? Each item was recorded on lists prepared by the office of the Custodian, with the exact date it was received, its condition and estimated value.

Photographer not identified. IDF and Defense Archive (received from David Elazar), no date

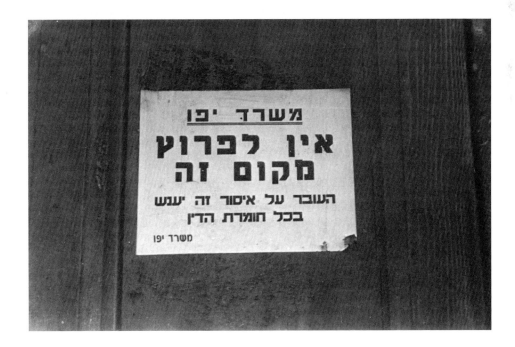

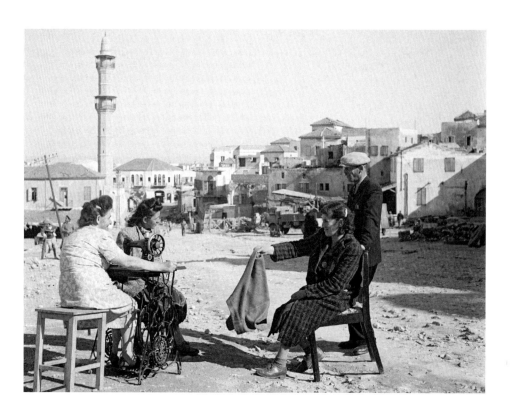

182 Yafa/Jaffa The ruins of the buildings on the border of the old city, near the al-Mahmudiya Mosque (Jam'a Yafa al-Kabir), haven't all been cleared yet, and their shattered remains are scattered everywhere. Bulgarian immigrants are already living in buildings the state decided not to demolish. It's hard for them to make a living, but they still have to pay rent every month to the office of the Custodian, which deducts income tax from the money it receives from "absentee property," as required by law. Not all the immigrants were also able to pay rent on a little shop. But it didn't cost much to buy tools like a sewing machine from the Custodian, and operate a small business even without a roof over your head. Thus, she could use her skills, relieve somewhat her loneliness as an immigrant shut in at home, and also earn a little money.

Photographer: Zoltan Kluger, Government Press Office, October 1, 1949

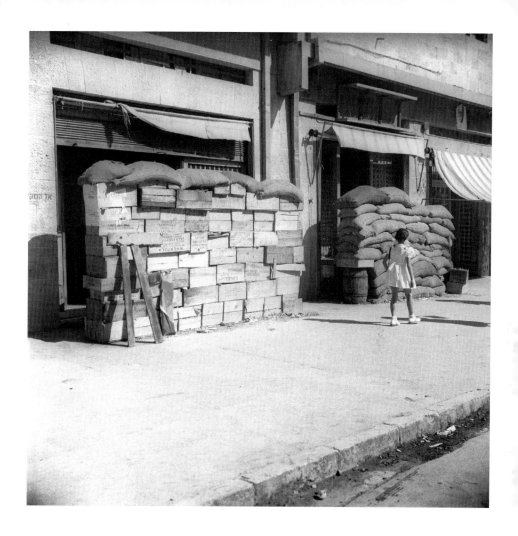

183 **al-Quds/Jerusalem** By July 1948, the office of the Custodian was determined not to leave goods unprotected. One shop was blocked with a wall of crates, a second by a barrier of filled sacks. When the Palestinians demand compensation one day from a different regime, and receive payment for the loss of homes, businesses and fields, they'll probably compromise over the lost merchandise.

Photographer: Yehuda Eisenstark, IDF and Defense Archive, July 28, 1948

184   Yafa/Jaffa Ajami ghetto is surrounded by a barbed wire fence which the Arabs were forbidden to cross. Arabs were set apart and the separation was manifest. The Arabs could see Jews moving about "freely," while the Jews saw the Arabs caged. To maintain this separation, some Jews moved freely from one side of the fence to the other. To reorganize the city, erase what should not be visible and make room for the new, to ease the distress of the uprooted Palestinian population whose needs must also be met along with those of thousands of Jewish immigrants, the military governor and his subordinates took advantage of the vast amount of material left behind by the Arab artisans who were employed in this broad boulevard lined with workshops. When they were expelled from Yafa, they left behind machines, tools, raw materials and special instruments that artisans improvise over the years to improve their work. The availability of equipment and raw material allowed investing a little time in painting authoritative signs, like "Exit," "Entrance," or "Parking," to demonstrate that someone is in control of the city space, and show who makes the rules. Until the soldiers learn everything they need to know to run the workshops, they require the help of skilled Palestinian workers. Is the Palestinian worker sitting outside the workshop taking a break, or are those inside discussing and doing things that are confidential, and have sent him to wait outside until they call him back in? The official caption isn't helpful, stating only, "An Arab, and a female soldier on duty."

Photographer not identified. IDF and Defense Archive (Mapping and Photographic Service), October 5, 1948

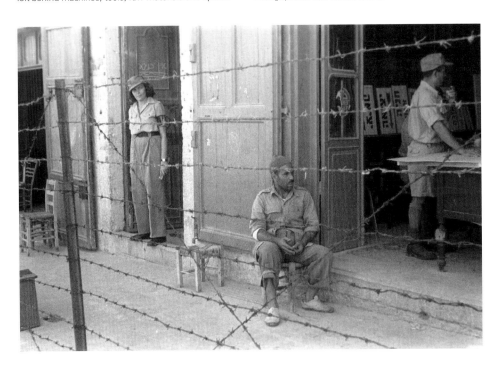

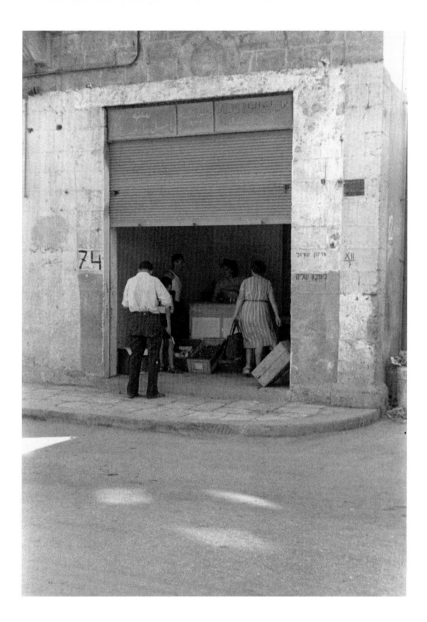

185 **Yafa/Jaffa** At a certain point, everything began going according to plan. First, stamping "State of Israel" on the items, then allocating them – "For immigrant housing," and only then moving immigrants in and opening up shops. Before the expulsion from Yafa the wholesale market was located here, selling vegetables, sugar, nuts, spices, dried fruit, oil, grains and legumes. The sign in Arabic – belonging to a shop selling candy and nuts (founded by Kamal in 1932) – isn't appropriate to its current use – selling vegetables – but a new Hebrew sign will soon take care of that.

Photographer not identified. IDF and Defense Archive, no date

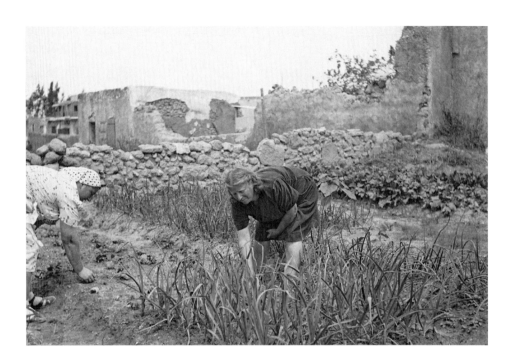

186   **'Aqir** When it was decided to settle Jewish
immigrants in the village whose 2,480 inhabitants had
been expelled, most of its land, which was known to
be very fertile, had been leased to the neighboring
localities. But next to each of the village's 400 houses
was a small plot that the Jewish immigrants who
moved in could immediately begin using to make a
living. A few of the houses had been repaired, though
most of them had been destroyed, and for a few
months some of the immigrants were employed to
remove the accumulated debris. Immigrant women in
the foreground plant vegetables. Behind them, beyond
the fence marking the boundary of the plot in which
they're working, two partially-demolished buildings
are visible. Even if their crop is small, they'll receive
full payment for it, which will be more than what Arab
farmers will get for a much larger crop.

Photographer: Zoltan Kluger, Government Press Office,
October 1, 1949

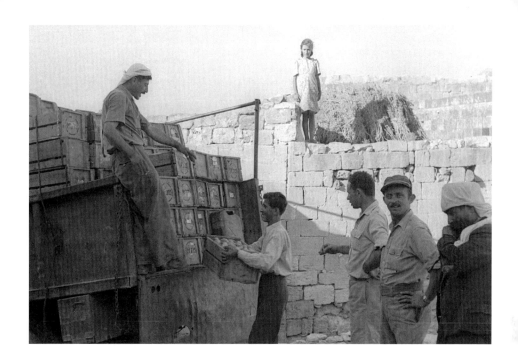

187   **Shafa-'Amr/Shfar'am**   The marketing of
agricultural produce was an additional area in which
official and semi-official Jewish organizations imposed
on Arabs conditions different from those enjoyed by
Jewish farmers, subordinating them. Often, when there
was a shortage of fresh produce, supply was directed
first to Jewish localities, even if Nazareth and Shafa-
'Amr were similarly distressed. The Jewish marketing
monopoly also discriminated against Arab farmers
in the payment they received for produce that was
identical to that supplied by Jewish farmers. Is the girl
looking down on what's happening below simply proud
of her father and the delicious vegetables that he grew
and is now selling to buyers from Haifa, or does her
expression already incorporate the civics lesson she's
learned about the economic and political significance
of fruits and vegetables whose marketing is also
subordinated to the line dividing Jews and Arabs.

Photographer: David Eldan, Government Press Office,
August 1, 1949

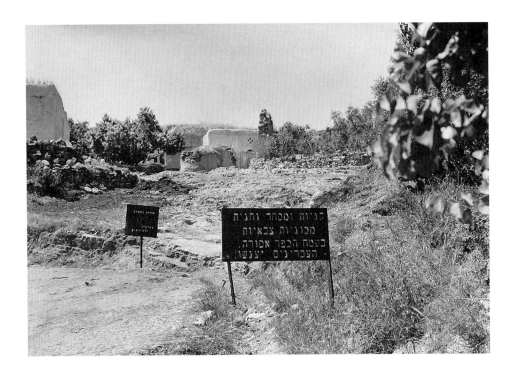

188 **Wadi 'Ara** Military government of the Palestinian population and a monopoly over the marketing of agricultural produce enabled the state to control the economic development of Arab citizens. The state also prohibited direct commerce between Arabs and Jews, explicitly prohibiting buying merchandise from the inhabitants. Signs placed in the entrance of many Arab villages warn civilians and soldiers not to enter: "Purchasing, commerce and parking military vehicles in the area of the village is prohibited. Violators will be punished." There was no discussion at all about whether Arabs would enjoy economic equality. The many discussions addressed the form inequality would take. Economic inequality was necessary to balance the Arabs' initial agricultural advantage – before 1948, about 70 percent of the farmers were Arabs, their produce was excellent and it was sold cheaply – and to prevent them from prospering, which might have enabled them to free themselves from dependency and subordination. The solution devised was to sell their produce in Jewish markets at full price, but in turn pay them much less than it sold for, not much more than their cost of production, so that they didn't receive the surplus value. The state took the difference and used it as it pleased, without, of course, involving Arabs in decisions regarding the money that had been stolen from them. A year later, when Arab Knesset members demanded that prices be equalized, it was decided to do so gradually, in order "to avoid disrupting the Arab economy."

Photographer: Beno Rothenberg, Israel State Archive, May 1949

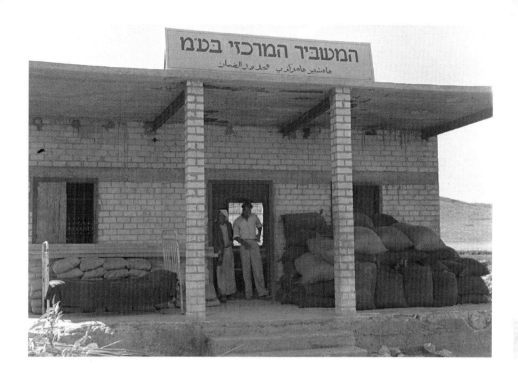

189 **Wadi 'Ara** The decentralized commercial activity among Jewish and Arab farmers and merchants, and among the Arabs themselves, that existed until the establishment of the state was subsequently centralized and administered almost entirely by a number of Jewish economic organizations like HaMashbir HaMerkazi. This was a veteran economic arm of the General Federation of Labor ("Histadrut") established some three decades prior to the establishment of the state. The Arabs who were now required to buy and sell products almost exclusively through these organizations were not Histadrut members. Only in 1959 did MAPAI consider allowing them to join. The local branch of HaMashbir HaMerkazi that opened in Wadi 'Ara served the state as a means to limit Arab economic development. The system of permits and roadblocks administered by the military government to limit Arab mobility was used as a control mechanism to insure that all transactions were mediated and supervised by HaMashbir HaMerkazi or by Tnuva.

Photographer not identified. Government Press Office, September 1, 1949

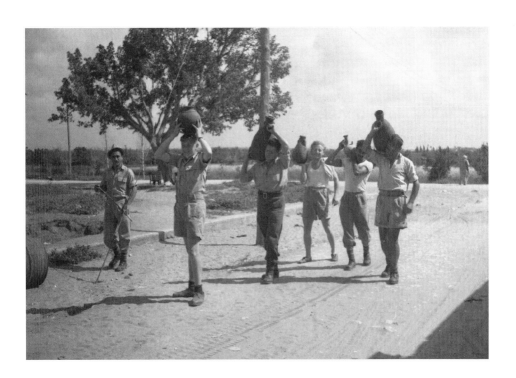

190 **Salama** Hast thou dispossessed and also emulated them?

Photographer: Beno Rothenberg, Israel State Archive, probably late April/early May 1948

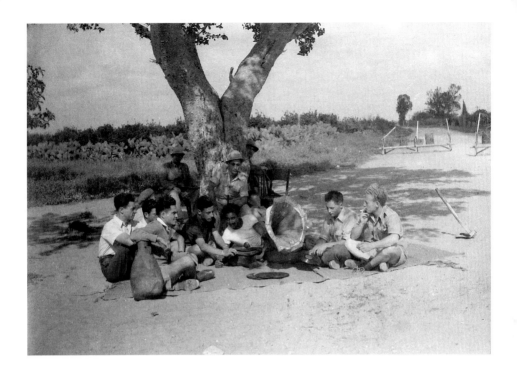

191   **Salama** Until the immigrants arrive, the
village is all theirs, and no one will disturb them. Soon
they'll complete their task and transfer all property to
the office of the Custodian. They'll take nothing for
themselves. Meanwhile they're resting, surprised to
discover that the villagers' musical taste isn't what
they'd expected, and they like it. It's just unfortunate
that the young man who's never before had a record
in his hands doesn't realize it's being damaged by the
way he's holding it with his greasy fingers. The owner
of the house, who certainly must have been very fond
of these records, would go out of his mind to see them
lying unprotected on the ground.

Photographer: Beno Rothenberg, Israel State Archive, probably late
April/early May 1948

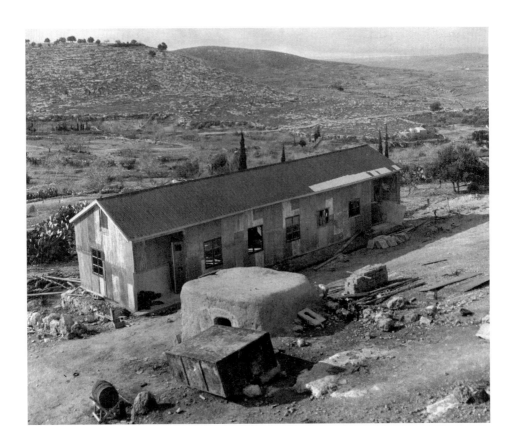

192 **Sar'a** Other than the clay oven, located between the dining hall that's just been erected to serve members of Kibbutz Tzor'a, and the overturned crate, nothing remains of the village buildings. Only the trees and prickly pear bushes scattered here and there hint that until a few months ago buildings also stood here. The kibbutz members could use the clay oven to bake authentic "Israeli" pitas. But the fact that they removed the chimney from the clay oven when they finished the dining hall supports the hypothesis that the members of the new kibbutz didn't retain the heating method used by the villagers – dried goat and cow dung.

Photographer: Zoltan Kluger, Central Zionist Archive, 1948

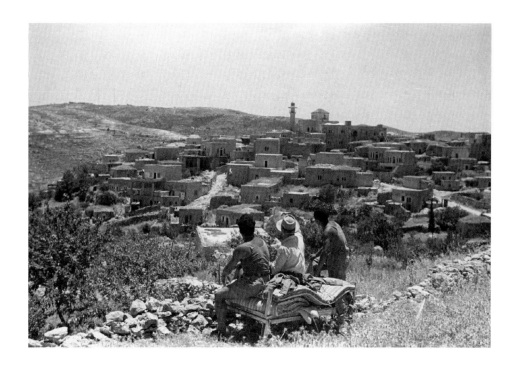

193   **al-Maliha** Even if now they're only figuring
out how long they still have to go, carrying two
beds provided by the Jewish Agency and a pile of
mattresses, they're already becoming familiar with
the hills' charms, the hidden lanes, the winding path
from the mosque to the well, learning to love nature
and the land, becoming people who know "their land"
intimately. Will one of the 2,250 residents of the village
who were evicted from the homes they're moving into
suddenly burst like a ghost out of one of the wardrobes
to tell them he'd been expelled?

Photographer: Fred Chesnik, IDF and Defense Archive, 1950

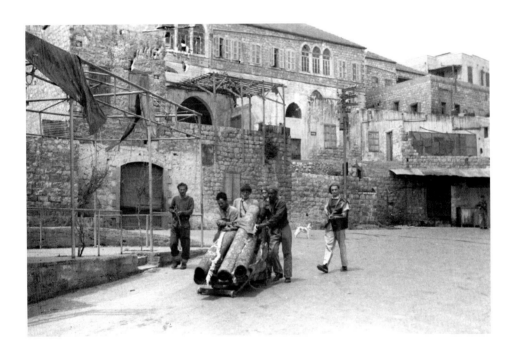

194   **Haifa** Are they being accompanied by two
members of the Haganah with drawn weapons
because they tried to resist being mobilized to remove
carpets from the homes of people who had been
expelled and transfer them to the Custodian?

Photographer: Fred Chesnik, IDF and Defense Archive, April 22, 1948

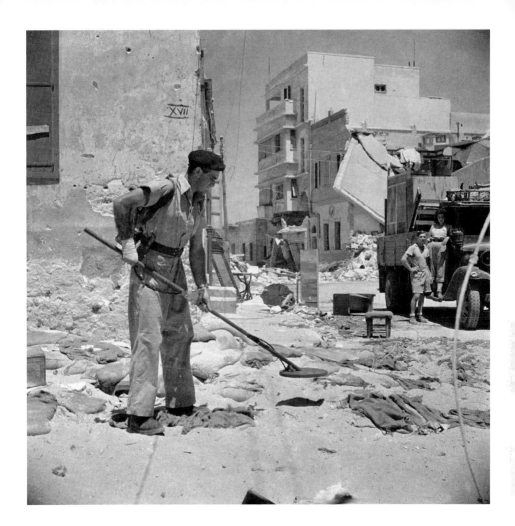

195 **Yafa/Jaffa** They were able to remove the
magnificent heavy mirror from the house next door.
They're waiting for the soldier on the left to finish
searching the area for mines before continuing to clear
the house. If the photograph bore an exact date we
could determine whether the truck which is almost
fully loaded is visual evidence of what the Custodian
and the Finance Minister described as "the army doing
whatever it pleases" – unauthorized transfer of property
to army units ("The army removed 1,800 trucks full of
goods from Lydda alone"), or is this a process conducted

"according to regulations," a combination of collecting
weapons, locating mines and collecting "absentee
property" from the houses and transferring it to the
office of the Custodian where everything would be sold
according to fair criteria which take into consideration
the needs of the various sectors of the Jewish
population. In two cases the weapons were sent to a
special "warehouse for confiscated items" and "divided
equitably" between the Haganah and the Etzel.

Photographer: Paul Goldman, (Israel Photo Art), 1948

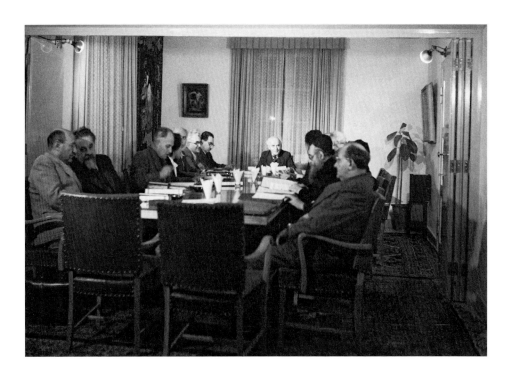

196   **Tel Aviv** On August 23, 1948, the Prime
Minister's Office sent a letter to the "Jaffa Office"
responsible for "abandoned property," requesting that
its staffers be permitted to "examine the carpets in
their warehouse in order to select carpets for the main
government building." In order to allay any suspicion
that these representatives are taking the carpets for
themselves, and to insure that the action is both legal and
coordinated among the various government ministries,
the letter continues, "After they select the carpets you will
receive instructions from the Finance Ministry regarding
their transfer and destination." Had this been a color
photograph, we could get an idea of their taste and their
color preferences. Carpets were also sold at that time to
the Soldiers' Welfare Committee, the Jerusalem Youth
Club, the Association of Oriental Women, Kibbutz Ramat
Rahel's kindergarten, the Ministry of Social Welfare, the
Town Military Officer, the Chamber of Commerce, the
offices of the Hebrew Encyclopedia, the office of the
Minister of Supply and Rationing. Zionist archives also
contain a long list of policemen and ordinary citizens who
purchased carpets that had been part of the abandoned
property. I won't mention their names.

Photographer: David Eldan, Government Press Office, January 19, 1949

CHAPTER 7

Observing "Their Catastrophe"

Most of the photographs in this book come from Zionist and government archives. The vast majority of them could easily have appeared in the "commemorative albums" published each decade – they contain nothing that the accepted discourse wouldn't recognize as another contribution to building the country and an additional point of pride. These photographs are public and accessible. Israeli citizens viewed these photographs or others like them, and didn't feel aghast or thought they were seeing a disaster. This book is a photographic archive that gathers items from different sources to make them visible in a new way. This archive allows a dual catastrophe to emerge from the photographs: the one imposed on the Palestinians and inscribed on the photograph's surface, together with the catastrophic blindness still inhabiting the souls of Israeli Jews. In other words, the book traces the process by which the catastrophe that occurred in Palestine from 1947 to 1950 is seen, when it is seen at all, mainly from the Palestinian perspective.

The book's final chapter presents photographs displaying this civil blindness in operation – despite the fact that the disaster is visible, participants don't notice it. The British policeman, the Red Cross nurse, the UN representative, the photographer, the journalist, the foreign observer – all playing their part in the catastrophe unfolding before their eyes, remaining passive, allowing the Israeli soldiers to complete the job. This disability became part of the Israeli Jews' consciousness of their civil behavior. Enough lies were available when this defensive armor threatened to crack – "there wasn't any expulsion," "they fled," "they missed their chance," and in any case, of course, "we had no choice – they threatened to destroy us."

Only a single Palestinian in the photographs is clearly shown bemoaning the disaster. He appears in the picture taken by a Palestinian photographer who lingered over his accusatory finger (el Haram el Sharif, Photo 204). But the accusing finger isn't necessary in order to see the catastrophe portrayed in this book. All that is needed to discern it is to describe what the photographs actually show, not that which during the subsequent decades became defined as "the unavoidable cost of the war."

Recognizing catastrophe – any catastrophe – for what it is: that is the necessary condition for renewing the possibility of observing, experiencing and responding jointly as partners to any disaster, rather than from opposite sides of the barricades. That's how the Jews and Arabs appear in the book's last photograph (taken in March 1947), side by side, watching the Haifa oil refineries burn following a Jewish terror attack against the British installations. They worked there together. The explosion shocked them all. Together they assisted the injured, watched the flames from afar. One day, a new form of civil partnership might emerge from the shared awareness of catastrophe.

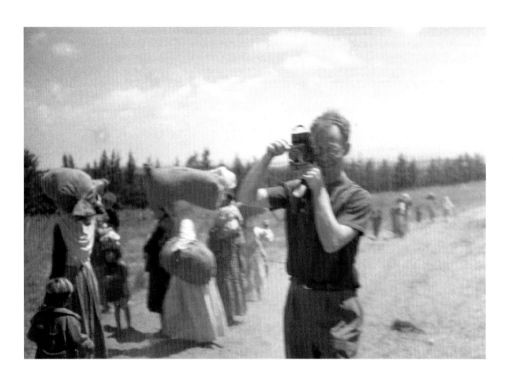

197 Deporting the women of al-Tantura

The photographed photographer – or maybe a cameraman if the instrument he is holding is actually a "standard 8" – stands very near the column of women who are now being permanently expelled to Trans-Jordan. The angle he chose has them passing before his lens one by one. If he were to look one day at the "rushes" he would undoubtedly be able to create a repertoire of the facial expressions of those being expelled. The photographer who appears in the photograph wasn't alone. The raw footage he and other photographers have tucked away in cartons or in drawers belong to the public. Displaying them is a necessary stage in reconstructing the constituent violence of the state of Israel's regime. Had these hundreds of portraits of people who were described as members of "murdering gangs" by those organizing the expulsions been displayed one next to the other before they were expelled, perhaps the state would have failed to mobilize the thousands of Jews who participated in the transfer, and without whom it would have been impossible to carry it out.

Photographer: Beno Rothenberg, Israel State Archive, June 18, 1948

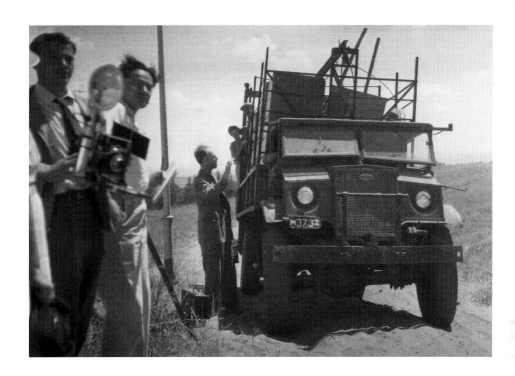

198 Deporting the women of al-Tantura A
journalist and photographer stand in the middle of
the road. Each readies his equipment – one holds an
open notebook and a pen, the other a camera with
flash attachment, his finger on the shutter release.
They haven't appeared by chance; the expulsion has
been underway for a few days, it had to have been
organized and coordinated among many persons and
organizations, and they – those documenting it – are
part of the event. The photograph has no date, and
the photographer's terse caption – "Transfer of Arab
women from al-Tantura to Trans-Jordan" – doesn't
allow us to situate it exactly within the chain of events
involved in the expulsion of Arabs from al-Tantura, who
were not sent directly from the village to Trans-Jordan,
but passed through a number of way-stations before
arriving there.

Photographer: Beno Rothenberg, Israel State Archive, June 18, 1948

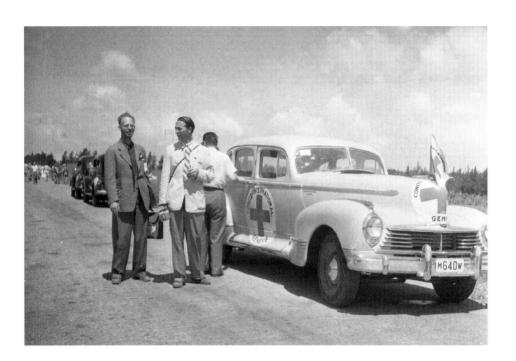

199 **Deporting the women of al-Tantura** From the
moment the inhabitants of al-Tantura were uprooted
from their homes and their surroundings, and were
no longer able to meet their own needs, they became
a burden. No state was willing to take care of them.
From the outset, the Jewish leadership that created
the refugees and turned them into a burden refused
to accept responsibility for them and tried to distance
itself from the problem. The Ministry of Minorities had
difficulty supplying their needs in Fureidis, which was
the first stop in their transformation into refugees,
since even without them the village weighed heavily
on its budget. The expellees weren't "prisoners of war,"
so they couldn't be dealt with as such. The Jewish
leadership did all it could to prevent their return to
their homes, so the only solution was to contact the
organization that had always proclaimed its neutrality
between the parties to a conflict – the Red Cross – and
invite it to participate in the expulsion and play its role.
Red Cross representatives arrived on June 18, and
promised to transfer from Fureidis to Tulkarm 1,086
women refugees from al-Tantura and elsewhere. Could
the Red Cross representatives have prevented the
deportation?

Photographer: Beno Rothenberg, Israel State Archive, June 18, 1948

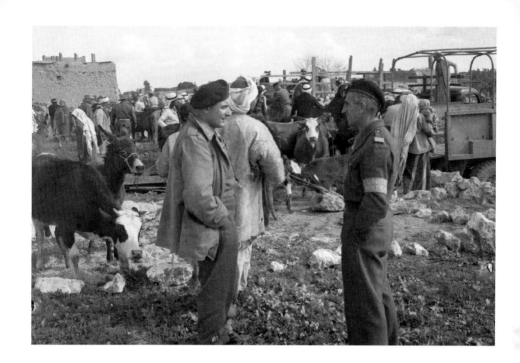

200   **'Iraq al-Manshiyya** The armistice agreement
between Israel and Egypt, signed under UN auspices,
stipulated that, after the evacuation of the Egyptian
army, the inhabitants of 'Iraq al-Manshiyya would
remain in their homes and Israel would protect
them and their property. The UN, which oversaw the
agreement, also oversaw its violation. The residents
appealed for help to the UN and to the Red Cross,
but the only aid it could guarantee was to help expel
the residents from their homes. UN representatives
converse among themselves, while in the background
soldiers are busy loading the Palestinians onto Egyptian
pickup trucks. Later they'll proudly report having
generously permitted the refugees to take some of
their property with them, since in any case their houses
as well as their land had already been lost to the
Israelis who would soon divide it among themselves.
Could the UN representatives have prevented the
deportation?

Photographer: Beno Rothenberg, Israel State Archive, no date

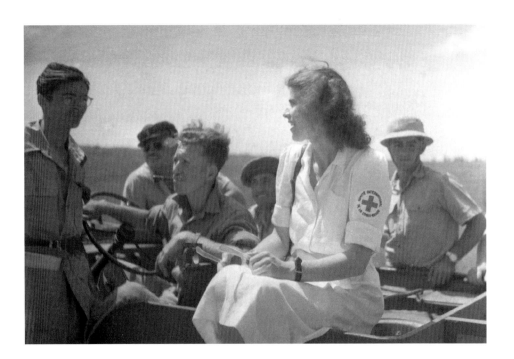

201   **Deporting the women of al-Tantura** On June
18, Red Cross representatives arrived in Fureidis,
accompanied by the Arab Affairs Advisor and a
representative of the Ministry of Minorities. The
Palestinians' distress and despair were apparently so
great that they put their hopes in the representatives of
the Red Cross and the UN, who lacked both the power
and the authority to assist them beyond assuring they
would not be harmed, at least while being deported.
Before the era of television, the deportees might
think that the clean, elegant image of a nurse in a
white uniform bearing the emblem of the Red Cross
would offer some protection, but it also allowed those
carrying out the expulsion to portray their actions as if
they conformed to international standards.

Photographer: Beno Rothenberg, Israel State Archive, June 18, 1948

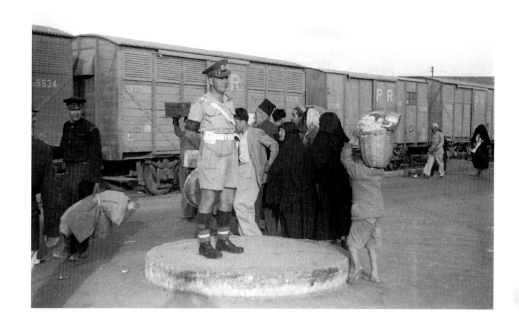

202 **Haifa** The British, who remained formally responsible for the security of the Palestinian residents, accepted almost without objection the new reality the leadership of the Jewish Yishuv had created by expelling them, and played the role of extras in the drama. The British supervising officer, standing on the small platform elevating him slightly above those being expelled, insures that the movement of thousands toward the railway cars proceeds in an organized fashion, while other soldiers, such as the one on the left, come over to help carry the few belongings the refugees were able to take with them.

Photographer: Fred Chesnik, IDF and Defense Archive, April 22, 1948

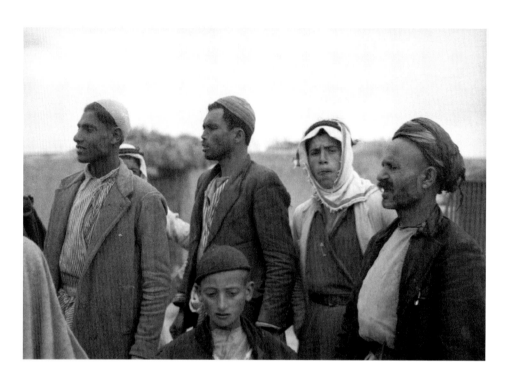

203   **'Iraq al-Manshiyya** Until a short time ago, while
they were still busy removing their possessions from
their homes, piling them up, even resting a bit on the
piles of belongings in front of their homes, or loading
them onto the trucks, they hadn't yet had time to
observe their catastrophe from "without." Now, when
everything's ready, and the first expellees begin to
leave, the three who are looking at the road on which
others are starting to move can't remain indifferent.
Their eyes narrow, their mouths open slightly, and the
faint, despairing sound of someone unable to bear
what he sees escapes their lips. The little boy drops his
gaze; the adult looks past the photographer's shoulder.
They do not yet see the photographer as someone to
whom they can turn for help.

Photographer: Beno Rothenberg, Israel State Archive, no date

204 **al-Quds/Jerusalem** The subject points his finger at damage to the courtyard of the al-Haram al-Sharif caused by an artillery shell that killed 14 people and wounded many others. There have been photographs of much greater damage, of more terrible destruction than what is shown here, that haven't included the pointing finger which has become so familiar since the 1980s. Nor is this the standard image, well-known to photographers and subjects alike, in which they stand opposite each other, the plaintiff and the damage he's suffered framed for the camera. The finger pointed here lacks the performativity of the later gestures, and looks more like someone pointing out the damage to an insurance adjustor. Even this gesture is absent from photographs documenting the nakba. Didn't the subjects wish to show the damage caused them? Or were the photographers who were present at the catastrophe, most of them Jewish, uninterested in recording that gesture, waiting instead to capture a frame portraying subjects who didn't seem to be protesting or composing themselves for the camera? Could it be accidental that the only two photographs (the other also taken in the same Jerusalem location) in which I noticed that gesture were taken by a Palestinian photographer?

Photographer: Ali Zaarour, with the kind permission of Zaki Zaarour, 1948

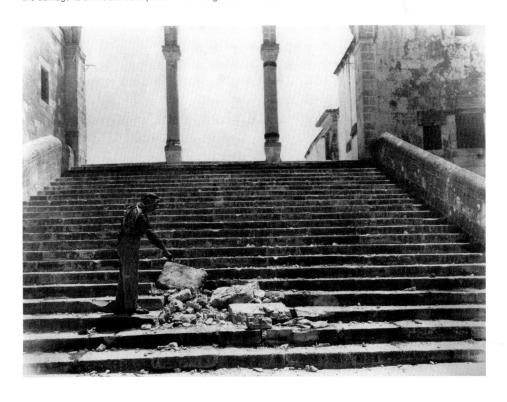

205 **Athlit prison camp** The accounts by Arabs
held in these camps focus primarily on the harsh
conditions, forced labor, distress, hunger. Memories of
entertainments, like the one shown in the photograph,
weren't able to tip the balance in their recollection
of what was more, and what was less, important.
The photographer and the Red Cross representative
were invited so that a different scene could be shown.
Prisoners wearing "traditional" clothing perform a
traditional dance in the middle of the circle. It isn't clear
who decided on the repertoire, and chose a dance
usually performed at engagements and at weddings.
Once the program had been selected, the jailers were
apparently those who provided costumes for the
prisoners, or at least garments for the female character.
She was played by a male Palestinian prisoner wearing
the clothes of a Jewish woman. While another prisoner
plays the flute, one of the jailers comes over to the
dancer and, like a devoted wardrobe master on a set,
arranges his garment.

Photographer not identified. Government Press Office,
November 12, 1948

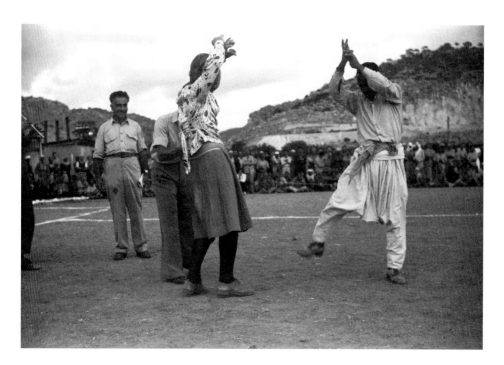

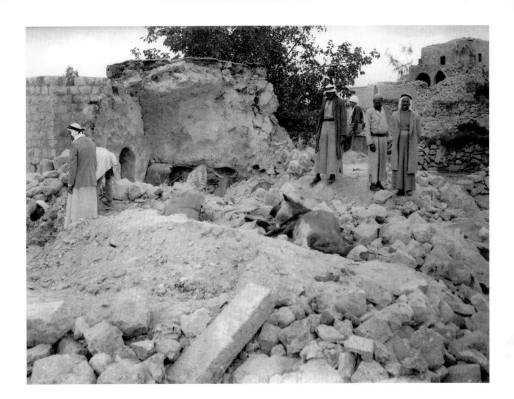

206　**Village not identified**　When the photographer
stood in front of them to take the picture, the man on
the right raised his eyes and smiled. Those standing
next to him continued to look at the donkey's carcass,
wondering whether it would be easier to lift if they
tied its legs together. Perhaps they also recognize the
shoe lying next to it, and that's what disturbs them.
Another group of men on the left remove objects from
the rubble. The name of the village and the date of the
photograph that could serve as the starting point of the
journey that would bring the information in the picture
to life, are written in the photographer's notebook
preserved inaccessible in the IDF archive. When it is
returned to its owner (the photographer's son) or made
publicly available, we will be able to determine whether
the Palestinians searching in the rubble are doing so
with permission or stealthily; whether they've been
forced to do so or are volunteers; is this the village from
which they or others have been expelled, a rehabilitated
village or one razed to the ground? The absence of such
photographs in state archives makes this one – taken
by a Palestinian photographer in a setting that was not
a photo opportunity set up by the army, and to which
Jewish photographers had not been invited – a unique,
if only a very partial, source of information about the
manner in which the Palestinians confronted the
remaining fragments of their catastrophe.

Photographer: Ali Zaarour, with the kind permission of Zaki Zaarour,
1948

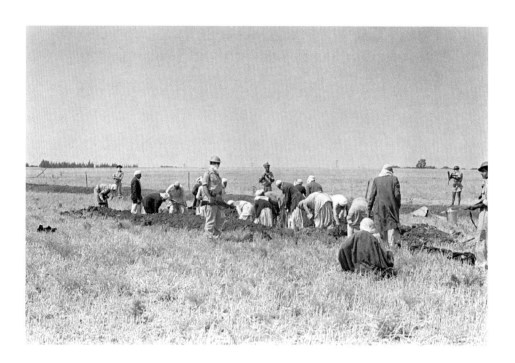

207 **"Afula"** The photograph in the IDF archive bears this caption: "Arab citizens harvesting crops in the fields; Haganah members guarding them." Those fields aren't Afula. They belong to Zir'in or al-Kafrayn or Abu Zurayq or al-Lajjun. The Arab citizens aren't gathering crops in the fields – they're digging a hole, one in which they stand up to their thighs. Had they been harvesting crops in the field they would have been surrounded by sacks and piles of produce, rather than by five Haganah soldiers pointing guns at them from five different directions. Were the air scented by the smell of fresh crops, the Haganah soldiers wouldn't have had to tie handkerchiefs over their noses. Eighteen Palestinian men were brought at gunpoint to the middle of this dry field (one was allowed to rest) and given hoes to dig a hole in which to bury a stinking secret. Had the photographer and the archive for which he worked not sequestered and masked the information, we could situate what the photograph shows in a specific place and time. The generality imposed on this photograph enables it to illustrate accurately repetitive Palestinian testimonies about the general recurrent procedure: a number of village men are taken under threat to bury those who had previously been shot during the fighting or during a massacre, in secret or before their eyes. Their testimonies are often supported by the heroic accounts of Haganah veterans. After all, someone had to have removed the dead Arabs. The soldiers weren't concerned about honoring the dead – or else they would have let the gravediggers take leave of their dead without pointing the muzzles of their guns at them. They were worried about the spread of odors, disease and incontrovertible evidence found on the bodies.

Photographer: Fred Chesnik, IDF and Defense Archive, 1948

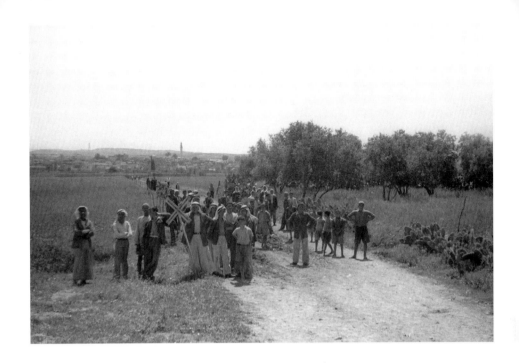

208   **Qalqilya** About a month after the signing of
the armistice agreement with Jordan, under whose
terms the area through which the road that ran
from Qalqilya to Tulkarm became part of Israel, the
photographer was apparently called to photograph the
fence erected along the border with Jordan. When
he arrived he was startled to see the residents of
Qalqilya "watching with amazement Israeli soldiers
erecting a barbed wire border fence," and that's how
the Government Press Office captioned the photo. In
a country like Palestine which had no borders, where
people traveled freely between Damascus, Alexandria
and Amman, and whose inhabitants hadn't been
trained to view fortified walls as a means of defense,
barbed wire was seen as a brutal instrument, amazing
and terrifying.

Photographer not identified. Government Press Office, May 7, 1949

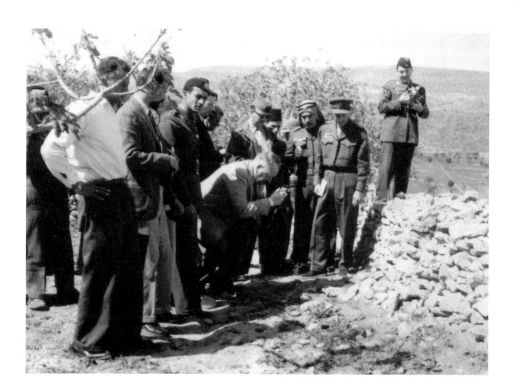

209 **The outskirts of al-Quds/Jerusalem** There were many cameras at the site of their catastrophe, but too few photographs testifying to it were published and disseminated. What did all those who were there, observing the catastrophe, in its presence, do with the visual evidence they collected? As he leans toward the traces on the ground not long after they were created, guided by eyewitnesses who can connect what they see to what they're reporting, he literally comes into possession of something that belongs to the public at large and not imprinted on his retina alone. There is an even greater need for such photographic testimony since most of the principal witnesses among the victims were exiled from their country, forbidden to return to testify, and most of the witnesses who carried out the ethnic cleansing that occurred prefer today to remain silent, stammer or prevent the others from testifying.

Photographer: Ali Zaarour, with the kind permission of Zaki Zaarour, 1948

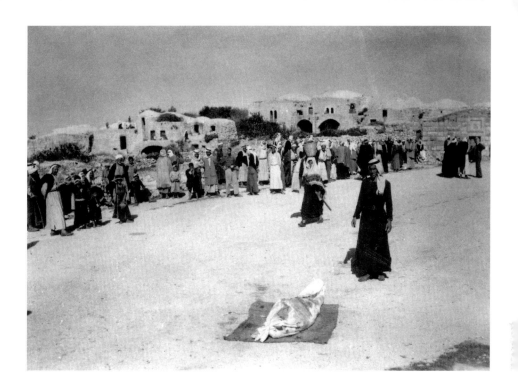

210   **Village not identified** The villagers form
a circle around the covered body. In another
photograph, taken at the same location by the same
photographer, which I chose not to display, the
body lies partially exposed on a sheet of cloth. It's
surprising that only the upper portion of the body is
covered by a piece of fabric. It appears as if those
who laid the body out in the center for all to see –
locals and foreigners alike – wanted people to look
at the pelvic region in order to understand the story
they wished to tell. The confiscated photographer's
journal, found in the IDF Archive, has not yet been
returned to his heirs. Only they can retrieve what
little information could shed some light on the
circumstances in which the photograph was taken,
or at least situate it in a particular place and time.
Even without being able to reconstruct exactly what
happened to the man now lying on a blood-soaked
cloth, from the fact of the photograph, which
appears to be a ceremonial display of evidence, and

the presence of the soldiers who are apparently
Jordanian (seen also in that other photograph), we
can infer that it was taken in Trans-Jordan, where
Palestinians were still able to present the damage
caused them as a catastrophe, one that did not yet
seem final. The other photograph shows many of
those watching from the circle covering their faces
with a handkerchief or with the kaffiyeh they're
wearing, as if they wished to shield themselves from
the odor and the sight. After the body was covered
the circle began to dissolve and some of those
present stood around in small groups discussing
what had occurred and what had been uncovered. A
photograph of the exposed body taken at the request
of the UN, was never made accessible or used as a
basis for appealing against the right of a sovereign
state to carry out such "acts of reprisal."

Photographer: Ali Zaarour, with the kind permission of Zaki
Zaarour, no date

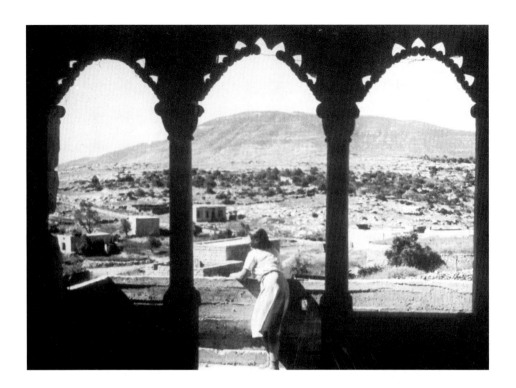

211 **Kufr Bir'im** Even at this early stage, the only way to see the catastrophe was to oppose the regime, oppose the field of view that it created.

Photographer not identified. The photograph was given to Nahida Zahra, a member of the second generation of those disposed from Kufr Bir'im, by a member of Kibbutz Bar'am (scanned with the compliments of Meron Farah, who is also one of those dispossessed from Kufr Bir'im), 1948

212   Kufr Bir'im The modern state adopted aerial photography from the moment it was invented in the nineteenth century, because of its military potential. This photograph of Kufr Bir'im was taken about one month after the state of Israel was established. But this wasn't the first aerial photograph Jews had taken of Arab villages. A Jewish "air service" had been operating in Palestine's skies since 1947 and contributed to the systematic generation of intelligence on the Arabs. It could do so because the British Mandate did not demand a monopoly of the skies. The lives of the people who've just finished harvesting their grain and bringing it to the threshing floor aren't visible in this bird's-eye view. Instead we see the environment of people's lives in military terms – access roads, emplacements, escape routes, firing positions,

etc. In 1953, five years after the state was established and two years after the first case was filed in the High Court of Justice asking that the uprooted be returned, all the buildings in the village were erased from the face of the earth, except for the ancient synagogue. The Arab Israeli citizens who were expelled from the village, still live nearby today. Had the rights stemming from Israeli citizenship not been applied differentially to different sectors of the population, they would long ago have obtained redress and compensation.

Photographer not identified. The photograph was given to Nahida Zahra, a member of the second generation of those disposed from Kufr Bir'im, by a member of Kibbutz Bar'am (scanned with the compliments of Meron Farah, who is also one of those dispossessed from Kufr Bir'im), June 25, 1948

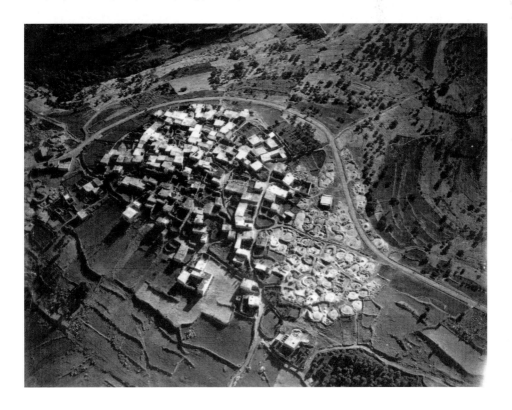

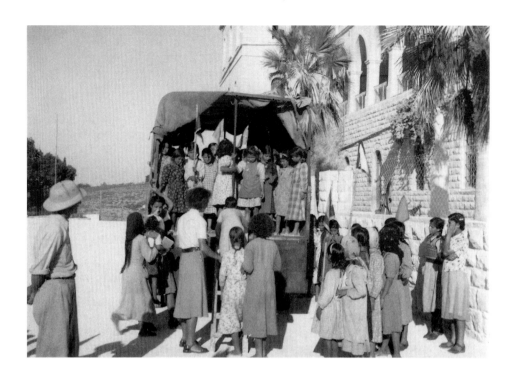

213   **al-Nasirah/Nazareth** Although they and their
parents were expelled from their home in 'Illut, they
remained in Palestine. For over a year they've been
living in the Silesian Monastery in Nazareth. They're
getting into the truck for a trip to Tabariyya transformed
into Tverya. Their parents and those in the monastery
do all they can to behave as if life goes on normally,
and make sure they don't miss any part of their
schooling, including field trips during vacations. But this
time, when they arrive there, they'll see an unfamiliar
landscape. Even if they don't notice it, the adults
accompanying them will surely see the rubble, the
Judaizing of space, the traces of the catastrophe that
are also imprinted on their own bodies. But they'll try
as hard as they can not to make a point of this, in order
not to undermine their education, and the girls will
wade and splash happily in the waters of the Kinneret
(Sea of Galilee).

Photographer not identified. The Monastery and School of
"Jesus Adolescent" (Don Bosco), Nazareth, 1948

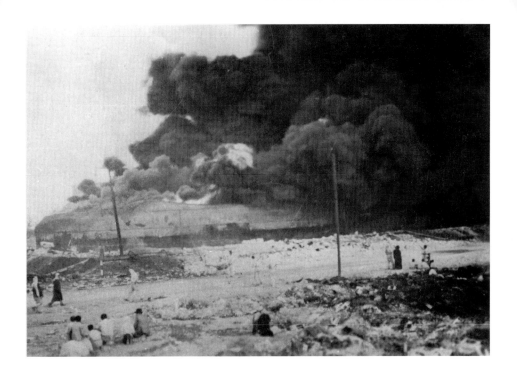

214 Haifa Citizens watching an apocalyptic scene together. Heavy smoke rises over the Haifa oil refinery following the bombing of three oil tankers by Lehi fighters. The flames that followed the explosions spread over a wide area of the refinery. Explosions continued to be heard for four days, the flames did not die out and smoke continued to rise. About 1,800 people worked at the refinery in 1947, about two-thirds of them Arabs and one-third Jews. At the time, relations between them were still good. They deteriorated only a few months later, following activities by the Etzel, whose fighters murdered a number of Arab workers waiting outside the refinery, and the response of the Arab workers, who murdered a number of Jewish employees. The attack documented in the photograph was directed against the British. It was part of a policy whose main component was causing damage to "British vital interests," in the course of which Jewish organizations had already tried to interfere with the regular flow of oil from Iraq to Haifa. The attack occurred a few months prior to the UN decision on the Partition Plan, before a clear line of division had been drawn between Jews and Arabs. The Jews and Arabs in the photograph are watching the disaster together. They can still see it in the same way. Among the Jews and Arabs gathered

in small groups where the disaster occurred are those who sit staring at the site; others are busy discussing it – one points in the direction of the burning oil while another listens to what he's saying, and some can be seen hurrying, perhaps because of what occurred before their eyes. Only a few of these observers are clearly identifiable as Arabs or as Jews, nor are there any traces of steps taken by a political regime to classify and separate Jews from Arabs, to distinguish between those who should be protected and those suspected *a priori* and viewed as a source of danger and therefore, vulnerable and abandoned. Recognizing catastrophe – any catastrophe – for what it is: that is the necessary condition for renewing the possibility of observing, experiencing and responding jointly to any disaster as partners rather than from opposite sides of the barricades. That's how the Jews and Arabs appear here, side by side. They worked there together. The explosion shocked them all. Together they assisted the injured, watched the flames from afar. One day, a new form of civil partnership might emerge from the shared awareness of catastrophe.

Photographer not identified. Jabotinsky House Archive, March 30, 1947

INDEX